TRAVELS THROUGH SACRED CHINA

TRAVELS THROUGH SACRED CHINA

MARTIN PALMER

Thorsons
An Imprint of HarperCollins*Publishers*

This book is for Lizzie Palmer,
a wonderful travelling companion and daughter.

Thorsons
An Imprint of HarperCollins*Publishers*
77–85 Fulham Palace Road,
Hammersmith, London W6 8JB
1160 Battery Street
San Francisco, California 94111–1213

Published by Thorsons 1996
10 9 8 7 6 5 4 3 2 1

A catalogue record for this book
is available from the British Library.

ISBN 1 85538 494 9

Printed in Great Britain by
Caledonian International Book Manufacturing Ltd, Glasgow

Photographs within the book © Circa Photo Library.
Temple plans drawn by Ranchor Prime, © ICOREC.

Frontispiece: Buddhist rock cut caves, Yungang, Datong, Shanxi province.

CONTENTS

ACKNOWLEDGEMENTS

This book arises from nearly twenty-five years of a love affair with China. This began when I was sent to work as a volunteer in a Chinese Children's Home in Hong Kong and the first acknowledgement is to the children of St. Christopher's Childrens Home, Tai Po, who taught me to see the world through different eyes. While there I met Chang Wai Ming and through her learnt to see the world the Chinese way and to see very critically my own culture. I owe her an immense debt of gratitiude, not least because she insisted I write to her in classical Chinese! To my sister Yan Chi, I owe the flame of interest in all things Chinese. To Kwok Man Ho my companion in so many books I owe my knowledge of the most fascinating aspects of folk religion.

But it is to Jo Edwards, Tjalling Halbertsma, Joanne O'Brien and Zhao Xiaomin, colleagues in ICOREC, that I owe most. Tjalling and Xiaomin for their company on the travels, for their research and for their willingness to track down obscure references. To Jo and Joanne, I owe the Gazetteer. When this book was almost finished I fell ill and Jo and Joanne finished it for me. To all four I express my abiding thanks.

INTRODUCTION

To travel through China is to walk on holy ground. Entering a Buddhist or Daoist temple is to voyage into a cosmic and salvationary drama, acted out not just by the statues and paintings, but by the very layout of the temple itself.

To undertake a pilgrimage to one of the sacred mountains of China is to travel back in time over three thousand years to the lands of the shamans and to experience today, the interplay between times past, present and future in walking the Dao, the Way of the mountains.

To understand the soul of China, you must see the Sacred in China which is there in the designs of buildings, the street plans of the cities, in the household shrines at the back of shops and in the concept that the very land, the very soil of China is itself sacred.

This guide book is a guide to the soul of China; to the vast religious and spiritual heritage of the many faiths which have emerged or interacted within China. It also enters into the spirit of the Dao, the Way, through which the culture and traditions of China are brought to life and the traveller becomes, once again, the pilgrim.

Martin Palmer

Research team, Jo Edwards, Tjalling Halbertsma, Joanne O'Brien and Zhao Xiaomin.

China
PROVINCES & CAPITALS

N

MONGOLIA

•Urumqi

X I N J I A N G

GANSU

Xining •

Q I N G H A I

INDIA

T I B E T

NEPAL

• Lhasa

BHUTAN   INDIA

0   500   1000 km

BURMA

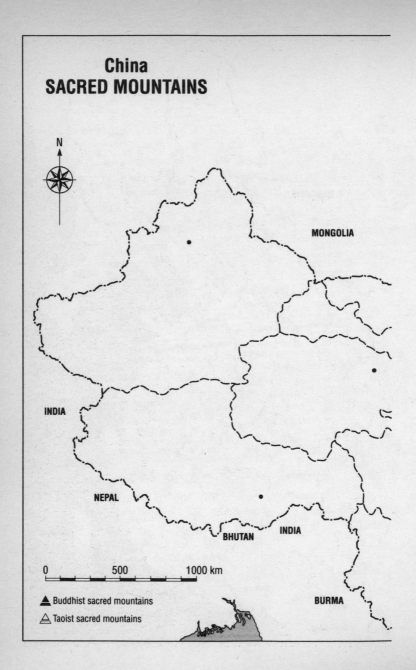

China
SACRED MOUNTAINS

N

MONGOLIA

INDIA

NEPAL

BHUTAN   INDIA

0   500   1000 km

▲ Buddhist sacred mountains
△ Taoist sacred mountains

BURMA

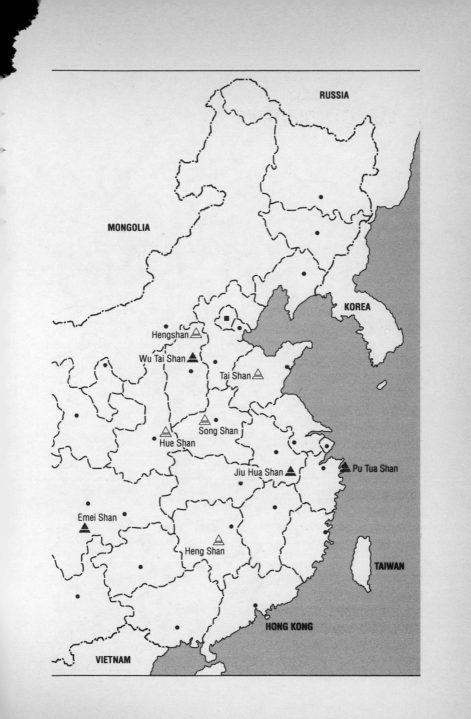

PART ONE

THE SACRED TRADITIONS

THE SACRED IN CHINA

In the summer of 1995 government officials moved in on a small town in Hunan Province. Their purpose was simple. It was to destroy a new temple which had been erected without official approval. The temple, a better word would be shrine, had been built over a matter of days by local peasants who had come to venerate the main image in the hope of wealth and success. In the rapidly changing China of today, with its fortunes to be made, many are being left behind in the race for prosperity. So the local people built this shrine. However, the government took exception to this temple and to its main image. For enthroned on a traditional altar at the heart of the temple was not one of the ancient gods such as the god of wealth, or the god of good fortune, but no less a person than Mao Ze Dong (Mao Tse Tung – please note: we use pinyin phoneticization as is standard in China today. Where appropriate we give the older style as well), founder dictator of the People's Republic of China and lifelong Communist!

Hundreds of miles away in Sichuan Province, in 1990, a visitor from southern China took a photograph of the giant seated Buddha carved from the rock at Leshan. When he got home and developed the photograph he saw that he had photographed two Buddhas. There was, of course, the great historic Buddha, carved in the 8th century AD. But there was an even larger Buddha. For the photograph showed that the island and spit of land surrounding the giant Buddha looked, when photographed from a certain angle, just like a person lying on his or her back. Today you will be shown not just the giant carved Buddha but also what is now called the Supine Buddha – the naturally formed Buddha.

In 1994, according to the China Daoist (Taoist) Association, a new or refurbished Daoist temple or shrine was being opened every day in southern China.

The sacred – and religion – is alive and well in China and as capable of creating new wonders, imparting the sense of the sacred – and at times the absurd – as it ever has been. China offers one of the most powerful sacred landscapes in the world. It provides one of the greatest meeting places of religions, ranging from shamanism through Daoism and Buddhism to Islam and Christianity. New religious groups are emerging every week and the rebuilding and reclaiming of China's sacred sites continues apace. From the reappearance of the humble shop shrine to the restoration of great temples, China is recovering its sacred traditions. But while the sacred and religion in China are being rediscovered, so much has also been lost in the political upheavals of the 20th century. In particular, China's absorption of Tibet has led to almost total destruction of that unique culture. However, I have not covered Tibet in this guide for it is so different from the rest of China as to require a book all of its own. The landscape of the sacred in China has been turned upside down since 1911 and today it faces perhaps its greatest challenge yet – indifference.

Yet to the discerning visitor, China can open up as a sacred landscape in a way few other countries can rival.

SPIRITUAL DIRECTIONS

The traditional maps of China differ in one very significant way from maps anywhere else in the world. On ancient Chinese maps, the south is always placed at the top, with north relegated to the bottom. This was no accident or quirk born of perverseness. The reason is simple. South is the direction of the Divine and the powerful. Only the Emperor was allowed to face south. All those around him had to face north.

In the West, we see the East as the direction of the spiritual – of Eden or the Holy Land; of India or the 'mysteries of the East' such as Egypt. In China, West is the direction of the spiritual – the great legendary teacher Lao Zi (Lao Tzu) 'went West' when he despaired of China, dictating his great classic, the *Dao De Jing* (*Tao Te Ching*) at the Gate to the West. When the Emperor Ming (58–75 AD) dreamt of a Golden Man in the West, he knew that this meant a new religion or spiritual tradition and duly, so the legend says, sent envoys to find this teacher. Back came Buddhism – from the West.

The sense of sacredness in the directions of the compass is reinforced by the two great Imperial temples in Beijing.

To the south of the imperial city stands the Temple of Heaven. Here all the buildings and the terraces for the performance of sacrifices and worship are circular, for Heaven is symbolized by a circle. South is the direction of yang, the male, fiery aspect of nature, which balances the yin, the female, cold aspect of nature. At the Winter Solstice, when the yang aspect is at its lowest ebb and the cold yin is in the ascendant, the Emperor offered sacrifices and prayers to ensure the return and revival of the yang.

In the north of the city, the yin direction, lies the Temple of the Earth. Here the main temple and the terraces are square or rectangular, as the square is the symbol of Earth. Each Summer Solstice the Emperor sacrificed and prayed here for the return and revival of the yin aspect, for at this point in the year the hot yang aspect is in the ascendant.

The Temple of Heaven is well known to visitors to Beijing, but not so the Temple of the Earth. Whenever I visit it it is almost always deserted, while you can barely move at the Temple of Heaven for tourists. Certainly the Temple of Heaven has grander buildings, but I love the quiet and simplicity of the Temple of the Earth – the yin of calm balancing compared with the yang of activity.

So there is Heaven and Earth, yang and yin, but what of us, of humanity?

Heaven and Earth and Humanity is the triad central to the Chinese understanding of the sacred. The circle of Heaven is above, the square of the Earth below and Humanity holds the tension between these two great forces. This symbolism, laid out in architectural terms to the north and south of Beijing was also encapsulated in the coinage of Imperial China, with its circular coins pierced by a square hole in the centre.

The land of China is intimately caught up in the notion of sacred. Its shapes, its rivers, its mountains, its diversity are all imprints of the sacred and vehicles to the sacred. From the soil of the land to the soaring mountains, China is sacred.

In the 'Zhou Li', the Records of the Rites of the Zhou dynasty, which dates from around 200 BC, there comes a clear picture of the interwoven nature of the sacred and the mundane in China. The Zhou Li lists sacrifices offered by the emperor to the following: 'the ancestral spirits of the people; the Heavenly deities such as the Supreme Heavenly Ruler, the Sun – great yang, and the moon – great yin, the major stars and constellations, such as the Great Bear; the Wind-Master Star and the Rain-Maker Star; the gods of the Earth, especially the Earth God; the gods of the Five Elements (wood, fire, earth, metal and water); the Five Sacred Mountains; the forests and rivers and marshes; and the One Hundred deities living in all directions.'

As will be seen from such a list, all manner of physical phenomena were worshipped, often in their own right, not because of some deity residing in them. Today this same sense of the whole of nature being inherently sacred continues – an unbroken though severely damaged line of descent links today's worshippers and believers with those ancient shamanic masters of the 3rd to 2nd century BC.

This all-pervading sense of sacredness was brought home to me most powerfully when I visited Hua Shan, one of the five Daoist sacred mountains (see chapter 7). I want to take you on a walk up this extraordinary mountain, because in doing so, we can encounter much of what makes China sacred.

I first visited Hua Shan in 1991 with my young daughter Lizzie. For reasons now long forgotten, we went in February. Don't go in February! We nearly died from frost, snow and wind, but despite this, or possibly because of this, the mountain climb left an indelible mark upon me. For in truth, to climb Hua Shan, or any of the great sacred mountains, is to climb the sacred history, philosophy and life of China.

At the base of the mountain, along the road leading to the formal entrance to the mountain proper, stand many stalls selling the usual paraphernalia of religious sites – prayer beads, horoscope books, divination texts, plastic images of major deities Daoist and Buddhist, amulets and so forth. There is a book waiting to be written on the universality of bad religious art and whoever does so should certainly visit the souvenir stalls of Hua Shan! Prominent amongst these trinkets were statues of the Earth god, Tu Ti. This deity is probably one of the earliest gods of China – he is specifically mentioned in the list from the Zhou Li – and until recently, was the most widespread. Every home, every shop or workplace would have one and he was worshipped first thing in the morning and last thing at night. It is by his permission that we are allowed to live and work where we do, it is his protection which ensures that we do not suffer and it is he who owns the land, not we.

This attitude has all but been swept away by the changes of the last 70 years in China. However, in places such as Hong Kong, Macau or Taiwan, the Earth god is still devoutly worshipped, and many homes in China have begun to put him back in his traditional place, particularly in the countryside. It seemed very appropriate to buy a statue of the Earth god while our feet were still firmly planted on the flat and level ground at the base of the mountain. Higher up the mountain we can worship the god of the Earth of Hua Shan in a strange little cave temple near the temple of the Immortals.

Moving through the gate we came to a small garden laid

out in the grounds of the Daoist monastery of Yu Quan Guan (Jade Spring Monastery) at the base of the mountain. Here great windblown rocks stand, looking like miniature versions of the sacred mountain itself. In fact they stand as treasured symbols of the forces of yin and yang – of the primal forces of nature. In their intricate hollowed shapes we can see the inter-action between that which is material and that which is spiri-tual – between the apparent hardness of the rock and the soft but persistent effects of the wind and water. The *Dao De Jing* puts this beautifully:

> The very softest thing of all
> can ride like a galloping horse
> through the hardest of things.
>
> Like water, like water penetrating rock.
> And so the invisible enters in.
> *(Chapter 43,* Tao Te Ching, *Kwok, Palmer and Ramsay)*

This notion of the greater strength of the weak or of the yield-ing is central to Daoist philosophy and to Daoist life. As the old saying puts it, the willow that bends in the wind survives; the willow that resists the wind, snaps. Daoism is about going with the flow, about being and becoming one with nature and with the Dao – the Way of Nature. In stressing this, Daoism sees itself as being very different from the rigidity of Confucianism or the dogmas (as they would put it) of the Buddhists.

To reach the monastery's main temple, we cross over water. The water is there to prevent the demons and evil spirits such as ghosts from entering this sacred place. They cannot travel across water, nor can they bend or turn in their travel path. This is why you will find short walls set up in front of or just behind the main entrances to almost all temples and holy places in China. Indeed, until recently, every Chinese home had such a devil wall, designed to deny entrance to trouble-some spirits. A particularly magnificent one is the Nine Drag-on Wall in the Forbidden City in Beijing.

7

At the main temple of the monastery stands the traditional three incense burners, the means by which an ordinary person can communicate with the spiritual world. Inside the temple, Daoist monks will ring the great bronze bowl to alert the gods to the fact that you are there to offer worship. However, they will only do this if you bow and are clearly there to worship. The casual visitor is ignored by both monks and presumably the gods.

FORTUNE AND CHANCE

You can also have your fortune told here. To do so, you take a container holding one hundred numbered sticks. After praying and thoughtfully composing your mind and your question, you shake the container until one or more of the sticks falls out. The numbers on these sticks gives you a reading which will then be interpreted by the Daoist monk in attendance.

When I first visited, I was keen to obtain a copy of the oracles which the priests used to do the readings. These are a fascinating subculture and I and colleagues have translated one such set of prophetic readings from the goddess Guan Yin (Kuan Yin – see *Kuan Yin*, by Palmer, Ramsay and Kwok, Thorsons, 1995). It took some bargaining but eventually I was given a set. The readings often contain some fine poetry, but become submerged under traditional interpretations which essentially cover the usual concerns of marriage, wealth, health and death.

Here again is a key principle of Chinese notions of the sacred – Chance. It is pure chance which stick falls out, yet it is interpreted as being revealing. Here is the key to the Chinese approach to the spiritual. What we try to do is of significance – after all we form the third member of the Triad of Heaven, Earth and Humanity. Yet what really counts is not asserting our own rights and powers but being in tune with the flow of Nature, with the Way of the Dao – the Path. It is in ultimately letting go of human attempts to control or even to understand.

In allowing chance to determine which sticks fall out, the person seeking help is allowing him or herself to be carried by the flow of Nature. By their inaction comes a response. This attitude of allowing chance to become your guide because it is directed by the Dao, is reflected in the name of the oldest divination system in China, the Yi Jing (I Ching) or Book of Changes. In the Great Appendix to the Yi Jing, supposedly written *c.* 5th century BC by Confucius (known in Chinese as Kong Fu Zi), the book is put into a cosmic context:

> Movement and rest have their constancy; according to these strong and weak are differentiated. Ways coincide according to their species and things fall into classes. Hence good fortune and bad fortune come about. In the heavens phenomena appear; on earth shapes occur. Through these, change and transformation become manifest.

The understanding of the way of the Dao as being chance is beautifully captured in the following lines from a poem by the 11th century AD philosopher Shao Yong, a Daoist who delighted in the chance of the Yi Jing, and whose words have a strange resonance with current language about the chaos theory:

> A butterfly circles the cold chrysanthemum.
> A cricket calls by empty steps.
> Within a dog lying before the gate,
> Without a guest coming throughout the day.
> Clear waves flow tranquilly mid-stream.
> White clouds rest quietly in clumps.
> How does Heaven's harmony arise?
> From time to time I drink a cup of wine.
> *(Adapted from the translation provided on page 231 of* Sung Dynasty
> Uses of the I Ching, *Smith, Bol, Adler and Wyatt)*

FOLLOWING THE PATH

The climb begins from the temple of the monastery. To climb the mountain is to rise to communication with the gods, for in classic Chinese belief, the mountain is a cosmic pillar, facilitating interaction between the material world and the spiritual. And the Path up the mountain, particularly on Daoist mountains, is part of the Path of the Dao. It is not just a route from monastery A to monastery B. It is in itself part of the adventure of being in the Dao. To climb the mountain, you must allow the Path, the Dao to take you where it will.

This walking the Path is fundamental to visiting a sacred mountain. Indeed, I have heard from Daoist monks that their main objection to the growth of cable cars on sacred mountains is that it not only disrupts the spiritual flow of the mountain – feng shui – but stops people walking. As one monk said on Tai Shan: 'You walk to know humility. If you fly to the top by cables, you think you are an immortal or a god. Well, you are not!'

On Hua Shan, the Path winds past the shrines to the local earth gods and the protector deities of the mountain. Legends and stories fill every turning in the Path, every large rock has its myth. These legends reflect the core beliefs of the mass of ordinary people, the peasants of China, for whom life has always been tough. In these legends, the powerful are outwitted and the poor protected. For example, on the early stages of the climb you pass close to a rocky outcrop called the Hairy Girl Peak, under which is a cave of similar name. The legend tells that in the time of the first true Emperor of China, the famous dictator Qin Shi Huang Ti (221 – 210 BC), a young girl called Yu Jiang, aged only 14, was chosen to be buried in the tomb along with the Emperor.

Yu Jiang was not very excited by this dubious honour, and along with six other girls, she fled the palace and sought refuge on Hua Shan. Here they subsisted on berries and mountain water. Yu Jiang lived all the remainder of her life on the mountain and never cut her hair. It grew long and beautiful, but because she lived in a cave, something strange happened. Her hair turned green and she grew into the very peak that can be seen today.

All along the path up Hua Shan you will find Chinese characters carved into the living rock. Often it will be a simple character such as Heaven. Other times it will be a poem, written by a famous poet and inscribed here by admirers. For the very characters of Chinese writing are in themselves sacred. They not only express the ideas contained within them, but are themselves part of what they express. Thus a character for Heaven is heavenly; a character for good fortune is in itself fortunate. In combining writing with landscape, the Chinese bring together two powerful strands of the sacred in a way which not only adds to the natural beauty of the climb but brings moments of reflection and introspection on a climb from Earth to Heaven.

However, I have to add that these poems and sayings also add to the length of the climb! My constant companion on climbs of sacred mountains is Zhao Xiaomin. He has a deep love and even deeper knowledge of classical Chinese and together we try to translate the poems or sayings while we climb. Thus it is that bemused Chinese pilgrims and tourists will have often seen an Englishman and a Chinese man standing arguing vigorously about how best to translate some Chinese phrase. We no longer measure the speed of our climbs by miles or metres, but by the number of poems per hour. One colleague has even suggested we should climb at night so we can't see the poems and thus be delayed. But that would cut out half the fun for me!

The tension between the world of human affairs and the world of the sacred is captured in two ways on this climb. The more devout Emperors made provisions for sacrifices to be made to each of the five main Daoist mountains, sometimes coming and supervising the sacrifices themselves, though usually from the comfort of a temple complex some four miles away, at the Xiyue temple. Today you can still see the poems and edicts written to celebrate these offerings, essential

11

elements of the regulation between the affairs of Heaven, Earth and Humanity, mediated by the earthly pillar of the mountain. Due respect for the Dao and for the twin forces of yin and yang determined this approach. Sacrifices to the mountains and to the primal forces and origins associated with them were an inherent part of Court ritual. The third century BC philosopher and Confucian scholar Xun Zi (Hsun Tzu) says:

> The li (rites) are rooted in three things: Heaven and Earth are the origin of life; our ancestors are the origin of our group; our rulers and teachers are the origin of ordered government. Without Heaven and Earth, how could there be life? Without our early ancestors, from what could we have sprung? Without rulers and teachers, how could there be ordered government?
>
> *(Page 353, Fung Yu-lan's* A History of Chinese Philosophy *vol. I)*

So at one level, the world of human affairs came to the sacred mountains to maintain the hierarchy of power and authority. But there is another, probably older tradition of the relationship between the world of human affairs and the sacred. It is the tradition of those who withdraw from positions of power to become hermits on the mountains; to pursue the quest for understanding and to achieve immortality – literal immortality – by retreating from the ephemera of the material world to the reality of the spiritual world. Many mountains tell stories of scholars and high ranking officials who suddenly realized the futility of material concerns and rejected privilege and power for the life of a simple hermit.

Hua Shan is no exception. Above Ziwei Cave is a vast rock which looks as if it was dropped there from a great height. This rock is associated with the stories of one such former scholar official who took to the mountains to find spiritual truth. Wang Changyue was a successful official who became disgusted with the state of the world and abandoned family and career to retreat to Hua Shan. The character for an immortal combines the characters for a person and a mountain. In other words, someone alone on a mountain. This is what Wang Changyue sought.

The stories tell that when he had been a monk for three years (some time in the 17th or early-18th century), he asked his Daoist teacher why he had not yet met a god. His teacher told him to continue to be honest and to maintain his prayers and recitations of the scriptures and one day he would certainly meet a god.

So Wang Changyue stood on the great rock day after day for a further three years and prayed and recited.

Suddenly, one day without warning, a thunderbolt crashed to earth and a brilliant light shone over him. Before his eyes a god appeared. He had three heads, eight arms and rode a terrible looking beast with nine heads. The god asked Wang what he wanted but Wang could not speak, he was terrified and stood quaking with fear. The god noted Wang's quivering body and feet and thought that Wang, who was incapable of saying anything, wanted a bigger body and larger feet. The god thus decreed that he should have them.

When the god disappeared, Wang found he fitted none of his clothes nor his shoes. He had nearly doubled in size! When his teacher saw him, he said, 'Obviously you have met a god and forgot to specify what you wanted. What a shame!' Wang was greatly embarrassed not to mention greatly enlarged, and determined that next time he would be prepared.

So he went back to the rock and spent another three years praying and reciting. Then, as suddenly as before, the brilliant light shone again and the god appeared. Wang was so overcome that despite his best intentions all he could do was stand shocked still and cover his mouth with his hand in astonishment. The god again asked what he wanted and again Wang could not answer. So the god saw Wang's hand over his mouth and concluded he wanted a beard. Low and behold a long and luxuriant beard appeared. Wang was overcome with mortification at this second failure.

For three more years Wang stood and prayed and recited on the rock. He was determined to be ready the next time and, three years on, when the brilliant light came again he was ready. Before him stood a goddess who asked what he required of her. Wang said he wished to find the true Daoist Way. The goddess told him to journey to the northeast of the mountain and there he would find the true Way. Wang followed her advice and came to understand all and to be united with the Dao and so became an immortal.

This story is typical of many Daoist tales in combining an element of humour with an element of instruction. The trials and tribulations of Wang are meant to entertain and to instruct. Looking at his rock, perched above the cave, one is reminded of the labours that are required to move from this material world to that of the spirit world. The retreat of the sage from the concerns and priorities of this world are a constant refrain throughout Chinese history and religion. They act as mirrors to the rest of society, asking what is really important in life. For example, divination text no. 63 from the *Poems of Wong Tai Sin* captures this:

> In a back lane, a sage quietly lived a simple life,
> having just enough food to keep himself alive.
> Poor and miserable though he might seem,
> yet he felt happy and held himself in high esteem.

Moving on up the Daoist mountain, we come to a temple dedicated to the goddess Guan Yin. Guan Yin is a Buddhist deity, the Bodhisattva of Compassion yet she is here, enthroned on the Daoist mountain. Buddhism and Daoism live side by side in most sacred places. Visit a Daoist temple and you will find Buddhist gods and Confucian heroes and morality tales. Visit a Buddhist temple and you will find immortals from Daoism cavorting around and deities from the popular pantheon of Daoism supporting the efforts of the various Buddhas and bodhisattvas of the temple. Sadly, the Buddhists tend to be rather down on the Daoists and to assign them lower places in their iconography. Thus in the Hua Yuan temple at Datong, there is a beautiful incense burner shaped like a pagoda which stands before the first hall. The burner has both Buddhist and Daoist deities upon it, but in a rather telling style. For while the Buddhist figures stand upon balconies looking serenely out, the whole edifice is carried upon the backs of the Daoist deities! I have never seen anything comparable in terms of Daoist art putting down Buddhist deities, though as will be explored later, Daoism has its own way of doing down Buddhism.

On Hua Shan, no one would dream of questioning what a Buddhist deity is doing here. For Guan Yin embodies a fundamental aspect of Chinese religion: the search for mercy and the longing for compassion. The physical world of China is harsh for most people. Their lives are a struggle. What they long for is release from this struggle and strife and a blessed rest in the afterlife and/or a good rebirth. Guan Yin embodies these hopes for she has delayed her own release into the no-thing-ness of Nirvana in order to save all who suffer. Her full name, Guan Shi Yin, means the One who Regards the Cries of the world. Her central text is found in the beautiful Lotus Sutra, where as the bodhisattva Avalokitesvara, a male version of Guan Shi Yin, he is described thus:

Who hears his name and looks to him,
Unremittingly remembering him,
Will end the sorrows of existence.
Even though men with ill intent
Cast him into a burning pit,
Let him think of the Cry-Regarder
The very fire-pit becomes a pool:
Or, driven along a mighty ocean
in peril dire of dragons and demons,
Let him think of the Cry-Regarder
And never will waves him overwhelm...

Every evil state of existence,
Hells and ghosts and animals,
Sorrows of birth, age, disease, death,
All will thus be ended for him.

15

True Regard, serene Regard,
Far-reaching, wise Regard,
Regard of pity, Regard compassionate,
Ever longed for, ever looked for
In radiance ever pure and serene!
Wisdom's sun, destroying darkness,
Subduer of woes, of storm, of fire,
Illuminator of the world!
Law of pity, thunder quivering,
Compassion wondrous as a great cloud,
Pouring spiritual rain like nectar,
Quenching all the flames of distress!
(Page 249–250, The Lotus of the Wonderful Law – Saddharma
Pundarika Sutra, *translated by W.E. Soothill)*

HERMITS AND SHAMANS

Away from the main pathway can be seen caves and crude
holes carved into the rockface or even cut into giant boulders
beside the pathway. These have been the dwelling places of
hermits over the centuries. Here, up almost inaccessible rockfaces, have lived men and women who have wished to escape
as far as possible from human contact. Because of the vastness
of the surroundings, it is often difficult to comprehend just
how inaccessible the hermit caves actually are. I recall on Hua
Shan how I and a colleague set out to climb up to one of these
– it looked to be an easy climb. In fact we chickened out after
just a few feet as the climb was in truth both long and very
dangerous!

Inside the caves or holes, are (or to be more precise on Hua
Shan, were) carved statues of the deities who have kept them
company over the years of solitude; for example, the three
great Bright Ones of Daoism, Guan Yin, the Future Buddha or
perhaps the Queen Mother of the West. Sadly the hermit caves
were a favourite target of the extremists of the Cultural Revolution who destroyed these statues or beheaded them. Slowly

16

they are being repaired or new ones made. Where new ones are made, they follow the same eclectic pattern of gods and goddesses from diverse traditions. A mixture of Daoist, Buddhist and perhaps even older deities. For these mountains have been sacred for thousands of years, pre-dating any of the existing formal religions, but perhaps owing their holiness to the earliest and perhaps earthiest of world religions – shamanism.

Today shamans can still be found in China. On Hua Shan there are a couple who come and go, depending upon the time of year and the attitude of the local authorities. To consult one, you need to be willing to wander a little off the beaten path, usually to some old, rather dilapidated temple or house. Here readings and communications with the spirit world can take place relatively undisturbed. On request and with suitable financial reward, the shaman will, if possible, go into a trance. While in this trance, he or she – about 40 per cent are women – is able to communicate with the spirit world and to mediate questions and enquiries to that world. The answers that come back are often difficult to understand and confront the questioner with the challenge of the 'otherness' of the sacred. Shamans have long been associated with rain making and still fulfil this function today. Their journeys whilst in a trance take them into Heaven itself and they become part of the world of spirits and deities with whom they commune. This is well expressed in one of the most famous of all Chinese shamanistic poems, the Li Sao poem in the *Songs of the South*, dating from *c.* 4th century BC:

First I would roam a little for my enjoyment.
I sent Wang Shu ahead to ride before me;
The Wind God went behind as my outrider;
The Bird of Heaven gave notice of my comings;
The Thunder God warned me when all was not ready.

I caused my phoenixes to mount on their pinions
And fly ever onward by night and by day.
The whirlwinds gathered and came out to meet me,

Leading clouds and rainbows, to give me welcome.
In wild confusion, now joined and now parted,
Upwards and downwards rushed the glittering train.
I asked Heaven's porter to open for me;
But he leant across Heaven's gate and eyed me
churlishly.

(Pages 73–4, Songs of the South, *translated by David Hawkes*)

Hermits, as one might imagine, do not like to be disturbed too often. Nevertheless, some are quite famous for their loquaciousness. On Qingcheng Shan I was once buttonholed by a hermit who insisted on giving me his own, personal philosophy of life. Totally incomprehensible and slightly alarming, for he fixed me with bright if somewhat demented eyes and ground his teeth at the end of each sentence. The holy and sacred are not always quite all there, or if they are, they sometimes seem to exist on a very different plane. It is rare to find one who can communicate easily the insights they have gained in their years of prayer and fasting. I recall one hermit on Mount Athos in Greece, an Orthodox Christian monk of quite extraordinary appearance. My friends and I met him on a bend in the path through woods near his cave. Lolloping up to us he thrust his head under the nose of our Greek translator and said 'Sniff that!' Dimitri duly did as he was asked with an expression of some consternation. 'What do you think?' demanded the hermit. Dimitri mumbled something noncommittal, whereupon the monk said 'Thirty years!' We enquired thirty years of what? 'Thirty years I haven't washed my hair you know!' And having imparted this gem of reflection, he ambled off down the path leaving us none the wiser.

Well, that is how it is with many of these wonderful characters on the sacred mountains of China. Don't expect great jewels of insight unless you have the time to stay and cultivate their friendship as Bill Porter has done in his excellent *Road to Heaven – Encounters with Chinese Hermits* (Rider, London 1993). In his interview with Master Hsieh of Hua Shan, Hsieh paints a sad picture of the decline of hermit life on Hua Shan due to the pressure of visitors. Yet tucked away, or occasionally encountered on the path, are still some determined souls who pursue this most ancient of ways of life on the sacred mountain.

Alongside the hermits there are of course the regular Daoist priests and monks. These you encounter at the temples where they look after you, albeit often in a rather off-hand way. But you will also encounter them on the Path, and that can be quite alarming, for there is a tradition of marathon monks in China. Marathon monks undertake punishing regimes in which they push themselves to the limits. The first time I encountered three such monks was on a very dangerous part of the climb. I was hanging on by my fingernails – literally – for we were climbing a sheer cliff face using shallow cuts into the rock. The Chinese have much smaller feet than me with my size 13 shoes. The cuts into the rock were, if anything, made for people with bound feet, so small were they. So there I was, in a howling wind, clinging to the rock face, inching my way up, wishing I was somewhere else. Suddenly there was a blur coming down the rock face towards me. Three monks were running down the rock face, seeming to touch upon the incized steps for only the briefest fraction of a second. On their backs they carried packs which I was later told by one of them contained heavy rocks. They shot past me as if just running along a road, rather than descending a sheer rock face.

Later on, they ran back up the mountain and came to rest where we were sitting. They will spend up to a month running up and down the mountain, not sleeping and pushing themselves to the extreme. This tradition of self-denial, almost self-abuse, came into Daoism from Buddhism where the rejection of any ultimate reality or significance in this physical world has often led to such acts of deliberate and excessive strain being placed upon the physical body.

IMPRINT OF THE IMMORTALS

Climbing further, we come to yet another reminder of the antiquity of sacred China. High on the side of a cliff on East Peak there appears to be a gigantic handprint. This is reputed to be the handprint of a giant sent to help the heroic demi-god Yu the Great. In one of the most popular of Chinese ancient myths, the world was threatened by massive floods. The Yellow River had burst its banks and was inundating China, sweeping away homes and farmland. The Emperor Yao, one of the hero Emperors of antiquity and a model for Confucian virtues, summoned Yu the Great to battle with these waters. Yu was almost certainly a shamanistic figure for he could turn into a bear at will. Together with his faithful friend the Dragon, he carved new pathways for the river; built dykes and dams to control the waters and eventually after ten years of unremitting struggle, channelled the waters of the Yellow River into a safe new course. In the process of doing this he had to split Hua Shan in half for it was blocking the new pathway to the ocean. On East Peak you can see the imprint of the hand of the giant sent by Heaven to assist Yu in dividing the great mountain.

There are literally hundreds of similar stories and personalities, gods and goddesses associated with different features and parts of this sacred mountain. At every turn of the Path there is a message for those who understand the traditions and iconography of the sacred – too many to encompass in this telling. The intention of making this journey has been to give glimpses of the diverse nature of the sacred in China. Let it end therefore by arriving at the peak, or to be more precise, at one of the five peaks of Hua Shan. For just as Chinese religion has not one belief system but at least three major ones and according to Chinese tradition, five, so the mountain also has more than one peak. This is important to remember about Chinese religion. There is no one answer. The Chinese operate happily with a variety of belief systems, combining elements of shamanism, Confucianism, Daoism, Buddhism and at times

Christianity as well. Asking which is the more important is often not appropriate, as in asking which of the five peaks of Hua Shan is the most important. They are all important because they are all different. Together they add up to the total experience.

On the upper reaches, between the South Peak and the West Peak is a temple to Lao Zi, the fabled founder figure of Daoism. Probably an historical figure of the 6th to 5th centuries BC, he later became mythologized into one of the Three Primal Beings of the Cosmos. In one of his forms, he is the maker of the pills of immortality which, once devoured, ensure everlasting life. Here in this simple temple are the remains of what is claimed to be the furnace of Lao Zi in which he made the pills of immortality. Here also he is supposed to have tried to destroy the Monkey King – at least this is what the very popular anti-Daoist, pro-Buddhist novel, *Journey to the West* claims.

Immortality – the quest for eternal life – is one of the high points of Chinese belief. It infuses the world with a special form of sacredness. Mushrooms growing high on the mountain are supposed to be an essential component of this pill, as is the climb itself. Yet the very nature of immortality is elusiveness. The Path seems to end at this temple, yet just beyond this high point it wanders on again. It is hard to tell when you have arrived at the end of the Path, the Dao of Hua Shan, for there are always paths leading on elsewhere. In this way it reflects perfectly the quest for the Dao and the elusiveness of that quest – indeed the elusiveness of the sacred itself. As Lao Zi's reputed book the *Dao De Jing* puts it:

The Tao that can be talked about is not the true Tao.
The name that can be named
is not the eternal Name.
Everything in the universe comes out of Nothing.

Nothing – the nameless
is the beginning;

While Heaven, the mother
is the creatrix of all things.

Follow the nothingness of the Tao,
and you can be like it, not needing anything,
seeing the wonder and the root of everything.

And even if you cannot grasp this nothingness,
you can still see something of the Tao in everything...
(Chapter 1, Tao Te Ching, *translated by Kwok, Palmer and Ramsay)*

THE RELIGIONS OF CHINA

SHAMANISM

Shamanism has been described as the oldest world religion. Its origins lie so far back in time that we know very little about when it began. What is known is that around 10,000 BC, shamanism had spread from its original homeland of Siberia, across the then existing land bridge between Siberia and Alaska, and was making its way down through Northern America. Here it formed the basis of Native American religion from Alaska to Central America. In China, we find shamanic practices in the earliest of the major cultures, especially that of the Longshan culture (*c.* 6000–3000 BC). Scapulimancy – oracle taking from the shoulder bones of ox or the shells of tortoises – a key element of shamanic culture in China, was being practised then. So too were various forms of ancestor worship. Shamanism underlies all these and more. By the time we get to the earliest recordable dynasties, such as the Shang and the Zhou, shamanism has become the state cult and its priests are the officials of the rituals of the dynasties. From *c.* 1750 to 500 BC, shamanism was the dominant religious force in China. Its decline comes with the increase in urban Chinese culture and the growth of Confucianism. The Confucians saw the ecstatic, religious and otherworldly nature of the shamans as counter to everything they wanted – order and control.

Shamanism is a belief in two worlds, the spirit world and the inferior material world which we inhabit. Communication between these two worlds is only possible for someone who is in a trance, opening them to possession by the spirit world. This is what the shaman is able to do. Through their mediation, the spirit world and the material world can be in touch. Help can be sought from the spirit world or the spirit world can say what has disturbed it about the actions of the material world. Hence the role of shamans in seeking oracles by scapulimancy and various other forms of divination – the Yi Jing being a classic example.

Shamans usually have an animal form that they can also take or through which they can communicate with the spirit world. Most common of these is the bear and this motif of the bear/human appears in a number of the oldest legends of China. For example, Yu the Great, tamer of the floods of prehistoric China is one such. Son of a demi-god who was also a shaman, Yu's father died and his corpse remained unchanged for three years while shamans sat around it. Then at the end of the three years, the corpse transformed into a bear. Yu the Great, whose labours in taming the floods and rivers of China are still celebrated today, could change into a bear at whim.

However, there is one big difference between shamanism and the later beliefs and philosophies of China. Shamanism does not see humanity as having a pivotal role in the cosmos. Instead, humanity is very much at the mercy of greater forces, including the animal world as represented in particular by bears, tigers and dragons. The idea of humanity forming the third leg of the Triad of Heaven, Earth and Humanity arose after the influence of shamanism had begun to decline.

Shamanism essentially presents a dualistic vision of the world, but one in which the two worlds can often overlap and the spirit world be perceived through the phenomena of the material world. This attitude has coloured Chinese understanding and relationship to the sacred. It has given the Chinese a sense that all nature is capable of being a reflection of the divine and that the human role is to be in relationship to the rest of nature, not in mastery over it. One of the oldest deities of China is the humble Earth god. He stands as a reminder that even the very ground we stand upon, build upon and live upon has meaning and purpose in its own right. It does not need human activity to make the land meaningful or purposeful. That is inherent. Thus human activity has to work with what already exists in nature, not superimpose upon nature.

CONFUCIANISM

Confucius was born in 552 or 551 BC, very close to the present day town of Qufu, Shandong Province. He later moved into the town itself and today half of the town is taken up with his temple and his House, while outside the town lies the large burial ground where he and his descendants are buried.

Confucius came from an old aristocratic family which had been in decline for a while. Some six or seven hundred years in fact! This gave Confucius a great nostalgia for the past and he despised the forces which had reduced his family so much.

The heart of his teachings was in fact a romantic vision of the past. He was the arch conservative par excellence. To him, the rulers of the past, especially the Five August Rulers who were supposed to have reigned from *c.* 2700 to 2200 BC, were the models which every ruler of his own age should follow. His model ruler is captured in this quote from *The Analects*:

Zi Zhang asked Confucius, 'What must a man be like before he can take part in government?'

The Master said, 'If he honours the five excellent practices and repudiates the four wicked practices he can take part in government.'

Zi Zhang said, 'What is meant by the five excellent practices?'

The Master said, 'The noble leader will be generous to the masses without being extravagant; works others hard without arousing resentment; has wants without being covetous; is magnanimous without being arrogant and is awe inspiring without being fierce.'

Zi Zhang said, 'What is meant by being generous without being extravagant?'

The Master said, 'To give to the masses that which benefits them, is that not being generous without being extravagant? For tasks to be undertaken, choose those who are capable of such a labour, so who will complain? If you wish to be benevolent, how can one be called covetous? The noble leader never dares to forget how to behave whether he is dealing with the masses or the select, with the young or the old. Is this not being magnanimous without being arrogant? A noble leader dresses according to tradition and looks the part. Is this not being awe inspiring without being fierce?'

Zi Zhang asked, 'What is meant by the four wicked practices?'

The Master said, 'To impose the death penalty without first trying to educate people about what is right and wrong, this is cruel; demanding things be done on time without giving due warning and time, that is tyrannical; to let things drift then demand action, that is to cause injury; to be mean minded when giving to others, that is to be bureaucratic.'

(Analects, *XX*, 2. *Author's translation*)

Confucius was hardly a bundle of laughs, a fact which Zhuang Zi, the 4th century BC 'Daoist' writer makes much of in his mocking prose. Yet ironically, Confucius was possibly more 'Daoist' than the 'Daoist' philosophers. In Confucius's writings, he frequently dwells upon the theme of the Dao. For the exploration of the Dao was central to most of the 'One Hundred Schools' of philosophy which sprang up between the 6th and 4th centuries BC. It was a remarkable time to be alive, those centuries, for suddenly China was producing philosophers and thinkers by the dozen. Its only parallel is ancient Greece at almost exactly the same time.

Confucius's teachings had four key strands, which can be summed up in the four Chinese words of Dao, ren, de and li. Dao we have already encountered, though in Confucius's thinking, the Dao is more properly to be understood as being the Way things ought to be done, indeed, were done in the time of the great ancient Emperors such as the Yellow Emperor or Emperor Yao. But at times, Confucius comes very close to the ideas in the *Dao De Jing*:

> When the Dao prevails in the world, the rites, music and punitive military expeditions are initiated by the Emperor (Son of Heaven). When the Dao does not prevail in the world, they are initiated by the lesser lords... When the Dao prevails in the world, policy is not in the hands of the Counsellors. When the Dao prevails in the world, there is nothing for the ordinary people to argue about.
> (Analects, *Book XVI, 2*)

Compare this with the *Dao De Jing*:

> The highest form of government
> Is what people hardly even realize is there.
> Next is that of the sage
> Who is seen, and loved, and respected.
> Next down is the dictatorship
> That thrives on oppression and terror –
> And the last is that of those who lie
> And end up despised and rejected.
> The sage says little –
> and does not tie the people down;

And the people stay happy
Believing that what happens
happens, naturally.
(Chapter 17, Tao Te Ching, *translated by Kwok, Palmer, Ramsay)*

Ren, the second concept, means benevolence. This underpins all Confucius's thoughts. If only people would act benevolently, then everything would be all right. Treat those below you with benevolence and they will treat those beneath them with benevolence and so on down the hierarchical order.

This was not an empty concept. For built into the notion of ren was the assumption that if someone above you did not act in a benevolent way, you could criticize them and remind them of their obligation to do so. Many great and compassionate Confucian scholars did exactly this at tremendous personal risk.

De, the third strand, means virtue and is the second word in the title of the *Dao De Jing*. De means virtue. Virtue was something to be developed so that people learned to control themselves and to understand their place within the greater order:

The Master said, 'Guide them by edicts, keep them in line with punishments, and the common people will stay out of trouble but will have no sense of shame. Guide them by virtue (de), keep them in line with rites, and they will not only have a sense of shame but will reform themselves.
*(*Analects *II, 3)*

Finally, Confucius taught the importance of li – rites or rituals. The word li has a broad meaning, ranging from rituals to do with religious ceremonies such as the sacrifices and prayers at the solstices of the Emperor, through to behaviour within the family and death rituals. Over the years li became an almost impenetrable web of correct behaviour which produced one of the world's most rigid and stratified of cultures.

For underlying all these four strands is hierarchy. Confucius taught that there is a natural hierarchy. At the top is the Emperor, below him his officials, below them the ordinary people. Each group must know its place and must be obedient to those above. Likewise the family has a similar structure, with the oldest male member being the head, his sons below him, their sons below them. The women are all subservient to the men.

When Kong died in 479 BC, he was to all extents and purposes a failure. Hounded from state to state he died at Qufu, Shangdong Province, with a handful of followers. Over the next few hundred years, his teachings were collected and his vision of a structured society began to be actually implemented.

By the time of the Han dynasty (206 BC–220 AD), Confucian teachings had become to all extents and purposes the state religion. The writings associated with Kong had become the set texts of the scholars and it was impossible to progress up the bureaucratic ladder without a deep knowledge of these books. The books fall into two main categories – the Five Classics and the Four Books. From the Han dynasty until the end of the Qing dynasty in 1911 – namely for some 2,000 years – these books formed the core of Chinese scholarship and all life was interpreted through the medium of these books – at least at an official level.

In the late Tang dynasty (*c.* 8th century AD), temples and cultic centres to Kong himself and to his main followers were erected and the official cult of Kong became a standard part of civic life.

In reaction to the mythologizing and spiritualizing of Kong and his teachings, there arose a renewed interest in a scholarly approach to Kong in the Sung dynasty (960–1280 AD) leading to the development of a fresh wave of Confucian thinking and teachings in what is known as Neo-Confucianism. This revitalized the system and opened the door to a wider interaction between Kong's teachings and the immense changes, material and spiritual, which China had undergone in the 1,500 years since Kong's death.

Today Confucianism has no functioning temples nor does it

play any official role in state affairs. The great Confucian temples of China are now silent of worshippers. Yet in becoming, as so many have, museums or libraries, they may have returned to a vision of the importance of learning which is actually closer to the heart of true Confucian values than was the ritual and ceremony of worship.

DAOISM

Daoism, in its two major forms, is a descendant of shamanism. It is the only indigenous religion of China, if you discount Confucianism as a religion. As such it is little understood outside China for it has never, as a religion, sought to convert outside China nor to have any role outside China until the last few decades. Yet one of its core books, the *Dao De Jing*, is amongst the most popular religious texts on sale in the West and its symbol of the yin/yang locked together has passed into Western culture to express a model of relationships which the West does not have, or has not expressed so succinctly.

At one level, Daoism reflects the anti-Confucian values of the shamans; the Way of those who reject hierarchies and controls; who mock 'success' and power; those who take to the mountains to meditate and those who listen to the voices of the spirit world. It is the Way of the spontaneous, the humorous and the quixotic. This is wonderfully captured in the book *Zhuang Zi* (4th century BC). In describing the conventional values of the Confucians who so revered and elevated the rulers of the past, the author, Zhuang Zi mocks them and their pretensions to wisdom and to the superiority of their ordering of life.

As was pointed out in the Confucian section, both Kong Fu Zi and his contemporary Lao Zi were followers of the Dao. It is only historic happenstance that led one particular branch of philosophy and later religious practice to be called Daoism. Lao Zi, Zhuang Zi and others of the era before 100 AD, did not think of themselves as Daoists. They were thinkers and philosophers, responding to the extraordinary outburst of religious and philosophical thought which blossomed from the 6th to 3rd centuries BC in China – the so-called Hundred Schools era.

Their link with shamanism is that they sought to grapple with the nature of Nature and its relationship to this material world and to the world of the spirits. They took the two worlds of shamanism and unified them through the overarching role of the Dao which in their thinking had moved far beyond the moral force of Kong to be the primal energy of the Origin of all beginnings.

The heart of Daoism is captured in Chapter 42 of the *Dao De Jing*:

> The Dao gives birth to the One, the Origin.
> The One, the Origin, gives birth to the Two.
> The Two give birth to the Three.
> The Three give birth to every living thing.

The two referred to here are yin and yang and the three are the Triad of Heaven, Earth and Humanity.

To understand Daoism, let's start with those ancient philosophers who first developed the notion of the Cosmic Dao as illustrated above.

Lao Zi

Lao Zi is possibly one of the most elusive of all religious founder figures. When the first great historian of China, Si Ma Qian (1st century BC) tried to write a biography of him, he says that he was mystified by the lack of any specific information. All he could record was that Lao zi was born sometime in the 6th century BC in a village in the state of Ch'u, became the state archivist in the state of Chou and that he met Kong – as described in the earlier account by Zhuang Zi.

Legend doesn't provide much more. The heart of the Lao Zi story is not really his life – with the exception of the story about his encounter with Lao Zi – but about his departure from China, or indeed possibly his death. It is said that Lao Zi despaired of the state of China and packed his bags to leave. Heading West – the direction of enlightenment as the East is for Europe – he stopped for the night with the gatekeeper of the Pass over the mountains to the West. The gatekeeper asked him to leave a message or teaching for those left behind and legend tells that Lao Zi wrote the *Dao De Jing* that night. Handing it over to the gatekeeper, he then departed West and was never seen again.

Who was Lao Zi was? Did he really write any or all of the *Dao De Jing*? Did he ever 'go West' or is that simply a term meaning he died? All these are unanswerable questions. They are then thrown into even greater uncertainty by the later traditions which make Lao Zi one of the three divine beings who have existed since before Creation – manifestations of the Dao as Origin of Origins.

It is perhaps of the nature of Daoism that such questions cannot be answered, for one key tenet of Daoism in its most philosophical phase – 6th to 3rd century BC – is the inadequacy of words to deal with the divine or the sublime. The *Dao De Jing* itself is quite clear about this,

> The Dao that can be talked about is not the true Dao…
> The name that can be named is not the eternal Name.

Zhuang Zi

Zhuang Zi, who lived *c.* 386–369 BC and is counted as Daoism's second greatest thinker, makes much the same point in his writings and adds to this the question, how do we know what reality really is anyway, even if we could find the words to describe it! The famous butterfly dream from chapter 2 of *Zhuang Zi* illustrates this:

> Once upon a time, I, Chuang Tzu, dreamt that I was a butterfly, flitting around and enjoying myself. I had no idea I was Chuang Tzu. Then suddenly I woke up and was Chuang Tzu again. But I could not tell, had I been

Chuang Tzu dreaming I was a butterfly, or a butterfly dreaming I was now Chuang Tzu? However, there must be some sort of difference between Chuang Tzu and a butterfly! We call this the transformation of things.

(Page 20, The Book of Chuang Tzu, *translated by Martin Palmer with Elizabeth Breuilly)*

Daoism as Religion

The quest for personal salvation and meaning in China only began to surface in the 3rd century BC. Prior to this it would appear that life after death was considered of less importance than just being an ancestor, and only the ancestors of the rich and powerful – especially the ruling families – were considered truly significant. The ritual actions of the emperors each year at the Temple of Heaven and the Temple of Earth, rituals carried out for over 2,000 years, right up until 1924, symbolize the old model of the human relationship with Heaven. Namely, all that was required was for the ruling Son of Heaven to speak on behalf of all people to Heaven and to Earth and all would be well. Individual meaning and purpose was to be found in one's place within the hierarchy of society and within the communal life of the extended family or clan.

The rise of a quest for personal salvation came at the time of the unification of China under the first true emperor of China, Qin Shi Huang Di, in 220 BC and the gradual collapse of local states and their cultures, including the old mythologies and beliefs of given areas. The unification of land undertaken by Qin Shi Huang Di was replicated by the unification of language carried out by order of Qin Shi Huang Di and the unification or suppression of local cultures and beliefs. These sweeping changes were instigated by the Confucian scholars, keen to superimpose a coherent ideology at a scholarly and official level. The resulting dislocation of people from their own local cultures is perhaps one of the reasons for the growth of a desire to find meaning in new forms, given that the older cultural expressions had collapsed into the vastness of the Empire of China.

Whatever the reasons, in the early 2nd century AD a new expression of religion arose, building upon the back of shamanism; drawing inspiration, imagery and eventually even gods from the philosophical writers of Daoism.

The origins of this religious development lie in the province of Sichuan, where a remarkable man called Zhang Dao Ling was born at some point in the 1st century or possibly even early 2nd century. A deeply religious individual, his early life is lost in a welter of legends, but it is clear that he was a remarkable child, reputed to have mastered and understood the *Dao De Jing* by the age of seven. At some point he retreated from ordinary life to the sacred mountain of Qing Cheng Shan in Sichuan where he meditated for some three years or so and then began to teach. The cave where he lived and from which he preached is still there and is a major site of religious pilgrimage, exuding a remarkable sense of peace and tranquillity (see page 296).

One day in 142 AD, Zhang Dao Ling received a most extraordinary revelation. Sitting meditating, he suddenly found Lao Zi standing before him.

Lao Zi gave Zhang the authority to organize religious communities, to forgive faults and sins, to heal and, most important of all, to exorcize ghosts, demons and evil spirits. Lao Zi also gave Zhang a demon-slaying sword with which he could cause any demon to be trapped and defeated. Zhang is usually depicted holding this sword, of very ancient design, as a badge of his authority.

Zhang organized the first full-scale religious expression of Daoism and his Five Bushels movement, named after the entry fee of five bushels of rice, soon spread across Sichuan and into neighbouring provinces. Zhang organized his followers, whose fee entitled them to forgiveness of their sins and entry into the cosmic Covenant established with Lao Zi, into parishes and dioceses, very similar to that of the Christian Church in its Roman Catholic or Anglican forms.

r the next 500 years, many different schools of Daoism arose focusing around revelations, healing, ritual, oracles, shamanic practices, developing monasteries and nunneries inspired by Buddhism, and establishing a network of temples or control over a network of temples throughout southern China.

By 471 AD Daoism was sufficiently developed to have issued its first Canonical selection of texts, which listed over 1,200 books. These books came from the three great traditions which had been established by then. These three still exist today and along with one other later tradition, constitute the four great schools of Daoism.

The Celestial Masters School

The first school is that of Zhang Dao Ling's descendants, the Celestial Masters' School, also known as the Orthodox Path Way – Zhengyi. Its main strength today lies in its network of 'parish priests' who minister to the faithful at the local level and who might be called upon to exorcise ghosts and demons, using the magic formulae of Zhang Dao Ling. The current Celestial Master, directly descended from Zhang Dao Ling, lives in Taiwan, whence the family fled after the fall of the Kuomingtang government in 1949. However, other members of the family continue to live in China and Zhang Ji Yu, 68th in descent from Zhang Dao Ling, heads a major research section of the China Daoist Association and has not only helped reprint the entire Daoist Canon, but also produced the first *Encyclopedia of Daoism*.

The Mao Shan School

The second school is that of Mao Shan, named after Mao mountain in Jiangsu Province. Its founder was a woman called Wei Hua Cun. She often went into shamanic trances and received revelations and visits from the gods. When she died her son continued her teachings and drew in one very important convert called Yang Xi. In 364 AD Yang Xi was summoned

by spirits to Mao Shan where he was visited by Wei Hua
With her were a host of immortals and deities and toget
they dictated a vast corpus of scripture which supplemented
that revealed to Wei Hua Cun in her lifetime. The texts are
known as the Shang Qing Scriptures and after many strange
and sad adventures, they have found a central place in the
Daoist Canon.

The texts are visionary, advocating long meditational practices and prescribing alchemical formulae for immortality.
These formulae have about them an eschatalogical quality, as
if the world was about to end, and tell how to escape the coming catastrophe.

The Ling Bao School

The third school is that of the Ling Bao tradition. Ling Bao
means 'sacred jewel' and this refers to the sacred texts at the
heart of the school. No revealer or Covenant with Lao Zi is
associated with these texts, for they are deemed to have a very
special history. Followers of Ling Bao say that when yin and
yang erupted into being at the start of time, and when the primal breath qi arose, at the same time the texts of the Ling Bao
came into existence written in golden letters on tablets of
purest jade. Preserved and studied by the gods, the texts were
at last handed on to Daoist adepts when the gods deemed
them ready to understand their profundity.

In fact the core of the Ling Bao tradition is that it makes the
more esoteric elements of the Celestial Master's school available, usable and comprehensible to the ordinary lay Daoist.
Through ritual, liturgies and popular texts, the Ling Bao tradition has fed popular Daoism with some of the fruits of the
Celestial Master's teaching.

These three schools merged in the thirteenth century and
although their separate traditions still exist and are referred
to as being distinct, they all function today as essentially part
of the Zhengyi expression of Daoism and are strongest in
the South of China. Their headquarters until recently was
Longhu Shan in Jiangxi Province, the legendary Dragon Tiger

mountain of the Celestial Masters, where the magic sword of Zhang Dao Ling hung until recently. The Celestial Family were evicted in 1927 but the temples and shrines have recently been restored and the mountain has once again become a Daoist centre.

The Quan Zhen school

The final school comes from much later and is primarily the work of two extraordinary men. The school is known as the Quan Zhen school and dates from the twelfth century AD. It stands apart from the Zhengyi tradition and is based in the north of China. Its founders were Wang Chong Yang and Qiu Changchun. Wang lived in the mid-12th century and in 1167 founded the Quan Zhen in Shandong Province. Wang claimed to have been given his teachings by one of the most famous and loved of the Eight Immortals, Lu Dong Bin (see pages 122–3), and for this reason Lu Dong Bin is held in highest regard by the followers of Quan Zhen. The school emphasizes retreat from the world and hence has a strong monastic dimension. It also practises quite extreme forms of meditation and self-denial. Wang is reputed to have stood for two years in a hole in the ground, ten feet down, in order not to fall asleep. See page 106 for further details of the beliefs of Quan Zhen.

The Teachings of Daoism

Having looked briefly at the main traditions, it is time to look also at what Daoism teaches and at how it manifests itself in the China of today – what you as a traveller can observe or participate in.

Daoism has four main strands, cosmological liturgy, magic, longevity and the quest for immortality.

Let's look first at cosmological liturgy.

Cosmological Liturgy

If you visit a Daoist temple, you will often find yourself in a microcosmic representation of the cosmos. This is especially true on sacred mountains such as Tai Shan. But more important than this are the cosmic liturgies which you will hear being chanted or, if you are very lucky, you might even see being enacted through dance and ritual.

The role of Daoist ritual is to retain and maintain the balance between yin and yang, Heaven and Earth, and thus ensure the continuation of life itself. Through ritual, Daoists act out the role of humanity in balancing the forces of the cosmos in order that yin and yang might be able to continue to spark the creation of life which arises from their dynamic opposition, but without burning out the cosmos.

Daoism lives out the core classic Chinese philosophy which chapter 42 of the *Dao De Jing* spells out – see page 31. Namely, it follows the Dao, from which all origins arise. From the Origin came yin and yang and from yin and yang came Heaven, Earth and humanity. This is the cosmic framework of Daoism, visible in its teachings and in its architecture.

In balancing yin and yang, Daoists seek to be true followers of the Dao, for the Dao is ultimately how existence is. To be a true Daoist, you need to go with the flow, not fight against it. If you go with the flow, you can achieve anything, but so much of human society is falsely constructed that this is very hard. Here we see the shamanic roots of Daoism. The worlds of material and spiritual must be kept in balance and it is only by sublimating the material world to the spiritual that success can be achieved. But the Daoists go beyond the shamans. The Daoists, through their liturgies, believe that they can shape and influence both the spirit and material worlds. Indeed, Daoism believes that through the liturgies, the whole cosmos can be shaped and affected, so long as this is done within the overall flow of the Dao.

A story might help illustrate this. Wang Chong Yang, the founder of Quan Zhen Daoism, was once teaching a certain Lady Sun Bu Er the techniques of Inner alchemy. He taught her to draw a circle which stands as the image of the matrix and of the world as chaos. In the centre he placed a dot, to represent Taiji, the Great Ultimate, the One referred to in chapter 42 of the *Dao De Jing*.

Lady Sun Bu Er went home and began to practise her meditations using this image. She fasted and ignored all around her for weeks, concentrating only on this image and its profound meaning.

One day, to her considerable astonishment, Wang visited her and came into her room, catching her in her meditations. He took one look at her and said, 'Well now! All ways are equally good, it is all really the same: let go, be spontaneous. You are trying too hard, sitting here by yourself in the cold. What is the purpose of all this? Eh! Do you not know that yin by itself cannot give birth to life; that yang by itself cannot find its heart, its centre? This way of yours, all by yourself, means yin and yang will never meet you now! However will you become pregnant and carry the child? Believe me, this here cannot exist without that there; and that there needs this here.'

Poor Lady Sun Bu Er was terribly embarrassed by all this but eventually she came to understand what Wang meant. To have balance within one's self, means you must be in balance with what is around you, your environment. Don't ignore or fight it. Become one with it. Do not go against nature, for that is to go against the Dao. Abandon yourself to where you are and through this you can transcend the here and now, move out into the whirl of chaos which is chance and finally emerge at the point of Taiji, of One and be united with the flow of the Dao which moves through and in all things.

This is what Daoist liturgy does at one level. It reunites you with the Dao, with the whirl of chance and the abandonment to nature. Yet it also structures and rebuilds broken relationships within the Dao. It asks you to halt your attempts to impose your order on chance and chaos and life – on the dynamics of yin and yang. Instead it asks you to let go, to float with the Dao and to be carried by it to who knows where.

Daoist liturgy also involves controlling those forces which threaten the flow and balance of yin and yang and the Dao. As such the liturgies become part of the dynamic struggle of existence, which in Daoist terms is translated into battles with evil forces and demons, adverse influences and inauspicious signs, which are combated by good forces, gods and goddesses, auspicious signs and helpful auguries.

You can observe these liturgies at all the major function- ing Daoist temples. For example, the White Cloud Temple – Bai Yun Guan – in Beijing has an impressive liturgy most days and especially at festivals such as New Year, Qing Ming or at occasions such as the ordination of new monks. But daily liturgy is performed and the temple has not only a magnificent choir but an orchestra as well. Recordings of the White Cloud Temple liturgies are on sale and are found at all the major Daoist sites.

On the Daoist sacred mountains, those which are still allowed to function, for example, Hua Shan in Shaanxi, Song Shan in Henan, Lao Shan in Shandong Province and Qing Cheng Shan in Sichuan Province, the liturgies can also be heard. Many of the mountains have special festivals associated with them which involve vast country fairs. At such times special liturgies are performed.

Visit a major Daoist temple such as the Temple of the Eight Immortals in Xian, the Temple of Eternal Spring – Chang Chun Guan – in Wuhan, Hubei or the Temple of Supreme Purity – Tai Qing Gong – in Shenyang, Liaoning, and you will be able to listen to the liturgies being sung each day. It is a matter of timing it right, and whilst generally early morning and late afternoon or early evening are the best times, this can differ depending upon which school runs the temple and what calendar day it is.

Magic

The second strand in Daoist teachings is magic. The magic of spells and incantations; of charms and amulets; of battling with evil cosmic forces and of dealing with disease brought about by bad influences and demons. This is still a very important aspect of Daoism. At all the major temples and mountains you can buy charms for exorcism, long life, good health and so forth. Most of these carry the picture of Zhang Dao Ling because he above all others is the great magician. He is usually depicted with his sword, though sometimes he simply holds the yin/yang symbol. Again, the reason why Daoists battle with evil and use magic is to restore the balance of yin and yang. Much of what the outside world sees as magic is to the Daoist simply the effect of tapping into the powers of the Dao and the forces of yin and yang and restoring the balance.

Longevity

The third strand is longevity, which can be combined with the fourth strand immortality, but I will treat them separately here. The quest for long life is one of the four cardinal hopes of the Chinese. A traditional blessing hopes that you will 'live long, grow fat, have many children and be wealthy'. Long life is associated with good deeds. Popular booklets at Buddhist temples teach this quite explicitly. In Daoism, longevity is linked to practices such as Taiqi with its physical and meditational techniques, with diet, with mystical processes involving invoking the gods and goddesses within your own body, and with balancing the yin and yang within ourselves – for all living things have yin and yang in balance within them.

Chinese religion and indeed Chinese home life and art are full of symbols of longevity. The crane, peaches, jade, mushrooms and bats are just some of the symbols of long life. Fascination with long life still influences China today, even in its most secular form. Travel through Peng Shan, near Leshan, Sichuan and you will find a vast Socialist Realist statue of the famous Peng Zi, renowned as the person reputed to have lived longer than anyone else in China and revered as a god of long life. Furthermore, the noodles of this area, which are reputed to confer longevity, are in great demand.

For many lay Daoists, the pursuit of longevity is the essence of their daily following of Daoism. It informs their diet, their lifestyle – to the extent that they have control over this – and their physical exercises. It is still common to find people of all ages, early in the morning or in the cool of the evening, doing Taiqi and other such systems of slow, meditative exercises, all designed to help the body last as long as possible and conserve and rebuild the essential breath of life within which is known as the qi.

Immortality

I was once in a Daoist temple outside Xian when an old monk approached me in a most furtive way. He told me in whispered confidences that he could bestow upon me for 'a hundred foreign dollars', the gift of immortality. Naturally I was intrigued. This is not the sort of offer one gets everyday! Indicating that I was interested to learn more, I was led away to the warren-like dwellings at the back of the temple where the monks live. A grubby curtain was pushed aside and I was ushered into a filthy little room. Declining his kind offer to sit in case I caught something lethal, he rummaged around under his bed and finally pulled out an old bag. From within this he extracted a wizened old fruit of indeterminate species and offered it to me. This I was led to believe was the Peach of Immortality, mine for just US$100! I declined as gracefully as possible and beat a hasty retreat.

But this quest for immortality is a central concern to this day of Daoism. Immortality is not considered some far fetched idea, but is in many ways the main goal of much of Daoist practice. Indeed, when the China Daoist Association produced their definition of Daoism in English for the Summit of Religions and Conservation at Windsor Castle in 1995, they pointed to the quest for immortality as being one of two main precepts of Daoism.

This is really the distinguishing feature of Daoism. For Daoism teaches that it is possible to live forever. What is fascinating about Daoism is that in teaching this, it does not adopt the usual stance of religions which is to see the soul as eternal and the body as temporary. Indeed some religions even see the body as a positive hindrance, an obstacle to true spiritual growth. Not so Daoism. In fact, quite the reverse. In Daoism, you can only achieve immortality if you can preserve this physical body and thus continue to exist in this physical frame.

The pursuit of immortality goes way back into Chinese history. One of the greatest of all Chinese sites is just outside Xian: the wonderful terracotta army of the first Emperor of China, Qin Shi Huang Di (died 210 BC). Surrounding his tomb

42

– itself a small hill in size – are thousands of terracotta models of soldiers. Buried in pits, they were placed there to protect the Emperor in death from attacks by the ghosts of the thousands he had had killed during his lifetime. This was but the last of a series of desperate attempts by this tyrannical but brilliant ruler to ensure his long life and then his immortality. Qin Shi tried every possible means to ensure immortality. He employed hundreds of shamans and alchemists to try and find magic mushrooms, elixirs of life and pills of immortality. He sent boatloads of people off into the oceans to try and find the magical islands of Peng Lai where the ingredients for the pill of immortality could be obtained. Following the advice of one of his advisers, who said the emperor would live for ever if he was never seen by his people, Qin Shi built over 70 miles of covered corridors linking his various palaces. He venerated the gods and goddesses of Tai Shan in Shandong, greatest of the sacred mountains of China, believing this would confer immortality upon him. All to no avail.

In building his tomb, Qin Shi hoped to protect himself in the afterlife. Being entombed meant of course that he had failed in his quest for immortality. He had died. Yet strangely enough, it is actually his tomb which has ensured his immortality as it has become the greatest tourist site in China after the Forbidden City and the Great Wall!

The historian Si Ma Qian (1st century BC) comments that all the emperors seem to have been obsessed with the quest for immortality, and vast fortunes were spent in the pursuit of this dream. Thus the quest for immortality pre-dates the emergence of religious expressions of Daoism, but is present in the writings of some of the Daoist philosophers.

As it developed in Daoism itself, and as it is expressed to this day, the quest took two forms, what one might call the External School and the Internal School.

Daoism, along with much of the rest of classic Chinese philosophy, teaches that the body is animated by containing the original breath, the breath of life – qi – which arises within the body at conception. If this breath can be sustained then the body will last forever. This is the focus of the Internal School of Immortality. Daoism also teaches that if the physical body can be made permanent, then one can live for ever. This means replacing the perishable element of the body with imperishable material. How is this done? Through ingesting imperishable materials. This is the External school.

While there are some who still practise aspects of the External School, it is unlikely that you will meet them. It is a system which has had many unfortunate consequences, as well as some unexpectedly significant consequences.

As I have mentioned, the aim of the External School was to replace the perishable parts of the body with imperishable materials. To do this Daoist initiates in this tradition ate gold, jade and mercury. These materials do not perish or tarnish. They seem indestructible. Hence their use in alchemical concoctions for transforming the body. Unfortunately, they can also be lethal, and many aspiring immortals died early and often painful deaths from these materials.

Less dramatic methods involved the use of herbs. None of these methods are actually credited with working. But their experiments produced interesting results. Through their alchemical work in trying to transmute their own bodies by metals, jade and herbs and in the quest for the alchemical formula to transmute base metals into gold, the early Daoists made many significant scientific discoveries. They developed methodological ways of testing and analysing the components of certain materials and observed the effects heat had on substances. However, in terms of the immortality they sought, it was a failure. But the attempt went on for centuries, resulting in a massive study of the available formulae produced in the mid-2nd century AD which was the first attempt to deal with the various traditions systematically. However, this book is virtually unintelligible!

Perhaps the best that can be said about this tradition in the quest for immortality, is to quote the wise words of one failed seeker after External transformation immortality, the Emperor Wu of the Han dynasty (ruled 141–87 BC):

If we are temperate in our diet and use medicine, we make our illnesses few. That is all we can attain to.

The second School, that of the Internal tradition is the one which continues to this day and exerts considerable influence over Daoism. Its main proponents are the Quan Zhen School of Daoism, though it is used by all the major Daoist traditions.

Quite simply, this School concentrated upon internal transformations. Rather than seeking to change the external body into an imperishable body through ingesting materials, this looked within and took a moral, ethical and practical line, designed to focus attention upon creating a purer being, whose body would thus be purer.

The heart of this tradition sees the body as being given life and as being sustained by two forces. The first and the most vital force is energy or breath which energizes the body. This is qi, the breath which enters the body at birth and which must be sustained. Daoism, however, identifies various kinds of qi in the body, not all of which are benevolent. Thus it is central to Daoist practices in the Internal School, to develop and aid those forms of qi which are benevolent, while suppressing those that are malevolent. In particular, attention is paid to the Embryonic Breath – the breath of your birth. To sustain and even increase this breath meant increasing or sustaining life. In classic Chinese physiological thought, the original breath entered at birth and contained all the breath that you would have to live with. Over the years, this breath gets used up and death comes when the last whiff of the original breath, the Embryonic Breath, passes from your body. Hence the concentration on breathing exercises in Daoism and on diet. Breath escapes not just through natural breathing. Eating the wrong kinds of foods can cause burping and farting. These are disastrous, not because of social embarrassment but because they are escapes of the Embryonic Breath and thus cut down on your lifespan.

Daoism has perfected many techniques for meditational breathing and with it many techniques for building up parts of

45

the body and of focusing upon the inner workings of the body. Through this, Daoism has contributed much to traditional Chinese medicine.

But perhaps the most famous way in which Daoism sought to create an internal body capable of living forever, is the attempt to form a new body, an Embryonic body within the old one. This involves the creation of an internal foetus within the human body which can emerge at the death of the old body and, with no break in existence, carry the soul of the individual onwards into renewed if not eternal life. In some traditions this was done by contemplation, by entering one's own body through meditation and beginning to create a new body. This is still a common form of the quest for immortality in China today, and one favoured especially by the Quan Zhen School. But there was, and perhaps still is one other way. This is known as the sexual technique.

The semen of a man is seen as being one of the two vital energy or life sources he is born with. Alongside the Embryonic Breath a man is born with his semen. This does not just create new lives through sexual intercourse, but it also sustains his own life. Thus, in classic Daoist sexual teachings, every time a man makes love to a woman, he loses something of his vital life energy. From this belief came the notion of activating and then retaining the semen within a man's own body. The semen was seen to be the vital yang force within a man which made him a man. The woman, as yin, was seen to desire this yang force to maintain her own life energy.

Daoism, like all major religions, is patriarchal and thus the man's need for regeneration of his creative energy was considered more important than the woman's. Techniques were developed whereby a man could climax sexually with a woman but retain his semen which then went to feed and nurture his embryonic body within. The Daoist Canon used to contain quite a number of texts explicitly detailing these sexual practices, but most of them were censored and removed over 600 years ago and the tradition is now quite limited in its scale and scope.

The Internal School combines its mainstream teachings with what can best be described as a moral dimension to the quest for immortality. Contrasting sharply with the earlier ethos of the emperors of the Qin and Han dynasties who sought immortality in order to continue to rule, Daoism developed a benevolent, compassionate dimension in its concern for immortality. Mirroring, indeed probably inspired by the Buddhist concept of the Compassionate Bodhisattva (see below), Daoism emphasizes that the moral worthiness of an individual is important in the quest for immortality. This is succinctly expressed by one of the greatest of all Daoist writers, Ge Hong (late-3rd to early-4th century AD) in his monumental work on Daoist practices, which stands as one of the key texts of Daoism today, the *Bao Pu Zi* – *Book of the Preservation of Solidarity Master*:

> Those who do not carry out acts of virtue and are satisfied only to practise magical procedures will never obtain life eternal.

This brings us to the text which has most shaped popular Daoism down the ages. The *Tai Shang Gan Ying Pian* – meaning *The Great Supreme One's* [Lao Zi] *Treatise on Response and Retribution*. Written in the twelfth century AD, this book, claiming to be a revelation from Lao Zi, has been reproduced more times than any other book in China. Merely to print or distribute copies of it was and is considered to be a meritworthy act which will ensure good fortune in this life and the next. It is essentially a book of morally improving proverbs, lists of good and bad acts and a collection of morality tales. The opening verses of the fourth chapter spell out its core philosophy – one which is still very much central to Daoism today:

> If you are with the Dao you will advance.
> If you are not with the Dao you will regress.
> Do not take the Way of evil.
> Do nothing wrong in the dark.

Accumulate virtue and increase your rewards.
Be compassionate to all creatures.
(Author's translation)

The quest for immortality fuses with this moral outlook to produce the notion of the Immortals themselves. These are the most common figures to be found in Daoist temples and monasteries and their importance is enormous. We shall encounter some of them later in this book.

Daoism Today

This century has seen more sustained attempts to wipe out Daoism than in the entire rest of the history of Daoism. Daoism has not been well considered by its own country since the coming of the Republic in 1911. Viewed by the West as little more than superstitious nonsense and without the links overseas of all the other faiths of China, Daoism has been deprived of most of its buildings, lands and prestige ever since 1911. In the south of China, many Daoist temples were destroyed by the Taiping rebellion from 1850 to 1864, which seized the whole of the south of China and very nearly toppled the Qing dynasty. Inspired by a fusion of Christianity and apocalyptic folk religion, the Taiping rebels took particular delight in destroying Daoist temples.

Today Daoism is recovering from the most terrible assault it has ever undergone. The two major traditions, Zhengyi and Quan Zhen continue to be the mainspring of Daoism and are working together to revive Daoism which nearly died out under the Cultural revolution of 1966 to 1975. Virtually all Daoist temples, monasteries and shrines were destroyed. Vast quantities of religious texts, statues and objects were smashed, burned or looted. Daoist monks and nuns were forced to return to ordinary life and religious practices were forbidden, or so severely restricted as to be virtually non-existent. Few places escaped the ravages at this time and where they did, it was usually through the bravery of local people who defended their sites (as happened to some degree on Qingcheng Shan in Sichuan).

But Daoism is slowly recovering. According to the China Daoist Association, a new temple or shrine – often in small villages or towns and associated with local cults – opens every day in Southern China, which is where Daoism is strongest. Many of the ancient sites have been returned to the Daoists, though without any of the control over the land or mountains that they used to have. Thus Daoist monks are at work on most of the great Daoist sacred mountains such as Hua Shan and Song Shan. But a mountain such as Heng Shan in Shanxi Province is still closed to monks, and the temples are simply used as tourist attractions and hotels.

The Daoist Association records a dramatic rise in the number of those being ordained. In 1985 there were 2,500 ordained monks. In 1995 there were 12,000. This is still a long way away from the pre-1949 number of monks, estimated at hundreds of thousands, but there does appear to be a genuine revival in interest in Daoism. Traditionally Daoist monks have come from Daoist families. As the monks and priests can marry (except in the Quan Zhen school) there is the possibility of hereditary monks. Many can claim descent from founder figures such as Zhang Dao Ling or Wang Chong Yang. However, with the enormous shake up of Daoism that has been the feature of virtually the whole of this century, the old established patterns have changed and monks are now being accepted from all walks of life. What remains to be seen is whether the growing interest in Daoism outside China will have an impact on Chinese Daoism and if so in what ways.

BUDDHISM

According to tradition, Buddhism arrived in China as a result of a dream. In the year 64 AD, the Han dynasty Emperor Ming (58–75 AD) had a dream one night. In his dream he saw a golden deity flying before his palace. The next morning he asked his advisers what this could mean. One of them, Fu Yi, said he had heard that in India there was a sage who had achieved

49

Buddhahood, who could fly at will and whose body was golden. Hearing this, the Emperor despatched envoys to India to bring back the teachings and statues of this deity. The envoys returned some years later, bearing with them upon the back of two white horses, statues and the text of the Forty Two Article Sutra (see Luoyang and the Ba Ma Si page 268).

Teachings of the Golden Deity – The Buddha

Historically, the Buddha was born around 560 BC in present-day Nepal. He came from the royal family and legend tells that his father tried to prevent him from seeing the realities of the world because of a prophecy given at his birth. It was said that the young prince would either become a great king or a great sage. His father wanted a king-son to succeed him. But his precautions were to no avail. One day, when Gautoma Siddhartha was in his mid-twenties and already married with a child, he persuaded his charioteer to take him out into the city.

When they ventured forth, Siddhartha saw four sights which he had never seen before. He saw an old man, a sick man, a corpse and a wandering holy man who had forsaken all life's pleasures. Realizing that the suffering he saw was part of life, he determined to find a way through such suffering. Leaving the palace and his family one night, he went into the forests to search for the true meaning of life. For many years he tried every known means of mediation and ascetic practices. He fasted until he was nothing but skin and bones, but then realized that this was as pointless as the previously luxurious and materialist life he had led in the palace. Eventually, when he was 53, he sat beneath a bodhi tree and sought the Middle Path between luxury and asceticism. Enlightenment came when he realized the Four Noble Truths and the Eight Fold Path.

The Four Noble Truths are:

1 That all life is suffering.
2 That we create this suffering for ourselves by trying to cling to passing pleasures which, because they are

ephemeral, die and leave us saddened, so we then start worrying about holding onto pleasures and suffer even more.

3 If only we could learn to let go of this craving or desire for happiness and stop clinging to that which will pass, we would stop suffering.

4 Through the Eight Fold Path, we can in fact do just this and thus achieve release from the wheel of suffering and of birth, death and rebirth.

The Eightfold Path involves having the right views; thinking right thoughts; making sure our speech is right; doing what is right – i.e. not killing, stealing or injuring; having a job which is right in that it causes no distress; having the right attitude to put the effort into living this path; having right mindfulness and finally having right concentration.

The Buddha taught for many years, eventually dying in his 80s. He ensured his teachings would continue by developing a body of teaching called the Dharma and an organizational structure of monks and nuns who would pass on the teaching, the Sangha.

This is the traditional picture of the historical Buddha in Theravada teachings. In Mahayana tradition, and as depicted in paintings in Chinese temples such as the Guan Yin temple at Datong, Shanxi Province, or carved into the walls of the Luoyang caves in Henan Province, the story becomes some-what more fantastic and cosmic. Sakyamuni has hundreds of previous lives, many of which are retold in legends known as the Jataka stories. In the era or aeon before this one, he was a bodhisattva. In this era he has come to recall people to the knowledge of their Buddha-nature. He is depicted in Mah-ayana scriptures as leading a cosmic life, moving from one vast gathering of the gods and deities to another, in a divine way, unlinked to any historical chronology. He transcends time and place in the Mahayana tradition.

At first Buddhism was taken to be a form of Daoism, for not only did the Buddhist translators use Daoist terms to try and express the complex Sanskrit teachings of Buddhism, but the Daoists added to this confusion by claiming either that the Buddha was none other than Lao Zi who, you will recall, left China and went West, or that the Buddha was a pupil of Lao Zi who didn't really grasp the finer points of Daoism and then set up his own School, which is how Buddhism came into being. Thus it was that for at least the first two centuries of its existence in China (1st to 2nd centuries AD), Buddhism was perceived by most as just another variety of the religious expressions of Daoism which also arose at this time.

However, by the 5th century, Buddhism was clearly seen and experienced to be a distinct religion and the rivalry between Daoists, Confucians and Buddhists which was from time to time to break into persecution over the next thousand years, was set.

By the 6th century Buddhism was an established part of the religious, philosophical and artistic world of China, with countless temples and hundreds of monasteries being established and embellished, but with the texts still coming primarily from India and having to be translated.

Schools of Buddhism

Dhyana
The original form of Buddhism to reach China is known as the Dhyana School which stressed individual effort and the suppression of passions as the way to release from the cycle of birth, death and rebirth. This drew its inspiration from the Theravada tradition of Buddhism. Theravada means the teachings of the Elders and is seen as the version of Buddhism closest to the teachings of the historical Buddha. The Theravada tradition teaches that personal effort is the only way to enlightenment and to release from the wheel of suffering and rebirth. It stresses suppression of desire as being the way to end the craving for permanence which feeds the wheel of suffering through karma. It focuses upon the individual following paths of meditation and concentration which bring the initiate

to enlightenment, or failing that to ensure that in his or her next life they can continue on this path towards eventual extinction of emotion, the ending of karma and thus release from rebirth.

Prajna

By the late-3rd to early-4th centuries AD, a second strand was appearing in China. This is the Prajna School, based upon the Mahayana tradition of Buddhism. While the Theravada stressed individual journeying along the path to enlightenment and release, Mahayana advocated the intervention of bodhisattvas – beings who had rid themselves of all desire, all karma. Beings who over countless lives had built up vast reserves of merit which they used to rescue suffering beings from the consequences of bad actions. In other words a salvationary form of Buddhism, designed to appeal to those who could not face, fund or endure the rigours of the Theravada tradition. The name Mahayana means the Greater Vehicle, for this tradition sees itself as offering a greater vehicle by which large numbers can be saved from the wheel of suffering and rebirth. They mockingly call the Theravada Buddhists Hinayana, meaning Lesser Vehicle, signifying their belief that that tradition can only save a very few.

While the Dhyana School in China produced some of the finest developments of philosophical Buddhism, in particular the Chan tradition, which when it was taken to Japan became known as Zen, it is the Prajna School which has most shaped popular Buddhism and still does so to this day. Of the traditions within the Prajna School, the most influential has been the Pure Land branch.

Pure Land Buddhism

The name Pure Land comes from the school's central text, the Sukhavativyuha, or Pure Land Sutra which focuses upon a discussion supposed to have taken place between Sakyamuni Buddha – the historical Buddha – and his favourite disciple, Ananda. They discuss a monk called Dharmakara who visited a former living Buddha (Chinese Buddhism believes there have been many 'incarnations' or manifestations of the Ultimate Buddha-nature in human form upon the earth). Dharmakara asked the Buddha for a description of the perfect Buddha world and the perfect Buddha. Having heard the descriptions, the monk then asked that when he had gained enough merit, he wished to be reborn as the Buddha ruling such a Buddha world of bliss, a Pure Land.

In the Sutra, we are told that Dharmakara asked his question countless aeons ago, innumerable lifetimes upon lifetimes ago. At some time in this vast immeasurable past, Dharmakara had his wish fulfilled and entered upon his last rebirth as the Buddha Amitabha ruling over the Western Paradise known as Sukhavati. To this wonderful place, Amitabha Buddha brings those whom he saves.

The promise of being rescued from the dreadful fate of constant rebirth and the awful punishments meted out in the Eighteen Buddhist Hells, was one which went down well with the faithful and especially with the not so faithful!

Boddhisattvas

Other Sutras and schools arose offering a similar hope. The Lotus Sutra, for example, is probably the most popular Sutra in China. In this lovely book, the Buddha discusses how those in turmoil and strife can be rescued by compassionate bodhisattvas. Of these, the most important is the bodhisattva Avalokitesvara, translated into Chinese as Guan Yin, the One who Hears the Cries of the World. See pages 91–8.

This tradition of compassionate beings, Buddhas and bodhisattvas forms the backbone of the majority of Buddhist temples and sites from the 7th century AD onwards. It is still the backbone of Buddhism in China today.

The rise of salvationary, compassionate Bodhisattva Buddhism was quite spectacular. It helped Buddhism to move from being a courtly and scholarly interest into being a mass movement.

Chan Buddhism

The exception to this rule of preference for Prajna is the growth of Chan and in particular the popularity of its founder, Bodhidharma – known in Chinese as Da Mo.

Bodhidharma was an Indian monk who, it is claimed in some sources, arrived by ship, landing at the southern port of Guangzhou around 520 AD.

Upon his arrival, he went straight to Nanking to visit the ruler of the State of Liang, China at that time being in a state of disunity with a number of rival states having come into existence.

Bodhidharma – Da Mo – had come to Liang because the ruler, Emperor Wu, was known as a protector of Buddhism. Da Mo lost no time in telling the Emperor that everything the Emperor had done to date was worthless because no matter how meritorious his actions, they were pointless because he did not have the crucial key to understanding. This key to understanding was that everything was nothing.

This is the core of the school of Buddhism that Bodhidharma developed, known as Chan Buddhism, or better known in the West by its Japanese name, Zen. The heart of his teaching is the rejection of sutras, discussions or academic study in favour of the exclusive use of meditation. Meditation in the Chan tradition is not just the means to an end. It is the end itself. It is believed to be the Ultimate realization itself. Rejecting books – it was even nicknamed the teaching not founded upon words or scriptures – Chan stresses teaching from mind to mind. Each novice is taken on by a master who instructs the pupil, but without reliance upon words.

Chan Buddhism teaches that the Buddha is within you, or to be more precise, the Buddha-nature which manifests itself in this time in the historical Buddha. Furthermore, the Buddha-nature transcends all that is, and can only be grasped or uncovered when the whole world of phenomena is seen to be nothing, empty of all meaning. Hence the development of statements known as koans, which are nonsense, such as 'Imagine the sound of one hand clapping', but which give the pupil something to meditate upon, for years on end, until finally the realization that what we construe as meaning is meaningless, breaks through. The aim is to break any attempt to understand or to reason your way forward. Instead you must dismantle all human attempts at control and meaning in order to allow True Enlightenment to break through or in.

Lama Buddhism

One last major tradition came to China, but it did so as the imperial cult of non-Chinese rulers and as such, whilst being very influential, has not made major inroads into the popular mind. That is Tibetan or Lama Buddhism.

When the Manchu emperors established their dynasty, the Qing, in 1644, they brought with them their allegiance to Tibetan Buddhism. Tibetan Buddhism had spread from its heartland in Tibet to convert the Mongolian tribes in the 12th to 14th centuries. The heart of Tibetan Buddhism is belief in the compassionate bodhisattvas such as Guan Yin. For example, the Dalai Lama is believed to be the reincarnation of this bodhisattva. Tibetan Buddhism incorporated many aspects of the older folk religion of Tibet, Bon, into its practices creating one of the richest and most intricate of Buddhist cultures. In many ways it owes as much to shamanic practices as to Buddhism and thus was of interest to the Mongolians because they were essentially shamanic, and found echoes in China because of Daoism.

When the Manchus conquered China in the mid-17th century, the then Dalai Lama was invited to come to the capital Beijing and to inaugurate Tibetan Buddhism into the life of the capital. Great Tibetan temples were established, such as the one created in the early-18th century in Beijing, the Yong He Gong – Palace of Peace and Harmony. Inside the Forbidden City, Tibetan Buddhism ruled the day, hence the degree to which its artifacts and shrines are present there and at places such as the Summer Palace.

Chinese Buddhism Today

Today, Buddhism is strongest in the north of China, and is still focused upon the old major centres such as the sacred mountains or the great metropolitan monasteries such as those in Beijing, Xian, Luoyang or Yangzhou. It is organized still through the two main traditions of Chan or Pure Land. As this book does not cover Tibet I am not including details about Tibetan Buddhism in the contemporary section.

Estimates of the number of Buddhists in China today fluctuates from somewhere between 70 and 120 million. It is estimated that there are some 9,000 to 10,000 temples and monasteries now functioning with about 90,000 monks and nuns. Of these, some 50,000 at least are nuns.

Lay Buddhism is visible through the throngs of visitors to all the major urban temples, where offerings, prayers and incense are offered almost without cessation. It is also visible in the many Buddhist household shrines within family homes where the family's favourite Buddha or bodhisattva is worshipped daily. In many shops and in vehicles such as taxis, amulets with Buddhas and bodhisattvas on them are to be seen. Intellectually, it is Buddhism and Christianity which today interests those students and young people who wish to explore the religious and spiritual side of life.

CHINESE FOLK RELIGION

Most Chinese would be hard pushed to define their religious allegiance. For many, the gods and goddesses, Buddhas and bodhisattvas, even the saints and Jesus Christ, merge into one big helpful or not so helpful family. Add to this the distinctive role of the ancestors as beings now observing the family from the Beyond, and venerated or worshipped at regular festivals through the year, and the picture becomes even more complicated.

This aspect of Chinese society has perplexed and infuriated Western visitors for centuries. How can the Chinese, it is asked, believe in ancestors and in reincarnation? How can you worship the Buddha of the Future and the Jade Emperor of Daoism? The West has always wanted China to have one major belief system so that it could understand spirituality in China. But China is not that simple, or perhaps, it is actually simpler than that.

For most people in China, religion, spirituality, call it what you will, is a matter of getting through the ups and downs of a capricious life. And this century has been more capricious than most! The role of most religion in China is to deal with the mundane while pointing to the profound. It is for offering compassion now and giving some hope for the future. Thus to combine gods who deal with illnesses from Daoism, exorcist masters from shamanism and Daoism and bodhisattvas from Buddhism who offer release in the next life, makes perfect sense. If having a crucifix helps ward off evil spirits as well, then fine.

If believing in the medicine of Lu Dong Bin, one of the Eight Immortals, is more reassuring than the dubious health facilities offered locally; if respecting the ancestors gives you a sense of being part of something much greater than just yourself and if offering Bank of Hell notes to the god of the Underworld will get you through the horrors of the Ten Daoist Hells or the Eighteen Buddhist Hells, then fine.

Much of Chinese religion is distinctly practical. It fuses elements of shamanism, Confucian values, ancestor worship, Daoism, Buddhism and even Marxism into a functional and primarily usable mixture, to be applied when and where necessary. The journey up Hua Shan with which this book opened took us from Imperial ritual through shamanic trances to Daoist immortals via Buddhist bodhisattvas. Such a journey makes perfect sense to a Chinese reared in the values of traditional folk religion.

This religion is magical, divinatory, dramatic, concerned with evil forces and good forces, humorous and occasionally philosophical. It centres around statues and offerings, around the dead and the deified. To try and place it in a straitjacket of

58

either one religion or another is to ignore its very essence, which is eclecticism. Thus our pilgrim ascending Hua Shan will buy and wear amulets inscribed with an image of Guan Yin; necklaces with the goddess of the Azure Clouds – the Grandmother of Tai Shan in another form; a crucifix on a chain and incense packets ranging from the Eight Immortals fragrant scent to the Future Buddha Happy Incense. All these, along with perhaps a photo of Grandmother who died last year, will ascend the mountain and each will have its place in the mystery of faith which is Chinese folk religion.

This eclectic mixture can be seen in temples where Buddhist temples have Daoist deities and Daoist temples have Buddhas. It can be seen in shrines in homes and shops where Guan Ti the god of fortune and a Confucian/Daoist mixture to begin with, sits beside Guan Yin who is beside the ancestor tablet with Mum and Dad inscribed upon it and their dates of death.

Ancestor Worship

Ancestor worship predates all the formal religions of China. Evidence of it comes from the earliest explicit religious scenes found in archaeology – dating from *c.* 3500 BC. And ancestor worship, while it has been used to bolster Confucian hierarchical values and to enforce Chinese family structures, or to back certain understandings of Buddhism or provide a backcloth for Daoist festivals of the Dead, has always remained of itself. There are few Ancestor temples left in China which can be easily visited. Most were destroyed by the Cultural Revolution and while many are being rebuilt, by their nature they are family affairs, and few visitors are welcome. Some can be visited in Hong Kong, especially in the old walled villages such as Kat Hing Wai or Shui Tau in the New Territories.

In Guangzhou, it is possible to visit one of the most magnificent of ancestor temples, that belonging to the Chen family – the Chen Jia Ci. While no longer functioning as a family temple, it offers a good example of the kind of layout of an ancestor temple, this one having been built in 1890–4.

Imperial ancestors were also of immense importance and there are a variety of sites to be visited which show how imperial families cared for their dead. One of the features of dynastic changes in China is that while you might depose the current, corrupt or weak emperor, you still made sure his ancestors were properly venerated so that they did not give you trouble. For example, when the Zhou overthrew the Shang dynasty *c.* 1100 BC, they enfeoffed to the relatives of the last emperor in perpetuity to continue to offer the rites and sacrifices to the Shang ancestors.

Two interesting ancestor temples with very different functions are the tomb and temple of Yu the Great at Shao Xing, Zhejiang Province and the Ming tombs outside Beijing.

The tomb of Yu the Great dates from *c.* 6th century AD, though the tradition that Yu died here goes way back into earliest Chinese mythology and historical accounts. I suspect that there was some form of shrine here before the 6th century. The design of the temple is that of a very elaborate ancestor shrine, for in effect, Yu is the Confucian founder figure of all the dynasties, and in particular he is held up as the model of virtuous and selfless service to the people. Set in graceful courtyards, the temples contains many steles describing the virtues of Yu and asking his favour as an imperial forebear. Offerings were made to Yu in the Central Hall and the whole site is designed to illustrate the importance of Yu and stress his virtue and his role as a model for rulers. It is an unusual site for few temples in China actually claim to have the tomb of their deity.

The Ming tombs – called the Shi San Ling in Chinese – were started in the early-15th century as the burial place of all the Ming Emperors – though the founder is buried near Nanjing and a couple who were considered failures are not buried here. Each tomb has a square courtyard in front, symbolizing the Earth, and a circular raised mound which is the actual tomb, symbolizing Heaven. This design stretches back to the earliest imperial tombs such as those of the Shang, Zhou, Qing and Tang dynasties near Xian. Serving all these tombs is the

Hall of Heavenly Favours. Here the ruling emperors came to offer sacrifices to the dead and to seek their guidance and protection. As with other dynasties, when the Ming fell and the Qing took over, descendants of the Ming were enfeoffed to conduct the sacrifices. The last such ancestor sacrifices to the Ming emperors by a direct descendant took place in 1924.

At a more humble level, family tombs and graveyards can be seen almost anywhere in the countryside of China, though the more visible ones tend to be in the increasingly affluent rural areas such as Sichuan or Guangdong Provinces. These tombs all follow a standard basic pattern, that is, their site will have been chosen for its feng shui – literally wind/water – or geomantic properties and will face an auspicious direction. Offerings of flowers and models plus remains of burnt offerings such as Bank of Hell money or models of houses, cars, videos, etc may lie around. As has always been the case and is increasingly so now that families can earn high incomes through the market economy, tombs declare as much about the wealth of the family as its devotion to the ancestor.

Chinese beliefs about life after death and funeral rites are very clear expressions of folk religion and of this deep seated ancient culture of ancestor worship.

Death and the Afterlife

According to classic Chinese philosophy, the body contains two kinds of souls, the hun, which are linked to Heaven and the po which are linked to Earth. There are three separate hun souls and seven po in each person. To some extent these are in conflict with each other and are part of the complex understanding of the physiognomy of the body and the flux between yin and yang that goes on within.

At death, it is believed that the hun souls are taken for judgement to the various Hells (see below) while the po souls remain with the body and in effect are the ancestor souls. However, whilst this is all very neat and precise in theory, in practice, most Chinese see the dead person as being an honoured ancestor, a frightening ghostly presence that has to be

61

kept content in the afterworld, and they believe that after 49 days the soul is reborn in a new form.

At Chinese funerals, all these elements come together. The name of the departed will be written on an ancestor tablet and placed in the family shrine as well as in the ancestral temple. These ancestral temples are located in the original home town of the family – a town which the descendants of a given branch of the family may have left ten or more generations ago. As the newly dead member is added to the family collection of tablets, the oldest tablet, usually seven generations ago, is quietly retired from the family shrine, for it is believed that their interest in this world and thus their power to influence it wanes over time.

At the same time, the family will be making offerings for the dead person to take with them into the Hells. These Hells are in fact known in Chinese as Earth Prisons and that captures their role. Daoism has ten of them, Buddhism eighteen, though usually only the ten are depicted in books, paintings and sculptures in temples. The soul has to pass through some if not all of these Earth Prisons to atone for sins committed in the past life. Thus, for example, in the Second Court of Hell, those who led young boys and girls astray but then entered the priesthood to escape punishment, those who steal books, those who know someone is about to marry a bad person and do not say, those who fail to ransom a slave when he can, etc are punished. The punishments vary from being stretched upon the rack, being hacked into pieces, pecked by chickens and boiled in a brazen cauldron of boiling water.

The other Hells are similar. In Daoism, there is the belief that you pass through these hells quite quickly. In Buddhism, there are some crimes which mean you are condemned to suffer for all eternity. This notion of hells and punishments was completely unknown to the Chinese until Buddhism introduced it in the 1st to 2nd centuries AD.

At the end of all these punishments, the soul is purged of any memory of its past life and is reborn in a suitable body. This belief has led to those born with a deformity or handicap

62

as being seen to have been very evil people in their past life.

However, all is not lost! For the Chinese have always viewed the afterlife and its administration – judges in this life often petitioned to be allowed to become a judge in the Hells at death – as similar to this world. Thus all officials are bribable and creature comforts can be afforded to those with the financial wherewithal to secure them. This is why at Chinese funerals, vast quantities of Bank of Hell notes are burned. These go straight to the 'credit' of the dead person in Hell and can be used to pay the bribes and to ease one's way in the afterworld. Likewise, paper models of houses, cars, videos, computers and any other modern luxury are burned, again, so that the dead person will have use of them in the afterlife in Hell.

These gifts to the dead are also believed to be used by the ancestors, who of course are not in Hell. Thus the dual understanding of the dead is reflected in a dual use of the same item.

The greatest fear of Chinese believers is that there are souls out there who do not have anyone to care for them and to make the offerings at the appropriate times through the year. These are called hungry ghosts because they are without any means of sustenance and thus haunt this world trying to kill and maim. Each year at the festival of the Hungry Ghosts, Daoist and Buddhist organizations combine and compete to receive funds to feed these hungry ghosts and thus to ensure that their potential for evil is removed.

I frequently horrify the drivers who take my Chinese colleagues and me around China, by stopping in the countryside to photograph or just visit tombs which we spot from the road. The drivers cannot understand why we would want to go anywhere near the dead, especially as they are not our dead. On one occasion, the driver insisted that we wash ritually before getting back in the car, for he didn't want evil spirits following his car and perhaps causing a crash. To be honest, I think my Chinese colleagues, even good Communist ones, are not entirely happy with going near tombs. On one recent trip, our local guide declared that no-one was frightened by ghosts these days. Yet when we spotted a particularly fine tomb and got out to investigate, he suddenly felt ill. The dead are a very powerful living force in China to this day.

At the time of death and at the funeral, Buddhist monks may well be invited to pray for the soul, adding their karma worthy prayers to the more material offerings of the family. If the family has Daoist links they may invite a Daoist priest to perform ceremonies which help the soul through the Hells – known as the Attack on Hell – as well as offer their prayers to assist the soul to a happy new life. Sometimes Daoist and Buddhist monks will be found sitting in the same room, chanting their various prayers. No one finds this odd.

The traditional colour of mourning is white and the coffin is accompanied to its resting place with drums and cymbals. It is not uncommon when travelling through the Chinese countryside to pass such a procession in a country lane. The dead are buried in the countryside but cremated in the cities. If the body is cremated, the ashes are then placed in a numbered drawer in one of the Memorial Halls attached to, primarily, Buddhist temples. Here the soul is prayed for by the monks for a fee and the family can come and offer worship. Vast drawer cemeteries can be found in Hong Kong, for example at the feng shui shrine at the base of the hill leading to the Temple of the Ten Thousand Buddhas, or in temples such as the Wen Shu Yuan – Temple of Manjushri – in Chengdu. In the street outside the Wen Shu Yuan, you can buy all the necessary equipment for a full traditional funeral – Bank of Hell notes, mock gold ingot bars, prayer papers, model houses, cars and so forth. Given that there must be about three quarters of a mile of stalls on either side, packed cheek by jowl with each other, this is a thriving trade.

In Guangdong Province, the province which has gained most financially by the increased market economy, funerals are very big business. The following report appeared in the *China Daily* of July 26 1995:

It is estimated that four large illegal cemeteries are operating in the province, plus numerous small ones in the

rural areas in the northern and western parts of Guangdong... Most people place their family member's cremated remains in their home or at ordinary public funeral
parlours at a cost of only 20 yuan ($2.40) a year.

Only the rich and some overseas Chinese can afford to
spend the 30–40,000 yuan ($3600–$4800) it costs for
plots in private graveyards.

A sign of the increased significance of funerals again in China,
is the fact that 'Guangdong has more than 40 public cemeteries, and half of them were built in the past three years.'

Feng Shui

In the countryside, tombs are aligned by feng shui (see also
chapter 6, page 153). This geomantic art is usually performed
by Daoists and involves aligning the forces in the ground with
the horoscope of the deceased in such a way as to ensure that
their final resting place is as auspicious as possible. The art of
feng shui originated with burials and has since grown over the
last two thousand years to provide a method for choosing the
site of any building, its colour scheme, internal organization,
height, and even the style of its gardens.

In recent years there has been an explosion of interest in
feng shui, and feng shui compasses, vital for making the calcu-
lations, are now easily available in China. Outside China, feng
shui has also become popular, not least for its combination of
spiritual, aesthetic and environmental factors. Sadly, it looks as
if the environmental insights of feng shui which led to such
beautiful cities and buildings in the past, is reviving too late for
the bulk of China. The horrors of Socialist planning and then
of free market development have removed much of the beauty of the old cities and created instead wastelands of concrete
and the universal appearance of white lavatory tiles on outside
walls. Now all buildings seem the same and the whole of
China appears to be a building site. As one Chinese friend put
it, 'In the past, the symbol of China was the phoenix. Now it is

the crane, and I don't mean the bird!'

Feng shui is a natural outcome of the yin/yang view of the world, rooted in the Daoist notion of the flow of nature being the essence of the Dao itself. Our role in building or burying is to be part of nature not apart from nature. As the dislocation from the sacred within nature, so violently expressed by Communist ideology and so relentlessly pursued by capitalism, begins to be critically examined by young Chinese, many are looking for a return to older styles and values and feng shui is part of that search.

RELIGIOUS FREEDOM AND CONTROL

Many people ask me what sort of religious freedom there is today in China. The answer is, quite a lot compared with the mid 1970s, but not as much as one might hope. As already stated, this book does not cover Tibet so we will leave that issue to one side. The Communist Party controls religious activity through the functions of the Religious Affairs Bureau. This sounds to many Western ears like a classic totalitarian system, but in fact China has always had such a Bureau, even in Imperial times. Its role is to oversee the proper conduct of religion in China. This of course is ambiguous, although in practice it means that all religious organizations have to be registered. They should then be offered protection, but this is patchy. While religious practice goes on relatively freely in many places, if a local party or provincial government becomes heavy handed or restrictive about religious practice, the Bureau often proves incapable of helping the religions.

The Catholics and the Christians – to use the Chinese terminology – seem to suffer greatest persecution and interference with religious practice. This manifests itself in disruption of meetings, demolition of churches and detention of clergy. Often this is directed against unofficial churches, but not always. Protests to the Religious Affairs Bureau rarely bring any changes. For details on Christianity in China, as well as

Islam, Judaism and Manichaeism, see Other Religious Traditions in China, pages 313–326.

The number of monks permitted to reside at a Daoist or Buddhist monastery is controlled very strictly by Government approved numbers. On average, permission is only given for about 30 monks or nuns to live in any one monastery. Were this restriction to be lifted or the numbers raised, it would appear that there would be no shortage of novices wishing to enter the orders. Again, this has to be put in context. The ordination of monks in both Buddhism and Daoism has always been supervised by Government officials, for it is a way of ensuring that unlicensed centres of ordination do not come into existence. China has a long history of religiously inspired rebellions, from the Daoists of the 2nd century, through to the Buddhist Secret Societies which overthrew the Yuan, and the Christian inspired Taiping rebellion of the mid-19th century.

The official organization for the different religions, such as the China Daoist Association or the Three Self Movement of Christianity, have a difficult role. They seek to make the best of opportunities afforded them legally, such as printing – for example the Daoist Association has been able to reprint the entire Daoist Canon and make this readily available to all the major Daoist centres – this has not been done for over 300 years – whilst also having to at times toe the Party line on, for example, peace issues. It is a very delicately balanced situation and, therefore, of little help to the major religions of China if outside people come in and stir things up. The situation is far from perfect, but it is improving all the time and will always be different from the way religion is practised and controlled in the USA or Western Europe.

Perhaps what is most significant about the sacred in China today is that it is re-emerging. The persecutions of the Cultural Revolution were an almost deadly blow to much of traditional religion and practice in China. What is re-emerging is different because it is in many cases having to be rediscovered, which always means, in part, reinvented. But what is driving this re-emergence is both the spiritual drive of the people themselves and, perhaps more importantly, the perennial sense of sacredness which is actually tangible in so many places in China.

PART TWO

THE DEITIES OF CHINA

THE HUMAN AS DIVINE

3

One of the key elements of the sacred in China is that it is obviously inhabited by a bewildering array of deities! Visit any temple and you will be confronted by snarling guardian deities; benign goddesses; heroic gods; vast Buddhas; rows of three gods or bodhisattvas; gods with faces of monkeys, oxen, horses; gods flying, sitting, jumping; gods and goddesses with attendants and mysterious sets of deities in rows of seven or eight or nine on either side of a hall, or possibly even sixty gods side by side.

Who are they and what are they about? When I first started visiting Chinese temples in the early 1970s, I felt as if I had entered a world without bearings. Nothing was familiar or recognizable. I knew nothing of the tales and legends behind these wondrous statues. Over the years I have come to know this extraordinary family of divinities; learned to recognize them by their symbols or stances; been told of their exploits or their powers. Like some Hollywood epic, Chinese temples have a cast of thousands. I want to introduce you to just a few of the key ones, while further information about some others will be found in the section on Gods and Goddesses.

THE ORIGIN OF CHINESE DEITIES

Chinese deities are usually historical figures who have been deified by popular acclaim and then elevated through the ranks of the gods by the Imperial decrees of ruling Emperors on earth. Thus the Chinese pantheon is a constantly growing one, even to this day, and to a very great extent, is explicit about how humanly constructed it is. Take, for example, the case of the god of fortune and war, one of the most popular of all the gods, Guan Di (Kuan Ti). I first met him as a patron deity of the local Kung Fu club near where I lived in Hong Kong. I then began to notice him everywhere – in shop shrines; on the altars of friends' home shrines; even in the newspapers. So who is he, this most ubiquitous of gods?

Guan Di starts life as an historical figure, the fighter and general Guan Yu, one of the three blood brothers who form the centre of the historical romance, the Epic of China, the Romance of the Three Kingdoms – San Gou Zhi Yan I. Guan Yu lived in the troubled times at the end of the Han dynasty c. 220–80 AD, and was a man of great honour and integrity. Many and varied are the stories of his nobility, his honour, his courage and his moral rectitude. Eventually he was captured, betrayed and executed. Within a few centuries he was being worshipped by the ordinary population as a god who could be trusted and who honoured his word and fought on the side of the oppressed and downtrodden.

Over the succeeding centuries, Guan Yu has become more and more elevated. In the year 1102, the Emperor granted him the title King of Military Pacification, in recognition of the struggle through warfare for justice and peace that was the hallmark of Guan Yu's life.

It was with the elevation to Grand Emperor of Heaven by Emperor Wan Li in 1594 that he gained his official title of Guan Di (Di means Heavenly Emperor). In 1813 there was an attempt upon the life of the Emperor Chia Ching. The assassins tried to murder the Emperor within the walls of his own palace, attacking the imperial quarters. When the attack failed, the guards swore that they had seen Guan Di himself, sword raised, standing at the entrance to the imperial quarters, defending the Emperor's life. Likewise, in 1856, Guan Di is supposed to have appeared in the Heavens, leading a Heavenly army during a great battle against the Taiping rebels who were seeking to overthrow the Qing dynasty. Such was the gratitude felt by the Emperor and the whole Manchu Court towards Guan Di that they erected temples to his honour in every town and the local officials were expected to go and pay their respects to him once every year.

But long before the Court had recognized his powers, Guan Di was already revered and worshipped by the ordinary people as a defender of the weak, the poor and the helpless against oppressors. In iconography he often stands beside Red Hare, his faithful horse, sword in hand. Beside him are his son Guan Bing, who carries the Imperial Seal of the Grand Emperor, and his faithful attendant Zhou Chang who carries a halberd.

Guan Di is not just revered as a god of war and of justice in this world. He is also one of the most powerful exorcists, and no ghost or evil spirit can abide his presence, whether in image or even when acted upon a stage. There are numerous stories of his powers, of which the following is but one.

The story of the Romance of the Three Kingdoms, the account of the struggles in which Liu Bei, Cheng Fei and Guan Yu were caught up, is one of the most popular subjects of Chinese theatre and opera. Thus every touring group of performers knows scenes from Guan Yu's life.

One day a group of famous performers in Beijing were rehearsing when a young man rode up with an invitation. The invitation, sent by a young woman of excellent birth, requested that the actors follow the servant and attend a great party which was to be held at a mansion near Beijing. Always on the lookout for a few extra coins, the actors agreed and following the servant, they travelled out of the city into the nearby countryside.

It was night by the time they reached the mansion. Set back from the road, it was ablaze with lights and filled with people, all of whom seemed young, happy and full of delight at being together. Upon entering, another servant took the actors to one side and said that his mistress had said that they were only to perform love songs and scenes of romantic love. Under no circumstances were they to perform any scene in which a god or goddess might appear, and most especially, no scene with Guan Di in it.

Agreeing to this, and looking forward to an enjoyable evening, for the wine was flowing freely and food was everywhere, the actors began to perform. The audience certainly seemed to appreciate their performances and called constantly for more. At first the actors thought that they would soon be fed or offered drink. But as the evening went on, they found themselves forced to perform but for no reward. Whenever they stopped, they were urged to continue. Whenever they asked for food or drink, they were told, later.

As the night turned towards morning, the actors were exhausted and very, very annoyed. Finally they decided that just to spite their hostess, they would disobey her request and perform a scene from the life of Guan Di. No sooner had the actor wearing the distinctive red face and full beard of Guan Di appeared on stage than the whole scene changed before their very eyes. Gone were the revellers; gone was the food and drink; gone were the bright lights; gone was the very house itself. To their astonishment and considerable consternation, the actors found themselves standing on top of a new grave. Leaping down, they read the inscription and discovered that they had been lured to perform by the ghost of a young woman who had died very recently. It was obvious that they had been entertaining the ghosts of those who die young and, without Guan Di's intervention, they might never have escaped from their clutches.

I want to now introduce you to a selection of my favourite deities, ones which can be seen in any major Chinese temple or indeed, on occasions, gracing the walls or shelves of Chinese restaurants or homes in the West. For me, half the enjoyment of visiting Chinese temples is in meeting with old divine friends, familiar characters in an ever evolving narrative. The smell of ancient wood, the layers of incense soot, the darkness caused by the grime of untold burnings of candles and joss sticks, provides one of the most evocative atmospheres imaginable. And there is almost always the surprise of encountering new deities, local gods and goddesses who are often only known in a given district. These, although I can but mention a few here, are perhaps amongst the most interesting, for they often represent the remains of very old belief systems, in existence long before Daoism, Buddhism or Confucianism took hold.

DOOR GUARDIANS

Entry into a Buddhist or Daoist temple is usually guarded by fierce figures brandishing weapons, or deities of the earlier shamanic cults of the area incorporated into the pantheon of Buddhism or Daoism. For example, at Baogua Temple on Emei Shan in Sichuan, one of the four Buddhist sacred mountains set in an area famous for its early shamanism and Daoism, I was fascinated to find the guardian deities in shrines outside the main door are gods of the ancient Shu kingdom, *c.* 400 BC. This pre-Daoist, shamanic and indigenous faith is represented by the Earth god of the Shu kingdom on the right (as you face the main entrance) and the Dragon king on the left. Both are unique and distinctive to this area and represent the older local faith in service to the incomer faith of Buddhism, which on Emei Shan actually pushed off the earlier Daoist temples and monasteries as it took over.

Usually there are either two or four guardians. If there are just two of them, they will probably be generals such as General Zhou, guardian of the East who is accompanied by General Zhu, the Red general or General Ji. These wear traditional armour, often with fierce faces carved on the breastplate, and they carry halberds, spears and long swords. They may also have coloured faces, red and green. One will hold a

74

thunderbolt, the other a club in certain traditions. One has an open mouth to depict the yang principle, one a closed mouth to represent yin. These are most commonly found at Daoist temples.

The custom of having door gods goes back, so legend asserts, to an actual event in the mid-7th century AD. The Emperor of that time was greatly disturbed by ghosts and evil spirits who began invading his bedroom at night, keeping him awake all night with fear. Week after week went by without the Emperor getting a decent night's sleep, and he was almost driven mad by the noise and fear these spirits created. One day, two generals of his private guard, Zhou and Zhu, offered to stand guard in full armour outside the door to the Emperor's bedroom and to scare away the evil forces. This worked until the evil spirits discovered another way into the bedroom. So a third general, Ji, took up his duties and the Emperor was able to sleep soundly at last. However, the three generals had to stand guard every night, for if they did not, the demons returned. After a month of sleepless nights for the generals, the emperor became worried about their health and ordered that life size sculptures – or in some tellings, paintings – be made of the three generals and posted up outside the entrances.

To this day, in many villages and towns in China, you will see posters of two brightly coloured guardian soldiers posted either side of the doorway into the home or shop. The tradition of using these two generals to protect you from evil is very strong, and while the third general is usually not used, in Buddhist and Daoist temples you can often see these two and occasionally the three, on duty.

THE FOUR HEAVENLY KINGS

In most Buddhist temples, you will find four very ferocious-looking door gods, often huge in size. If there are four door guards, then these are the Four Heavenly Kings, the Lokapalas, whose duty it is to protect the temple from all directions. They each have their symbol.

- The Heavenly King of the East, Dong Fojiao Denggao Gangshen Yi – also known in Sanskrit as Dhrtarastra – carries what looks like a parasol or umbrella.
- The Heavenly King of the South, Nan Denggao Gangshen Er – also known as Viirudhaka – carries a snake in his right hand.
- The Heavenly King of the North, Bei Denggao Gangshen San – Dhanada – holds a lute-type musical instrument.
- The Heavenly King of the West, Xi Denggau Hangshen Si – Virupaksa – holds a sword.

In having Heavenly Kings of the four directions (there is in fact a fifth one, for the Centre, who is associated with sacred mountains) the Buddhists took over the importance of sacred directions and protectors from traditional Chinese belief. As early as the Shang dynasty there are records of gods of the five directions and originally the five Daoist sacred mountains related to the five directions.

SYMBOLS AND SIGNS
OF THE GODS OF CHINA –
A QUICK REFERENCE GUIDE

3a

This chart of the signs, symbols and appearances of the major deities of China is designed to help you identify who is who in Chinese temples. Full details and stories associated with each of these deities are given in chapters 3 to 5, or in the appendix on Minor deities.

Buddhas

Amitabha Buddha. Forms the centre of a threesome, with Guan Yin the Bodhisattva of Mercy on his left and Dai Shi Zhi – Mahasthamaprapta on the right.

Future Buddha, Mi Lo Fa, Maitreya. Usually shown as a fat bellied, jolly, bald man, seated with one leg bent upwards. Sometimes surrounded by five children. He holds a hemp bag and a string of prayer beads. Also shown in stern mode, seated with legs hanging down rather than in lotus position. Sometimes surrounded by lions and holding a vase and wheel and a lotus flower.

Gautoma Siddhartha. See **Sakyamuni**.

Sakyamuni, the historical Buddha, Gautoma Siddhartha. Sometimes shown as a half-starved man, during his search for enlightenment. Sometimes he lies on his side, supporting his head on one hand – the parinibbana mode. Often to be found as the central statue of the three main statues as the Buddha of this age. His hand touches the ground. Occasionally represented by two footprints or by a wheel.

Set of Three Buddhas. Central to all Buddhist temples will be three large, almost identical statues. These can represent the Buddha of the Past: hands resting in lap; Present: Sakyamuni, one hand pointing to the earth, and future: Maitreya Buddha, hand raised as in teaching. The same hand gestures are also used by another threesome, the Three White Buddhas: Yao Shi Fo the healing Buddha; Sakyamuni; Amitabha Buddha.

Boddhisattvas

Di Zang, Kshitigarbha, Bodhisattva of Hell and the Dead. Very bald and elongated head. Carries a stick with rings looped through the top.

Guan Yin, Bodhisattva of Compassion, Buddhist. Probably the most common Buddhist statue and the only significant woman present in Buddhist iconography of China. This makes her easy to spot! Her major forms are:

- holding a rosary and a vase, with a bird flying above her head. Sometimes accompanied by a boy and girl, perhaps with a dragon under her seat.
- a white statue of the goddess with flowing robes or seated with one knee bent, usually holding a rosary, a vase or a book.
- holding a child.
- sitting or standing with a willow tree behind her or a willow branch in her hand.
- seated with two other 'Buddhas' in the main threesome, either beside Sakyamuni or beside Amitabha Buddha.
- with many arms, each of which has an eye in the hand. This is the Thousand Arm, Thousand Eye Guan Yin and occasionally she will have exactly that, but usually around thirty to forty arms, each holding

a symbol.
- Guan Yin of the Seas, riding upon waves.
- with a peacock.
- fully armoured and holding spears, swords and other weapons.

Manjushri. See **Wen Shu**.

Samantabhadra, Pu Xian or Pu Sa, Bodhisattva of Perfection, Buddhist. Rides an elephant.

Wen Shu, Bodhisattva, Manjushri, Buddhist. Rides upon a lotus, set in the middle of a lion's back, who is standing. Holds a sword and a book. Sometimes just holds a blue lotus.

Gods

Children, God of. See **Zhang Xian**.

Door Guards/gods. On ordinary houses, two armoured warriors – Generals Zhou and Zhu, folk religion and Confucian. Two deities just inside Daoist temple doorways – Blue Dragon and White Tiger.

Earth gods, folk religion, Confucian and Daoist. Old man holding a staff and golden bar.

Four warrior door gods – the Four Heavenly Kings, Buddhist, wearing antique armour and holding an umbrella, a snake, a lute and a sword.

Guan Di, God of War and Literature, Daoist and Confucian. Very popular. Heavy black beard which he is stroking, and often holds a sword or a halberd. Wears antique armour. Seated, with horse and son beside him. Son holds Imperial Seal.

Heavenly Kings, Four. See **Four warrior door gods**.

Kitchen god, folk religion and Daoist. Seated often with a cat and dog beside him.

Literature, God of: Wen Chang, Daoist and Confucian. Formally dressed and accompanied by two others, one looking deformed, the other dressed in red.

Long life, happiness and fortune, Gods of: folk religion and Daoism. Usually shown as three old men together, the god of long life has a bald, elongated head and holds a staff and a peach; the god of wealth wears a winged hat; the god of happiness sometimes holds a book.

Medicine, God of. See **Yao Wang**.

Sixty year gods, folk religion, Confucian and Daoist. Any room filled with sixty gods all looking rather the same is bound to be home to the gods of the sixty years of the Chinese calendar.

Sun and Moon, god and goddess of. The Sun god has a quiver and bow and the sign of a raven. The Moon goddess has the sign of a rabbit.

Warrior gods, Four. See **Four warrior door gods**.

Yao Wang, god of Medicine, Daoist and Buddhist. Standing or seated, has a dragon whispering in his ear and two assistants holding boxes.

Zhang Xian, Daoist, god of children. Old man pointing an arrow at a dog in the sky.

Other

Apsaras, Buddhist. Angel type beings.

Bodhidharma, Buddhist. A famous monk of very fierce, wild appearance, with thick eyebrows and beard. Often shown crossing a river on a reed.

Deva Kings, Twelve. See **Twelve Deva Kings**.

Eight Immortals, Daoist. Usually pictured as a group though a few have shrines on their own. One woman, one transvestite and six men, often in a boat or on a bridge. See chapter 5 for details of who is who.

Fu Xi, Confucian and Daoist. The first ruler of earth. Sometimes shown with sister Nu Gua as half-serpent, half-human. If alone, usually holds eight trigrams and looks wild.

Great Disciples, Ten. See **Ten Great Disciples**.

Hell, Ten Kings of. See **Ten Kings of Hell**.

Immortals, Eight, See **Eight Immortals**.

Jade Emperor, Daoist. Seated on Dragon Throne, wearing imperial clothes, with a thick black beard in the shape of a spade and a flat square hat with a bead fringe.

Lao Zi, Daoist. If alone, shown riding an ox. He has long bushy eyebrows and a bald head. Often holds a book. Sometimes shown seated holding a fan.

Li Nuo Zha, Daoist. A hero god, shown riding a spinning wheel or circles and holding a flashing ring of metal and a long spear. His hair is in two bunches either side of his head and he is young looking.

Li Tie Guai, Daoist. One of the Eight Immortals. He is crippled and has a crutch.

Lohans, eighteen, Buddhist. Eighteen monks, all with bald heads and strange gestures. Usually standing nine each side of major statues. See Minor Deities for symbols and appearances.

Lu Dong Bin, Daoist. One of the Eight Immortals but renowned as god of medicine. Has a large sword slung over his back and a fly whisk.

Ma Ni Li, Daoist. A form of Mother of the Bushel also known as Queen of Heaven. Can have eight or sixteen arms and three heads. Rides a charging pig and one of her faces is porcine. If she rides a chariot, this is pulled by pigs as she also represents the sun riding across the sky.

Manjushri. See **Wen Shu** (boddhisattva).

Mother of the Bushel, Daoist. Eight arms and sometimes four heads. Holds the sun and moon above her head(s).

Pure Ones, Three. See **Three Pure Ones**.

Queen Mother of the West, Daoist. Statuesque and wears a strange crown. Usually shown with two maids, one holds a fan, another a basket of peaches. Sometimes flies upon a crane. If riding a carriage, this is drawn by a stag or white dragon.

Shen Nong, Confucian and Daoist. First farmer, wears leaves and holds a sprouting staff.

Ten Great Disciples, Buddhist. Monks, each with their own symbol, see appendix on Minor Deities.

Ten Kings of Hell, Buddhist and Daoist. Enthroned, usually with followers, and holding tablets of authority. They may have the Ox-faced and Horse-faced gods with them, who can easily be identified!

Three Pure Ones, Daoist. These are the three large statues in Daoist temples and represent:

- The Primordial Heavenly Worthy One, Ling Bao Heavenly Worthy One and the Supreme Dao Heavenly One, who is Lao Zi. Apart from Lao Zi who has a long white beard, the others look very similar, expressionless and vast.
- The Primordial One, the Yellow Emperor and Lao Zi. The Yellow Emperor is usually dressed as an emperor, with a flat, square hat with beads hanging down to form a fringe. Can be confused with the Jade Emperor or the God of Tai Shan.
- The Jade Emperor, the Celestial Being of the Jade Dawn and the Golden Gate.

Twelve Deva Kings, Buddhist. Represent the directions and elements, each with their own symbol, see appendix on Minor Deities.

Wei Tou, Buddhist. Leader of the 32 generals who defend monasteries, he is found in the first hall or gate, standing, dressed in armour, holding a large sword, often across his chest, while his hands are pressed together in prayer.

Xu Kong Zang – Akasagarbha, Buddhist. Essence of the world, shown holding the sun on a lotus growing from behind his shoulder, and can be male or female.

Xuan Zang, Buddhist. Historical figure, a monk who travelled to India to collect scriptures. Dressed as a monk, he has four companions – Monkey, Pigsy, Sandy (a giant wearing a necklace of skulls) and his white horse. Monkey often carries a long stick and Pigsy a rake.

Yellow Emperor, Daoist and Confucian. Sometimes shown riding in a chariot which is a form of compass, drawn by a dragon, or he can be riding the dragon.

Zhang Dao Ling, Daoist. Founder of magical Daoism. Shown with a sword and usually riding a tiger. Has a long black beard and fierce expression.

Zhang Guo Lao, Daoist. One of the Eight Immortals, usually shown riding a donkey backwards and carrying a strange musical instrument with long pipes.

THE SACRED ONES OF BUDDHISM

The next two chapters will look at various key deities within each faith, a sort of family tree of the divine if you like. What is important to recall is that for the ordinary believer in China, these deities are significant not because of the specific faith they belong to, but for their powers and attributes. Most family shrines will have a mixture of deities from at least two faiths if not more.

The Future Buddha

On sale throughout the Chinese world is a funny looking figure of a fat, pot bellied, bald old man with a great grin; the Laughing Buddha as he is often called. He is usually to be found at temples, in the centre of the entrance hall, seated on a cushion and flowing in all directions. This is Mi Lo Fa, the Buddha of the Future, Maitreya. He is always accompanied in such a position by the four Heavenly kings. Maitreya Buddha is the Buddha who will come after 5,000 years have passed since the historical Buddha, Sakyamuni, and Maitreya will descend from his Kingdom of the Future Paradise, Tushita, and bring peace and harmony to the world.

Maitreya has undergone almost as dramatic a change in China as Guan Yin has. Originally, the statues of Maitreya showed a severe image. Maitreya, being the successor to

Sakyamuni, is often shown in such statues as looking very similar to the historical Buddha, very human. The distinctive feature is that Maitreya always sits like a European, his legs hanging down in front, not folded under as with most Buddhas. He is often shown on a throne supported by lions and holds two symbols – a vase and the wheel of truth. These may be resting on long-stemmed flowers which he holds, bringing the vase and wheel level with his face. In his hair he has a stupa.

How did this austere Buddha become the fat laughing Buddha who greets visitors to the temple? It appears that it is a clear case of adoption. Legend says that in the 10th century AD there lived a man of such portly shape and geniality in China. He was apparently able to foretell the weather, and seemed oblivious to all discomfort. Always jolly, he loved the company of children. Jokingly he used to refer to himself as Mi Lo Fa, the Future Buddha and somehow this stuck. When he died, stories grew that this was indeed Maitreya, come in the form of a fat fool, to wander the world seeing if it was time for his rule of peace and harmony to come. Presumably, given that he lived 1,000 years ago, he concluded it was not and so the Future Buddha remains a promise of a better world yet to come.

Mi Lo Fa always holds a string of prayer beads, each bead representing 100 years and signifying his waiting for the time to come when he will appear, and a hemp bag. This reputedly is the bag into which the fat man of the 10th century used to put any gifts he was given. It is also, according to some, the bag containing the Original Qi (ch'i), the Primal Breath of creation, which he holds in order to bring new life to the world. This shows the way in which Buddhism has tried to absorb older Chinese philosophical and cosmological ideas. Because of his distinctive hemp bag, he is sometimes called the Hemp Bag Buddha.

Today Maitreya Buddha is usually portrayed thus and it is very common for children to be lifted up to sit in his lap. His distinctive pose, with one leg bent at the knee but upright, almost supporting his fat belly, and his torso naked to his waist, is sometimes added to by having five children climbing over him as he laughs. I enquired of a Chinese Buddhist friend, Chang Wai Ming, why this was. She told me that these five children symbolize the five religions of the world – according to Chinese definition these are Daoism, Confucianism, Buddhism, Islam and Christianity – and that when these five religions can all work together, then the Future Buddha will come to reign in peace and harmony.

The Bodhisattvas Wen Shu and Weitou

Immediately behind the Future Buddha there will usually be one of two statues. Either Wen Shu, Manjushri, the Bodhisattva of Wisdom, or Wei Tou – known as Skanda in Sanskrit – who is the protector of Buddhist monasteries and the leading general of the 32 generals under the command of the Four Heavenly Kings. Dressed in full armour, his hair pulled up to form a peak on his head, he carries a large sword, usually laid across his chest and supported by his hands and arms which are pressed together in a position of devotion. He is always standing and is often lifesize. He backs all the major statues in the centres of Buddhist temples. Find the major image in a temple hall, walk round the back and there will be Wei Tou – Skanda.

If it is Wen Shu, Manjushri, he is usually seated upon a standing lion, resting upon its middle back. Born, according to legend, from inside a lotus flower, he is usually seated upon one on the lion's back, and carries in one hand a sword and in the other a book of scripture. With the sword he cuts apart ignorance and the book is the Treatise on Transcendent Wisdom. He can also be depicted holding the sword and a blue lotus, symbol of the Buddha's teachings or, sometimes, just the lotus.

Wen Shu, Manjushri, is often depicted to the side of Sakyamuni and opposite Pu Xian, Samantabhadra, the Bodhisattva of Perfection, who can be identified by the mace which he carries. Samantabhadra is sometimes to be found at the rear of

Sakyamuni figures, guarding him, or guarding Guan Yin. The most famous statue of Samantabhadra shows him on his usual mount of an elephant, and is the vast bronze statue cast in 979 AD, housed in the extraordinary brick hall of Wannian temple – temple of Ten Thousand years – on Emei Shan. Indeed, the whole mountain is dedicated to this bodhisattva, who is the patron of those who believe the Lotus Sutra (see above page 54 and section on Emei Shan on pages 202–6).

The Lotus Sutra we have already encountered in the story of Guan Yin. To understand anything of popular Buddhism in China, you need to understand the appeal of the Lotus Sutra, the Pure Land Sutra and the worlds of compassion and mercy which they offer to the ordinary believer.

The name Pure Land comes from the school's central text, the Sukhavativyuha – Pure Land Sutra. The core of the text (there are both a short and a long version of the Sutra) is a conversation which is supposed to have taken place between Sakyamuni Buddha – the historical Buddha – and his favourite disciple Ananda. In this delightful discussion, Sakyamuni Buddha tells of a monk who lived thousands of years ago called Dharmakara. At that time, an earlier historical Buddha was living (Chinese Buddhism believes there have been many historical Buddhas, each appearing to his own era), whom Dharmakara visited. Dharmakara asked this Buddha for a description of the perfect Buddha world and the perfect Buddha who might rule over such a world. Having heard the description, Dharmakara determined that even if it took untold lives to achieve it, he would seek such perfection that he might be finally born as the Buddha of the longed for perfect Buddha world.

Well, the Sutra goes on to describe how, countless aeons ago, the monk made this vow and how over untold, unimaginably numerous lifetimes, he achieved his goal at last and was finally born as the ruler of the Buddha world of Bliss, the Pure Land. This Pure Land lies in the West and is often called the Western Paradise. Here rules one of the most popular figures in the Chinese Buddhist world, Amitabha Buddha – the monk

87

Dharmakara, reborn at last in the desired role of ruler of Paradise. To this Paradise, Amitabha Buddha gathers all those who, according to the long version of the Lotus Sutra, believe in Amitabha's saving powers and do good, and according to the shorter version, all those who simply believe in the power of Amitabha Buddha to save them.

The Lotus Sutra depicts the Buddha giving a lecture and discussing how those in turmoil and strife can be rescued by compassionate bodhisattvas. A bodhisattva is one who has reached the stage of such perfection and negation of karma that they could choose not to be reborn but instead slip into the state of nothingness – Nirvana. But instead of doing so, they choose to use their vast reserves of merit to help save those who are suffering.

I was introduced to the beautiful imagery of the bodhisattva by a Chinese friend whose whole life was a reflection of the search for some meaning in the midst of deep troubles, physical and psychological. A tormented soul, she was prey to many fears and anxieties which caused her to sway dangerously close to mental breakdown a number of times. What stopped her, as a devout Buddhist, was belief in Guan Yin and in the compassionate nature of bodhisattvas. To her, all that lay between total fear of the future and of life were these words:

A Bodhisattva resolves: I take upon myself the burden of all sufferings, I am resolved to do so, I will endure it. I will not turn or run away...

At all costs I must bear the burdens of all beings, in that I do not follow my own inclinations. I have made the vow to save all beings. All beings I must set free. The whole world of living beings I must rescue, from the terrors of birth, of old age, of sickness, of death and rebirth, of all kinds of moral offence, of all states of woe, of the whole cycle of birth-and-death, of the jungle of false views...

(Sikshasamuccaya, Vajradhvaja Sutra)

That quote, combined with chapter 25 of the Lotus Sutra, part of which was given on page 54, is what stopped my friend from total despair. Nor is she alone. The image of the all-saving Amitabha Buddha or the compassionate bodhisattvas such as Guan Yin, are as central today as they have been since they first rose to prominence in China in the 7th to 8th centuries. Their images are to be found all over China, from the great temples to the images hanging down in the front of taxi cabs. If you have ever been driven by a Chinese taxi driver, you will understand the need for mercy!

In the temples, it is often hard to work out quite who is who. Normally, however, if it is a Buddhist temple, the bodhisattvas and the Buddhas of the Western Paradise or of the Future Paradise are seated either side of the historical Buddha, Sakyamuni. The sets of three great statues dominate the central hall of Buddhist temples and at first glance, appear to be identical. Usually painted or covered with gold, they are models of serenity and expressionlessness. Some can be ten metres high or more, such as the magnificent new set at the Temple of the Ten Thousand Buddhas in Shatin, Hong Kong, the renewed set in the Tanzhe temple, Beijing, or the enormous set in the Da Fo (Great Buddha) monastery on Qiluan Peak, Leshan, Sichuan Province.

The sets of three statues express fundamental Buddhist teachings in the Mahayana tradition of Buddhism. The most common forms of the three are the Trikala Buddhas, of which there are two main versions.

The first set of Trikala – Trikala means Three Ages – Buddhas has Sakyamuni in the centre as the Buddha of the Present. To his left (as you face the statues) is Ding Guang Fo, Dipamkara, the Buddha of the Past and to his right, Mi Lo Fo, Maitreya, the Buddha of the Future. It is customary to make all three statues look almost identical, with just differences in hand gestures. Usually Sakyamuni has one hand pointing downwards to touch the ground, from the story that he called upon the earth to bear witness to the truth of his teachings. The Buddha of the past will often have his hands resting in his lap, a sign of completion, while Maitreya Buddha has his right hand in the gesture of making a point while teaching.

In the Luoyang caves, Ding Guang Fo, Dipamkara, the Past Buddha, is a popular figure, and there he is portrayed as having his shoulders covered but his chest bare and his left hand holds his robe at the shoulder or at the knee.

These three are sometimes referred to as the Three White Buddhas.

The second Trikala Buddha set consists of Sakyamuni in the middle, with Yao Shi Fo – Bhaisajyaguru or Pindola Buddha – on his left (as you face the statues) and Amitabha Buddha on the right.

Yao Shi Fo is known as the Medicine Buddha or Healing Buddha and is venerated for his ability to cure and heal. Legend says that he ruled as Buddha when the historical Buddha was still only a bodhisattva and had many more lives to go before he became a Buddha. Yao Shi Fo ruled the Eastern Paradise, which is why he is paired with Amitabha, who rules the Western Paradise (see above page 87). These three are also seen to represent the Three Jewels of Buddhism, namely the Buddha himself, the Dharma or teaching and the Sangha, the community of monks who pass on the teaching.

Again, all three look the same, except for the hand positions which parallel those of the other Trikala Buddhas.

One other set of three warrants introduction here, for it expresses most clearly the vision and hope which Mahayana Buddhism offers.

In the centre is not Sakyamuni, the historical Buddha, but Amitabha Buddha, the Buddha of the Western Paradise – known in Chinese as O Mi To – who also combines the attributes of another Buddha, that of Eternal Life, Amitayus – Chang Sheng Fo – for both are concerned with the fortunes of the soul after death. Amitabha saves from the horrors of death and rebirth, while the Buddha of Eternal Life offers exactly that. By combining the attributes of both into one statue of Amitabha, the statue is saying here lies salvation and eternity in one. This is why he is usually accompanied by Avalokitesvara – Guan

Yin on his right (as you look at them) and Dai Shi Zhi – Mahasthamaprapta, on his left.

Guan Yin we shall look at in much greater detail in a moment, but Dai Shi Zhi – Mahasthamaprapta is probably almost totally unknown in the West. He is mentioned in the Lotus Sutra and is thus considered to be a salvationary bodhisattva alongside Guan Yin. In Chinese tradition, he is understood to be a manifestation of the wisdom of Amitabha Buddha.

Salvationary Buddha, rescuing bodhisattvas. Here in a set of three you have the heart of Chinese popular Buddhism. And of all these, Guan Yin – Avalokitesvara – is not only the most important, she is also the most ubiquitous and deeply loved of all the deities of China, male or female, Daoist or Buddhist. We need to meet her properly if we are to come close to the real life and beliefs of sacred China.

Guan Yin, Bodhisattva of Mercy

Guan Yin is the most important of all the deities. Her image is to be found everywhere and her role in Chinese life is similar to that of the Virgin Mary and Jesus rolled into one, in Catholic countries. She inspires a devotion and affection which is without parallel in Chinese society, and her miracles are countless.

Once I was climbing a very difficult mountain in China and the weather was bad. My companions and I reached the safety and shelter of a rock ledge which afforded some protection against the wind and rain. We were not the first to find this place a shelter for three others were already huddled there. As we shuffled in, it was clear that two of those already there were praying. I caught the sound of Guan Yin's name. When they stopped, I enquired as to why they had been praying to Guan Yin. Did they hope she might come and rescue them? No, came the reply. They had got themselves into this mess by setting off in bad weather. What they prayed for, was that Guan Yin would forgive their foolishness and tame the weather so they could finish their journey.

This captures Guan Yin's special role. She is a miracle worker, but she works miracles with what we are. She cannot or will not change us or save us from our own stupid actions. But she will rescue us from the full consequences of our stupidity, arrogance, pride or whatever it is that drives us to do what is wrong. She redeems us if you like, by bringing out the very best of what we are and could be.

A very dear friend of mine in Manchester, England, has a remarkable story to tell about her. Let us call him Chang Wing. Chang Wing was a very successful lawyer in the UK. He was also a very powerful Master of Kung Fu. On top of this he loved fast cars and reckless driving. Although brought up as a Buddhist, he had turned his back on this as material pleasures took over.

One night, having drunk too much, he drove too fast. His car crashed and killed two other people. Chang Wing was paralysed from the neck down and the doctors despaired of his ever recovering at all. One night as he lay in the hospital bed, he began to pray to Guan Yin. Her image had adorned his family shrine throughout his childhood. Night after night he prayed to her for help and apologized for the deaths and suffering he had caused. One night he awoke in the early hours to see a woman in white drift through the end window and come towards him. He immediately recognized her as Guan Yin. Unable to move, he lay there as she came up beside him. She touched his arms and chest and then disappeared.

The next morning, feeling and movement had returned to his arms and to his body above his waist. He has never regained use of his legs. Chang Wing's understanding of what happened is that Guan Yin gave him back as much as she could. But because he had caused death and suffering through his own stupidity and pride, she could not or would not restore him completely. He has to live with the consequences of his actions, but she gave him back the possibility of a life again.

There are countless stories of Guan Yin and I have covered some of these in the book *Kuan Yin*, published by Thorsons, 1995. Here I want to introduce you to some of the forms in which you might encounter her in the temples and homes of China, and to explain a little about the traditions and stories which lie behind these forms.

In temples, the figure of Guan Yin will often form its own set of three, depicting the goddess in the centre, whose signs are a rosary either held in the hand or in the beak of a bird overhead, a vase, or a scripture, being the Lotus Sutra. The Lotus Sutra refers back to the origin of her powers and compassion. The vase symbolizes her pouring out her compassion upon the world. On either side of her, obviously as attendants, are her two companions, Shen Cai, a boy or young man, and Long Nu, a young woman. She is often depicted with a dragon under her throne.

The two attendants of Guan Yin came to her when she lived in the physical form of the Princess Miao Shan. Born the third daughter of a very belligerent king, she soon showed that she was different by her intense piety. Refusing to marry, she infuriated her father even more by insisting on becoming a Buddhist nun. The king tried everything to dissuade her, eventually sending troops to burn down her nunnery and kill her. She escaped and meditated for many years upon a mountain top until she achieved perfection. Here she was joined by her two assistants. Shen Cai was a worthy young man whom she chose to protect her. One day she got the local gods to pretend to be pirates and to appear to attack her. Shen Cai, seated on an opposite mountain peak flew to her rescue. When Miao Shan had convinced him she was in no danger, she took him to the edge of the peak and showed him his physical body lying broken on the rocks. In coming to her defence, he had overcome his physical nature and achieved eternity.

Long Nu was the daughter of a dragon god. Her father was caught in the shape of a fish in the nets of a fisherman. Guan Yin rescued him and put him back into the waters. In gratitude Long Nu came to serve Miao Shan and has remained with her ever since.

Returning to the story proper, Miao Shan's father fell ill and was told by a wandering monk that only the free gift of a living person's eye and arm, used as basic ingredients of a medicine, could cure him. Asked where such a person could be found, the monk directed the king's servants to the peak where Miao Shan lived. She willingly gave up both her eyes and her arms to save her father. He recovered, came to thank this wonderful person who had saved him and realized it was the very daughter he had tried to kill. Needless to say he converted to Buddhism, gave up all his bad ways and everyone lived happily ever after. When the king realized who Miao Shan was, she then revealed herself to be none other than Guan Yin.

This story is one of the best known and most loved of all the stories associated with Guan Yin.

Probably the most famous and widespread image of her is that of the White Clad Guan Yin. This image appears to date from the earliest centuries of her development. Powerful modern versions of this can be seen at Pu Tuo Shan. It pictures her in the most simple of poses and in the simplest of clothes. At its most pure, for example in Sung dynasty sculpture, Kuan Yin sits, sometimes with her right leg raised upon her left, draped in white. Her head is often covered and the cloak flows to the ground, covering her completely. As before, in one hand she usually has a rosary, while in the other she holds either the Lotus Sutra or a vase. It is also usual for her to be seated or standing upon a lotus flower, or to have such a flower in her hand or nearby. The lotus is of course one of the most important of Buddhist symbols. It stands for the flowering of the mind and being freed from the murk of this world. For just as the lotus flower is rooted in the mud and dank waters of the pool but flowers only in the light, so through Buddhist teachings can the individual reach enlightenment, especially if helped by a compassionate Bodhisattva.

The statues of Guan Yin as a Child Bearer vary enormously. Sometimes this is simply a variation of the White Clad Guan Yin. In such instances, she usually has a child with her, either in her arms or running beside her – normally a boy, this being what most Chinese families wanted – and still want! She is invariably accompanied by her rosary, though sometimes this will be in the beak of a bird which flies above her serving her, and she also has a willow branch and the Lotus Sutra. Beside her often stand her two helpers, Shen Cai and Long Nu, the Heavenly Brother and Sister.

Still within the basic form given by the White Clad Guan Yin, there is her role as the Willow Branch Guan Yin. The willow branch is an important Chinese symbol of Buddhist virtues. It is renowned for its ability to bend in the most ferocious winds and storms and to spring back into shape again. The 'weeping' willow also symbolizes the compassionate concern for the ills of this world which are exemplified in the Mahayana teachings of Buddhism, most notably in the Lotus Sutra. The willow is also an ancient Chinese symbol of femininity and as such was naturally ascribed to Guan Yin, who is often pictured with what is known as a willow waist. But the willow also has magical powers. It is used in exorcisms for it is believed that demons cannot bear the presence of the willow. Interestingly, it is also a key element in shamanistic practices and a means by which the shaman in China can make contact with the spirit world. For all these reasons, it has become one of the key symbols of Guan Yin.

There is also the Thousand Arm, Thousand Eye Guan Yin. These images are truly extraordinary. In some cases Guan Yin will literally have a thousand arms and hands, and in the centre of each hand there is an eye. There are two somewhat different stories of why she is depicted thus. The most common one is that it represents her all-embracing compassion for the world, and her constant gaze upon the suffering of all. For this, a thousand arms and eyes is just sufficient. However, there is a second story which I have heard enough times in different settings to think it worth telling!

As briefly outlined above, when Guan Yin lived upon earth in her form as Miao Shan the king's daughter her father rejected her completely and even tried to kill her. She survived but he fell ill. Being told that only the freely offered arm and eye of one without anger could cure him and being told that such a One lived on a sacred mountain, the king sent a messenger to ask for the arm and eye. It was of course his daughter Miao Shan who offered not just one arm and eye but both arms and both eyes. The king was cured, came to visit this extraordinary being only to discover it was his rejected daughter, now without arms or eyes. The story goes that after she had revealed herself to be Guan Yin, the king ordered a statue to be made of her. Wishing to emphasize the sacrifice that she had made, he ordered that the statue be made bereft of eyes and arms.

Now, in Chinese the sound for 'bereft' or 'deficient' and for 'thousand' are virtually identical. At some stage in the transmission of the message to the sculptor, these two words became confused. For months the sculptor worked away, desperately seeking some way to capture imaginatively in stone the wish of the king for a statue of a goddess with a thousand eyes and a thousand arms!

At last the grand day of unveiling came. With immense pride the sculptor brought the statue to the palace and the king came to unveil it. Imagine his surprise at finding that, far from having no eyes and arms, Guan Yin now had a thousand of each!

In fact, most Thousand armed, Thousand eyed Guan Yins have slightly less than that – anywhere from thirty to fifty. This is because of various mathematical formulae which enable the figure of one thousand to be reached. For example, many will have forty arms, for each arm is capable of saving twenty-five worlds or timespans, thus making a thousand. Other combinations of numbers will relate to the various symbols associated with Guan Yin. In China, forty-two hands are frequently shown, each holding a symbol.

The most common such symbols range from those we have already encountered such as the willow branch, the lotus, the Lotus Sutra and the rosary, through to the thunderbolt of enlightenment, a statue of the Buddha and the axe for cutting free from attachments, or the divine creatures of the sun – a crow – and the moon – a rabbit. Each symbol reminds the worshipper of the powers and compassion not just of Guan Yin but of Buddhism itself. They are visual representations of the teachings of Buddhism and draw us back more than many other statues of Guan Yin do, to the bodhisattva origins of the goddess and to her roots in Buddhist philosophy and teachings.

Yet another popular style is that of Guan Yin of the Southern Ocean or Sea. Here the slender form of the White Clad Guan Yin is combined with swirling waters, leaping fish or placid seas. The cult of Guan Yin, arising in the late-9th century in the far northwest of China spread eastward away from the high mountains of the northwest to the coasts. Here her cult absorbed many of the more ancient sea goddesses. The stories linking her to the seas and especially to the seas around Pu Tuo Shan, her sacred mountain off the coast near Ningbo, are multitudinous. And the Southern Seas Guan Yin is a very popular image to this day. It can often be seen in the homes, shops and workplaces of those Chinese who have migrated from the coastal regions of China, such as Shanghai, Hong Kong or Canton. For to these people, it is as the protectress on the Seas that Guan Yin is most important.

Guan Yin is frequently pictured standing with a peacock, for again, her role as protector of all creatures is one which is stressed time and time again in popular legend, song and theatre. The story goes that after Creation, Guan Yin ruled amongst all the creatures upon Earth. To her they brought their troubles and squabbles. But she had to leave them eventually. As soon as she did, arguments broke out. Guan Yin returned, sorted them out and left again. But to no avail, for yet more disputes broke out. When she came back again, the creatures begged her to stay. This she told them she could not do. But to remind them that she cared for them all, she gave the peacock a hundred eyes to watch over all creation for her.

The protection afforded to all creatures on Pu Tuo, and in the seas around the island, was frequently commented upon by visitors in the past – and devotion to Guan Yin is often linked to taking up a purely vegetarian diet. Chinese folk Buddhism is not in essence vegetarian. But devotion to Guan Yin

97

often carries with it the assumption that you will be mostly if not wholly vegetarian. The statue of Guan Yin and the peacock reminds us of her role as protector of all life, and of the Buddhist teachings about the importance of all lives, in whatever form or shape.

This aspect of her role as protector and ruler over creation is the basis for another of her forms. In this form she rides upon a strange looking creature which looks a bit like a lion but is called a Hou. In this guise she is ruler of the Earth, as its protectress and guardian.

Another form is that of the Armed Guan Yin. In these depictions, Guan Yin looks like a rather overloaded medieval warrior, clutching and firing a cross bow and carrying a fierce looking shield. This represents Guan Yin's role as protectress and combatant in the struggle against evil, demons and ignorance. The Chinese Buddhist world of popular belief is infused with evil spirits, devils, ghosts and other beings opposed to the wellbeing of humans. To protect them from such forces, the Armed Guan Yin comes riding to their rescue. But at a deeper level, these same weapons are used to symbolize the need to kill off the powers within one's self which restrict the ability of the soul to rise above the material and mundane and reach towards the light of salvation offered by Guan Yin.

Sakyamuni Buddha

It might seem odd to some that the historical Buddha is only now being properly introduced in this section. Yet this reflects the fact that Sakyamuni is not all that important on his own. His significance comes from being part of the sets of three and in being a bridge between cosmic worlds of the past and future. Indeed it is possible to visit some Buddhist temples and never see a statue of the historical Buddha at all.

When travelling with Western Buddhist friends I have been intrigued by their reactions to the demoting of the historical Buddha. In the West I suspect that we have been oversold the pure philosophical Theravada Buddhism because it appeals to a post-Christian world view in which deities and the supernatural are seen as out of date. Yet worldwide, be it in China or Thailand, Sri Lanka or Ladak, India, it is the supernatural, deified Buddhas and their vast court of saviour figures, demons, ghosts, spirits, angels and suchlike which command the love and affection of the people. Personally I have little difficulty with all this, for it reminds me of the vast and wondrous depths of Celtic and early Medieval Christianity in the West, or the ranks upon ranks of saints, miracle workers and holy men and women which populate the world of the Orthodox Christian believer, complete with the elevation of the historical Christ to the position of the Pantocrator, Creator of All, cosmic being beyond all beings.

In other words, popular Buddhism in a place like China is much closer to popular Catholicism or popular Orthodox Christianity than it is to the philosophical ruminations of most Western Buddhists or, indeed, most Western Christian theologians. And I know which model I would put my money on for surviving into the future. The world of popular belief seems capable of withstanding any amount of attack. All over China I am struck by first the scale of destruction of images which the Cultural Revolution brought, and then by the speed and scale of the restoration of these images by ordinary people today. In temple after temple, new statues are being installed, at considerable cost. And it is the salvationary, magical, supernatural aspects of Buddhism which are being restored first, by popular acclaim.

With regard to Sakyamuni, his importance comes from his having brought the eternal teachings to this era, but he himself is not considered capable of saving people from rebirth or from suffering. This, as we have seen, is the role of the other, non-historical, eternal Buddhas and the bodhisattvas.

The name Sakyamuni means the Sage of the Sakyas, the clan from which Gautoma Siddhartha came.

In early Buddhism – c. 500–150 BC – the Buddha was never shown except as a pair of feet or by the symbol of a wheel or some other such device. It is only when the Greek city states founded by Alexander the Great on the edge of India became

Buddhist, that statues appeared. The Greeks modelled the Buddha on their god Apollo, who wore a Greek toga and had a halo as he was the sun god. This is where the basic elements of what we now think of as standard iconography of the Buddha came from. Take a good hard look at an early statue of the Buddha or at a classic Buddha statue. His features are Western; his clothing is a Greek toga; his head is surrounded by a sun halo and his body shape is that of a well-built Greek! This Greek influence can be clearly seen in the Buddhist caves of Datong and Luoyang, where even the greenery and palaces in which he is depicted look like details from the Parthenon in Athens.

The Eighteen Lohans

In the main halls, accompanying the major statues and arranged in neat rows along the walls, you will find sets of statues of exactly the same number each side. If there are nine on each side, showing eighteen bald headed monks, then these are the eighteen lohans or arhats. These are the eighteen monks who have reached the stage of ending the Eight Fold Path and who have not only perfected and enlightened themselves, but can also help enlighten others. It's a sort of pre-bodhisattva condition and is a reminder of the earlier form of Buddhism, Theravada, where the Path was one which each individual had to walk to find enlightenment and release. The arhats – lohan is the Chinese term for them – are examples of that tradition. The number eighteen is odd, for originally there were sixteen, all of whom are recorded in the original scriptures and are Indian in origin. The Chinese seem to have considered that you can never have too much of a good thing, so they added two more. The eighteen each have very distinctive appearances and symbols and a full list of them is given in the section on Gods and Goddesses.

There are traditions of the Five Hundred Lohans – for example, as used to be seen in the Hua Lin temple in Guangzhou before the Cultural Revolution and may be again soon if restorations continue apace, and in the Bi Yun temple in Beijing, which have survived intact. It is said that in the Guangzhou temple, one of the Five Hundred Lohans was Marco Polo, identifiable by his broad brimmed hat!

The Ten Kings of Hell

The Ten Kings of Hell appear in some Buddhist temples, being identifiable by the fact that they are usually holding official tablets of office (long rectangles which are peaked at the top), with the number of their Hell inscribed beside them – going from one to ten. They may have with them the two key attendants who drag unwilling souls to judgement – the Ox-faced god and the Horse-faced god (see chapter 5).

The bodhisattva of Hell is Kshitigarbha, in Chinese, Di Zang, who delivers souls from the torments of Hell. He cannot change the judgement of the Kings of Hell but he can help people to realize their better nature and thus earn pardon for their sins. He is very distinctive, often with a very bald and elongated head, and carrying a special staff which has rings looped onto the end. This stick he uses to force open the gates of the various Hells, or to translate more faithfully from the Chinese Earth Prisons.

Bodhidharma

The distinctive image of Bodhidharma (known in Chinese as Da Mo) is often to be found in temples of the Chan tradition, with his stern looks, black curly beard, heavy eyebrows and distinctive pose. In popular iconography his distinctive looks are often to be found. I have noticed that even in Government-run gift shops and craft centres in China, he is a favourite topic for scroll painters and sculptors. So who exactly is this peculiar individual?

By the 6th century, Mahayana Buddhism in its Prajna, salvationary mode, was swiftly rising to be the most popular form of Buddhism in China. It seemed as if the more austere, self-disciplining form of Buddhism was on the wane. Then the Indian monk Bodhidharma burst upon the scene.

According to one main legend, around 520 AD, Bodhidharma

101

arrived by ship from India or possibly from southeast Asia, at the port of Guangzhou. His arrival made quite an impact for he is famously described as one of the ugliest men the Chinese had ever seen, and hairy to boot! His striking, crumpled face, usually scowling, heavy bushy eyebrows, and thick curly beard, still adorn all pictures of him to this day. Nor did his appearance belie his personality. You did not tangle with Bodhidharma lightly.

Upon arrival, he made straight for the court of the ruler of the Liang State, Emperor Wu, who was renowned as a supporter of Buddhism. As the Buddhism which Emperor Wu supported was mostly Pure Land and Lotus Sutra influenced, Bodhidharma lost no time in telling the Emperor that everything he had done so far was useless because no matter how meritorious his actions, they were pointless because he did not have the crucial key to understanding. This key to understanding, said Bodhidharma, was that everything is nothing.

Bodhidharma was thus not inclined to debate with Emperor Wu. Having made his case and the Emperor Wu having been less than impressed, Bodhidharma shook the dust of Liang from his feet, floated across the Yellow River on a reed (a frequent subject for paintings or statues of him) and took up residence at the monastery of Shao Lin Si – Little Forest Monastery – near Deng Feng in Henan. Here, on the slopes of the Daoist sacred mountain of Song Shan, he sat in Chan meditation staring at the back wall of a cave for nine years. The cave is still there today and can be visited.

Bodhidharma died around 535 according to the major legends and traditions surrounding his life. His tomb can be visited at Shao Lin Monastery. However, as will have been gathered from the description of his passage across the Yellow River on a reed, Bodhidharma was no ordinary man. He is reputed to have left his tomb and to have limped home to India. He limped because he left one of his sandals in his tomb on Song Shan!

Whatever the truth about Bodhidharma, he is a central and popular figure throughout China today. Shao Lin Si is of course famous not only for his life there but because of the martial arts developed there by the monks, who would travel out to fight for whatever cause they felt was worthy. Indeed, in the White Drapery Hall of the monastery can be seen a fresco dating from the Ming dynasty (1368–1644 AD) showing an emperor being rescued from his enemies by the battling monks. Because of the popularity of kung fu movies and novels, Shao Lin Si is now a very busy and popular site, especially with overseas Chinese. Monks still train there in the traditional arts and around them have grown up many training schools in Kung Fu and Qi Gong, where the art and its religious roots are taken very seriously. The largest of the schools there has over six thousand pupils.

Xuan Zang

The monk who went to India to collect the Scriptures and around whom a whole host of legends have grown.

If Bodhidharma is the hero of Chan, then Tripitaka, Xuan Zang, is the hero of Prajna, Pure Land school. In the year 629 AD, Xuan Zang slipped illegally out of China and headed for India. He wanted to collect answers to questions that had arisen in his studies and, I suspect, he loved travel! He was away for sixteen years, returning in 645 when he returned with 520 chests full of sutras and statues. He was a living witness to the power of faith in the protecting powers of the Buddhas and bodhisattvas, for he had many adventures and was nearly murdered a few times and on one occasion was about to be offered up as a sacrifice by bandits in India when he prayed to Maitreya Buddha. Suddenly a terrific wind descended upon them and the bandits were sufficiently terrified to allow Xuan Zang to go free.

Xuan Zang recorded his journeys in a fascinating book called the Da Tang Xi Yu Ji – *Records of Travels to the West*. Equally importantly, he translated many of the sutras he had brought back. The Emperor was so impressed with his exploits that he established the monk in the newly established monastery of Great Goodwill – Dacien si – in Xian, Shaanxi.

Here Xuan Zang worked in a translation hall until his death in 664. The most notable feature of the Temple of Great Goodwill is its magnificent early pagoda. This was built at Xuan Zang's request, by the Emperor, to house the sutras and statues Xuan Zang had brought back. Founded in 652, it fell down within a few decades and in 701 the seven-storey edifice which you can see today was built to house this extraordinary collection.

The travels of Xuan Zang passed into folk Buddhism and by the twelfth century, plays based around his journey were features of many Buddhist fairs. Gradually he acquired a group of fellow travellers who were supposed to have shared in the journey and its risks with him and to have protected him by their powers. Finally, in the 16th century the great novel, *Journey to the West* – Xi You Ji – was written, which brought together the various traditions and stories into one of the most delightful collections of myths and legends imaginable. In this novel, Xuan Zang, sometimes called Tripitaka, travels to India to bring back the life-giving scriptures which will help to free people from the wheel of rebirth. To accompany him he has four creatures who have committed heinous crimes and who need to atone for them. Each has been offered the opportunity to do so by the goddess Guan Yin, who promises that if they escort the pilgrim monk, not only will their sins be forgiven, but they will attain nirvana – release from the wheel of rebirth.

The four creatures are: Monkey – also known by his own boastful title as Great Sage Equal to Heaven; Pigsy – a gross, greedy pig; Sandy – an ogre monster who lived in the river of flowing sands and killed travellers, who is usually pictured wearing a necklace of skulls; and a dragon who, having eaten Xuan Zang's horse, is turned into a horse upon which the pilgrim monk rides to India.

These five form one of the most popular and common of scenes in Buddhist temples. They will crop up anywhere from the base of pagodas to the embroidered cloth hanging from an altar to moving models in a Disney type freeze in the temple grounds. Despite the book's overtly anti-Daoist line, they also

104

appear at times in Daoist temples, so popular are they in the folk religions of China.

He is always depicted with his three companions, Monkey, Pigsy and Sandy and always rides the fourth companion, his white horse. Usually he is shown wearing simple Buddhist robes and a flat hat. Quite often he is depicted with a bundle of books, or there are panniers of books on the back of the horse. Monkey normally precedes him, holding his famous staff which could expand in size rapidly and with which he defended his master. Monkey frequently has an iron band around his temples by which Xuan Zang could control him. Pigsy is usually dressed in a long coat while Sandy wears his distinctive necklace of skulls – signs of a dissolute youth!

Often, the scenes from the *Journey to the West* are carved as a series around the base of a pagoda or along the walls of a temple. There is a fine set at the base of the pagoda in the Wen Shu Yuan – Temple of Manjushri, in Chengdu, Sichuan.

One of the joys of staying at monasteries in whatever religious tradition, Buddhist or Christian, is the tradition of storytelling in the evenings. Guests are expected to contribute to the round of stories. I have heard the Monkey stories told in so many different ways by the light of candles in remote monasteries. The narrative of Monkey is a living one, as vital today as it has ever been. I have even added to their number, for my children loved the Monkey stories when they were young, and I often made up new adventures of the friends to entertain them. Some of these I have been made to tell again to devout monks in monasteries in China and wonder if they have now become part of the repertoire of present day Chinese storytellers! I hope so.

THE SACRED ONES OF DAOISM

5

For many years, the magnificent Daoist Palace of Yong Le Gong, north of the town of Rui Cheng in Shanxi Province, lay forgotten and neglected. By happy chance, the building of a dam in the area required the evaluation and then removal and preservation of this unique set of buildings. For here, on the site of the old village of Yong Le was the birthplace of one of the most important of the Eight Immortals, Lu Dong Bin, and the Yuan (Mongol) Emperor in 1247 gave permission for the already existing monastery to be massively expanded to create a Palace for Lu Dong Bin. At the time, the Quan Zhen school of Daoism which traces itself back to Lu Dong Bin, was in the ascendancy and Qiu Chang Chun had just returned from his successful visit to the Emperor, Genghis Khan, who had made him head of all religions in China

The Quan Zhen school is one of the last schools of Daoism to emerge. It was founded in the 12th century AD and its stronghold has always been in the north, while the other traditions have been in the south. This is the tradition with which I have personally had most dealings, especially through their main temple, the Bai Yun Guan – White Cloud Temple in Beijing.

Its founder was Wang Chong Yang who lived in Shandong Province and in 1167 founded the Quan Zhen after receiving

106

revelations from Heaven. These revelations were given by one of the greatest of Chinese popular religious figures, the immortal Lu Dong Bin. For this reason, Lu Dong Bin is held in the highest regard by the school to this day, and a magnificent new statue of him can be seen in his own special hall at White Cloud Temple, Beijing.

The central tenets of the school remain today what they have always been. Namely retreat from the world wherever possible; celibate monasticism (the other traditions allow monks to marry), some quite extraordinary forms of meditation and a strict code of self-denial. Wang set an example in this by standing for two years in a hole in the ground, ten feet deep, in order not to fall asleep. I am glad to say that my friends in the school today are not so extreme, though they are renowned still for the rigour of their observations of fasting and of physical exercises.

However, it was Wang's disciple Qui Chang Chun who really launched the Quan Zhen school into the big time. Indeed, he launched Daoism into the big time as well. His impact was such that to this day, it is still the second most popular and powerful school in Daoism, the most powerful being a combination of all the other major traditions into the Zhengyi school of Southern Daoism.

When Genghis Khan seized the north of China in the first two decades of the 13th century, Qui Chang Chun was head of the Quan Zhen school. The invasion threw the whole of northern Chinese society into turmoil. Indeed, at one time, Genghis Khan planned to destroy every city and turn the whole of northern China into a vast pasture for his horses. In the swiftly changing social and power structures of that turbulent time, Qui Chang Chun showed he was equal to the task and sought to debate Daoism before Genghis Khan himself. Permission was given, and guided by a Nestorian Christian Mongolian chieftain, Qui Chang Chun was brought to the tent camp of Genghis Khan, in order to debate against Buddhist leaders, the relative virtues of Buddhism and Daoism.

Qui won, claiming that, 'If the conqueror respects Daoism,

107

the Chinese will submit.' At Qui's suggestion, Genghis Khan appointed him not just head of all the Daoists, but head of all religions in China, including the arch-rivals of the Daoists, the Buddhists. Such a position had never existed before, and was never to exist again. But as a result, Qui was able to obtain for the Daoists in general and the Quan Zhen school in particular, immense power, finance and prestige. The whole extraordinary story of Qui is recorded in one of the books of the Daoist Canon, entitled Xi You Ji, and written by a young monk who accompanied Qui. The White Cloud Temple in Beijing is but one of the fruits of this journey, for it was originally an imperial palace which the Daoists were given as the headquarters for Qui in his role as Supremo of Chinese religion.

In Quan Zhen Daoism, we find Daoism at its most developed, cosmologically and theologically, and it is this high point of Daoism which is captured in the incredible Yong Le Palace.

Built at the zenith of Quan Zhen power, the Yong Le Palace was a triumphant expression of Daoism at its political peak. The real heart of the Palace itself is the Hall of the Three Pure Ones (see below). Here, covering the walls of this vast Hall, is the complete Daoist pantheon with magnificent paintings of 286 deities. This unique expression of Daoist power and authority offers us a picture of the pantheon of Daoism as expressed for hierarchical and power reasons. Today, the number of deities has grown beyond easy reckoning and the order of priority has changed a bit. But essentially we see here an expression of the cosmic model of Daoism – which is replicated in architectural and theological terms at the Qing Yang Gong in Chengdu.

Central to it are the Great Emperors of the South, East, and North, with the Queen Mother of the West – related to stars but also to the four Daoist sacred mountains associated with these directions. Trailing in their glory come the teachers of Daoism, such as Lao Zi, Zhuang Zi and Lie Zi. The Jade Emperor of Heaven and his Empress of the Earth sit beside immortals. The gods of the Great Bear constellation form part of a whole collection of deities associated with the planets, the sun

108

and moon and the 28 constellations of Chinese astronomy and astrology. It is a vast, bewildering array of deities.

Many people find the sheer scale of Daoist deities over-whelming. There are so many of them and particularly at local sites, there are so many distinct local deities, that it seems almost impossible to get a handle on them. In this section I will only be telling the stories of the major deities and their place within the logic of Daoist cosmology and salvation drama.

The Three Pure Ones

The focal point of most major Daoist temples is the Three Pure Ones, sometimes called the Three Heavenly Worthies, the Three Elements and so forth. Essentially, the number three is key and around this has accumulated any number of titles and descriptions.

In its purest, philosophical form, these Three, usually look-ing very similar and being in imitation of the Buddhist sets of three statues, express the notion of the Dao as the universal, cosmic force that manifests itself in particular ways at particu-lar times.

The pattern of a threefold revelation is spelt out in what is in effect the credal statement of Daoism. When Man Ho Kwok, Jay Ramsay and I were translating the *Dao De Jing* a few years ago, I was particularly struck by chapter 42, especially once we had freed it from verses which did not belong to the chapter originally. As we worked on the translation, and in the light of my other translations of Daoist texts, I began to feel strongly that if Daoism had a core statement, then it was chapter 42 of the *Dao De Jing*.

Imagine then my delight when I visited one of the greatest of Daoist temples, the Qing Yang Gong – Purple Sheep Temple – in Chengdu, Sichuan Province and found that this was so. There, in a temple which is itself a map of the Daoist cosmos, is the text of chapter 42. Not just written up, but written in vast letters. It is to be found painted onto the 20-foot high reverse of the shrine of the Thunder god of Sichuan, who has become the guardian spirit of the temple. It was written and placed there after a disastrous attack on the temple during a siege, which ended with the temple being consumed by fire. As if defying such destructiveness, the rebuilt temple had chapter 42 of the *Dao De Jing* placed at the very entrance to the complex, written around a large yin yang symbol, an affirmation of core Daoist teachings in the teeth of violence and oppression.

To understand chapter 42 is to begin to understand Daoism. I have translated it as follows:

The Dao gave birth to the One, the Origin.

The One, the Origin, gives birth to the Two.

The Two give birth to the Three.

The Three give birth to every living thing.

The two referred to here are yin and yang and the three are the triad of Heaven, Earth and Humanity.

Yin and yang are a uniquely Chinese model of how the world works, indeed how the whole cosmos works. Yin and yang originate in the words for the dark side of a mountain and the sunny side of a mountain. Gradually they came to represent complete opposites, not just in terms of a mountain, but in terms of all aspects of life. Today they are often defined as yin – female, cold, damp, dark; yang – male, fiery, hot and light.

I often hear people in the West talking of yin and yang as a symbol of harmony. They are not. They are violently opposed to each other, but are incapable of conquering each other for each contains the seed of the other within it and thus involuntarily gives birth to the other. One of the best examples of how yin and yang interact is that of the seasons. Autumn and winter are yin. Yet when winter and darkness reaches its peak at the solstice in December, that is exactly the point at which yang begins to re-assert itself – the evenings begin slowly yet surely to get lighter and eventually spring and summer – yang – emerge. Likewise, when summer and light is at its peak – the summer solstice in June – that is when yin begins to emerge, and so on ad infinitum. The balance that exists in the universe comes from the constant struggle of these two cosmic natural forces, which are present in all aspects of life – including us – to overcome each other. The yin yang model is not a New Age harmony notion. It is a violent struggle for supremacy which can never be won, but which can disturb the balance of the universe unless care is taken.

This is where the triad of Heaven, Earth and Humanity come in. Heaven is yang, Earth is yin and humanity is both and has the crucial role of maintaining the balance between these two. This used to be enacted symbolically by the Emperor, as described at the opening of chapter 1. Today Daoists see the responsibility as having devolved onto us all.

The Three Pure Ones are to some extent a reflection of this notion of humanity being in a pivotal position, and the Three Pure Ones reflect Daoist belief that there is an Ultimate beyond the Origin; an Origin and a manifested form of the Dao which brings guidance to us as to how to live. How do we fulfil our unique role as preservers of the balance of yin and yang, of the dynamic struggle of existence and of being within the flow of the Dao? It is in this context that one needs to approach the Three Pure Ones.

The first of these is the Primordial Heavenly Worthy, the origin of origins, also called Da I, the Great Unity. In him is the Dao of cosmology expressed. He equates to the Dao itself, before all, even before the Origin.

Next comes the Ling-bao Heavenly Worthy, who links Heaven and Earth. The Ling-bao Heavenly Worthy is in effect the Ling-bao Scriptures which, being revealed Scriptures, are the link between the cosmicness of Heaven and the materialness of Earth. It takes the place of the shaman at one level, in being able to bridge Heaven and Earth and reveal in a transcendent yet material way the teachings of the Dao. The Ling-bao therefore acts as the bridge between the Ultimate and

Original beingness of the Primordial Heavenly Worthy and the third expression of these forces, the embodiment in a human form of the Dao.

Finally there is the Dao De Tian Zun, the manifest form of the Dao, which in this aeon has appeared in the form of Lao Zi.

Lao Zi. What an enigma! Ironically, the best known 'Daoist' in the world was never a Daoist and may not have even existed! If he did, he would, I suspect, be astonished at what Daoism has made of him over the centuries.

Lao Zi is reputed to be the author of the basic classic of Daoism, the *Dao De Jing*. He was not, though it is highly likely that at least seven of the chapters, the so-called 'I' chapters where the text speaks in the first person singular, are from his pen. He is said to have lived in the 6th century BC and to have encountered Kong Fu Zi – Confucius. Yet when the great historian of China, Si Ma Qian (1st century BC), came to try and write a biography of him, he says that he was mystified by the lack of any specific information. All he could record was that Lao Zi was born sometime in the 6th century BC in a village in the State of Ch'u and became the state archivist in the State of Chou. He also records the meeting with Confucius. The *Dao De Jing* is supposed to have been written by him when, as an old man (his name simply means Old Master) he despaired of China and 'went West'. At the mountain pass to the West he was persuaded to write his thoughts down in one night. This he did and handed the resulting text of 5,000 characters to the gatekeeper. This is how legend says the *Dao De Jing* came into existence. Having finished his text, Lao Zi 'went West'.

Whatever else the *Dao De Jing* is, it is not a text written in one night! It is in fact a collection of wisdom sayings with brief commentaries, collected together and published under the name of Lao Zi in order to give it greater authority. It dates from the 4th century BC.

The little that is known of Lao Zi has in no way prevented the growth of a cult of Lao Zi. Indeed, so strong is this to even now, that there is a major battle raging at the moment between two sites which claim that they are each the birth place of Lao Zi. For centuries, the town of Luyi in Henan Province has claimed to be his birthplace, even boasting his tomb as well – which is odd when you think he is supposed to have disappeared into the West. But in 1993 another place set about claiming Lao Zi. The account of why they think their site is the true one makes for a very interesting story, as I discovered when I learnt of their discoveries from the local school teacher of history, Ma Han Min.

The villagers of Zhengdian in Anhui Province are convinced that theirs is the true site. To back this up they tell the following story of Lao Zi's birth.

Once there lived in the village a beautiful young woman, who on Lantern Festival night, the 15th day of the first month, went for a walk. Drawing near to a plum tree she saw that, as it was still winter, the branches were bare. She longed for the winter to be over and the plums to be hanging upon the tree. No sooner had she thought this than a shooting star flew overhead and the very next moment, a big red plum appeared hanging on the tree. The young woman picked the strange fruit and bit into it. But before she knew what was happening, the entire plum had rolled down her throat and into her stomach. The next day she realized she was pregnant.

But this was no ordinary pregnancy. The pregnancy lasted 83 years! The reason was simple. Every few days the baby in her womb would ask, 'Has Heaven become firm?', to which she replied 'No'.

One day, when she was a hundred years old and still pregnant, she shouted, 'Yes' and the 'baby' erupted from her. But the 'baby' was already 83 years old and so emerged into the world an old man – hence his name Lao Zi, Old Master. His personal names were Li, meaning plum and Er meaning ear.

At the moment that Lao Zi was born, nine dragons (a very auspicious number) erupted through the earth and sprayed the 'baby' with water to refresh him. It is the nine wells created by these dragons which Zhengdian village claim they have rediscovered and which prove that this is where Lao Zi was born.

113

They have also found evidence of a vast Lao Zi temple complex and are now building an enormous new temple. So tall is it that it will be the second tallest temple hall in China, rivalled only by the Hall of Heavenly Peace in the Forbidden City. The reason for such a vast hall? Well the name of the village means Main Hall, and as Ma says, this must have referred to the fact that the main hall of Lao Zi's temple once before stood here.

But if Lao Zi's birth has become mythologized, his life after 'going West' has its own corpus of stories.

Rivalry between Daoists and Buddhists has a long and not very honourable history in China. The low point was reached in the great Daoist persecution of Buddhists, Christians and Manichaeans in the Great Persecution of 841–5 AD when thousands of temples and monasteries of these three faiths were destroyed and monks and nuns joined the lay community. Usually, imperial authority prevented such violent outbreaks and thus the warfare between the faiths was conducted via books and pamphlets. In trying to discredit the Buddhists, Daoists came up with the following story.

When Lao Zi went West, he arrived on the borders of India. Here he set up a school and taught those who sought knowledge and understanding. One early pupil was an arrogant young prince who came for a few lessons and then left, thinking he knew it all. He didn't. His name was Sakyamuni and the Daoists claim, what the Buddha taught was nothing more nor less than a badly understood version of Daoism! I have to say that sadly this sort of nonsense is still being taught today, but not often in China. Instead, the West has become the most recent producer of such rubbish. For example, American Daoist groups publish the Hua Hu Ching – one of the books which puts forward this notion, as if it were actually a book by Lao Zi. This does little to enhance Daoism in the West or interfaith understanding and I find it most regrettable. (See for example *The Complete Works of Lao Tzu – Tao Te Ching and Hua Hu Ching*, translated by Ni Hua-Ching, published by The Shrine of the Eternal Breath of Tao, California 1979.)

But this is as nothing to the divinization of Lao Zi. In later

Daoist thought (*c.* 8th century AD onwards) he is considered to be the main physical manifestation of the Eternal Dao and to have existed before all time and to exist beyond all time. This is why he appears in the Three Pure Ones. He is often to be found in Daoist teachings making the pill of immortality and, as I pointed out in chapter one, you can even see his furnace where he makes the pill on Hua Shan.

The Three Pure Ones have further versions and combinations. In the other most popular form there is still the Primordial One, the absolute principle of Dao, but with this come a variety of other members of the triad, ranging from Lao Zi and the Yellow Emperor, to the Jade Emperor and the Celestial Being of Jade Dawn and the Golden Gate. The various contenders for these posts all go under roughly the same overall term, namely the Three Pure Ones are: the Pure One of Jade Purity; the Pure One of Supreme Purity and the Pure One of Great Purity.

These deities will be found in the main hall of most Daoist monasteries and temples, and even the local monks may be vague as to which is which. The point, however, remains the same. They represent the notion that the Dao reveals itself to humanity as part of the balance of Heaven and Earth. The triad of Heaven, Earth and Humanity has here been turned into a process of revelation which serves the same purpose of linking all three in a cosmic tie.

Each of the three named people, Lao Zi, the Jade Emperor and the Yellow Emperor often appear by themselves as well.

Lao Zi

Lao Zi is usually depicted either riding on an ox, which is how, traditionally, he left for the West. He is often given long, bushy eyebrows and a bald head and can look a bit like a more serious and elderly version of the Happy Buddha, Mi Lo Fa. In his hand he holds a book, the famous *Dao De Jing*. Other statues have him seated in a chair, holding a fan.

The Jade Emperor

The Jade Emperor – Yu Di – is usually shown seated upon a dragon throne, wearing formal imperial clothes. He has a thick black beard, which is usually cut straight, making a spade shape. He is deemed to be the king of Heaven and under his rule come all the bureaus and administrative departments of Heaven. The Daoist Heaven is essentially the earthly imperial order, elevated to divine status.

The Yellow Emperor

The Yellow Emperor – Huang Di – is a quasi-historical figure. Supposed to have reigned *c.* 2500 BC, he is counted as the first of the Five August Emperors of antiquity. He is not dissimilar to a Moses-type figure, hazy and mythologized, but probably originally a powerful shamanic ruler who brought some order to the petty feuding and primitive lifestyle of ancient China. He is recalled as a mighty warrior who brought order to the world and established many of the facets of civilization which continue to this day, such as metal working, pottery and weapons. As such he is almost the Supreme Ancestor of the Emperors and through them of the Chinese themselves.

His tomb lies just to the north of Huang Ling, Shaanxi Province, which means, Yellow Tomb. On Qiaoshan, the pathway winds up past a temple dedicated to the Yellow Emperor and reaches his circular tomb at the top, set of course within a square surround – Heaven and Earth combined (see page 249). He is shown riding in a special chariot which is also a form of compass, indicating the direction South, the imperial direction. This is sometimes drawn by a white dragon or he rides upon a dragon, with arrows falling around him. He symbolizes the Centre in the five directions and is sometimes grouped with the gods of the four directions (see below). He also represents the element Earth in the five gods of the Five Elements (see Gods and Goddesses, page 221).

Heaven, Earth and Water

In a few places, there is a third form of the triad, namely the god of Heaven, the god of Earth and the god of water. Heaven always takes the centre position, holding a traditional sceptre of office, with water to his right and earth to his left. These are held to be bringers of great good fortune.

Gods of Long Life, Happiness and Fortune

Which brings us to another collection of three, and these three can be seen all over the world where the Chinese are to be found. They are probably the best known of the Chinese gods. They are the god of long life, the god of happiness and success and the god of fortune. The god of long life is the most distinctive, for he is bald and old, with a long white beard, and carries a wooden staff in his left hand and a peach of immortality in his right.

The god of wealth is dressed as an official, with usually a winged hat to show his high status, for in Chinese thought, wealth comes from a good position.

The god of happiness and success is dressed as a minor official and sometimes holds a book in which is recorded the fortunes of those who seek his help.

Goddesses

In the cosmological world of Daoism, the feminine is powerfully present in two key goddesses: the Queen Mother of the West and the Mother of the Bushel.

The Queen Mother of the West

The Queen Mother of the West – Xi Wang Mu – is the most powerful and probably the most ancient. References to divine Queens of the East and West are found on the oracle bones of the Shang dynasty and the first mentions of the Queen Mother of the West come in the *Dao De Jing* and the Zhuang Zi. The Zhuang Zi has a most powerful evocation of her mystery and antiquity:

> The Queen Mother of the West obtained it [the Great
> Dao] and was able to take her seat on Shao Kuang Moun-
> tain – no one knew her origin, no one knows her end.
> *(Chapter 6, from* Chuang Tzu, *translated by Martin Palmer with*
> *Elizabeth Breuilly)*

She is also described as a shamanic deity in the extraordinary
4th century BC book, *Shan Hai Jing – Classic of the Mountains and
the Seas –* where she is described thus:

> Another 350 li [Chinese mile] to the west is a mountain
> called Jade Mountain. This is the place where the Queen
> Mother of the West dwells. As for the Queen Mother of
> the West, her appearance is like that of a human, with a
> leopard's tail and tiger's teeth. Moreover she is skilled
> at whistling. In her dishevelled hair she wears a sheng
> headdress. She is controller of the Grindstone and the
> Five Shards Constellation of the heavens.
> *(Transcendence and Divine Passion – The Queen Mother of the*
> *West in Medieval China, by Suzanne E. Cahill. This is a fascinating*
> *and excellent study of the Queen Mother of the West.)*

Her statues show her either seated with two maids, one with a
fan, the other with a basket of the peaches of immortality, or
she is flying on a white crane. She is sometimes accompanied
by five immortal maidens or by two azure winged birds. When
shown riding in a carriage, this is pulled by either a stag or by
a white dragon. She is almost never depicted alone.

As one of the few deities to survive virtually intact from
shamanic times, she is of considerable interest. This is no light-
weight goddess; nor is she an Earth Mother. There is no evidence of Earth goddess worship in China. All the goddesses are
associated with Heaven and are quite remote. The Queen Mother of the West is an awesome figure and this is added to by the
later legends which say she has the power to bestow immortality on mortals. In her palace, she grows the peaches of immortality. To consume one of these confers instant immortality.

The Mother of the Bushel

The other great goddess of Daoism is the Mother of the Bushel, the Queen of Heaven, Tian Hou, meaning Heavenly Ruler. The bushel refers to the Dipper, the seven stars of the Great Bear, central to Daoist astrology. She is the goddess of the North Star and is sometimes described as the Dao Mu – Mother of the Dao. She is believed to be the Mother of the Jade Emperor. The seven stars of her constellation are an old Daoist symbol, and can be seen today on banners and paper charms at Daoist temples. Her traditional style is as having eight arms and, on occasions, four heads, one facing in each direction. In her hands she carries the sun and moon at the top, and all sorts of diverse symbols in the remaining six, ranging from the peaches of immortality to swords, bows and other devices taken over from Buddhism.

She is usually flanked by the Queen Mother of the West on her left and the Goddess of the Earth on her right. Thus again, she stands as a symbol of the triad but this time in female form – namely, Heaven, Earth and Humanity. On either side of her hall will often be found the fourteen gods of her constellation, with the seven gods of the north to her right and the seven gods of the south to her left. North symbolizing death, there is often the Dark Emperor, god of the North, in attendance and then six other gods. South being the direction of life, the god of longevity is often shown with the six other star gods.

The Mother of the Bushel plays an important part in what is the other great precept of Daoism, that of cosmic balance.

Earth Gods

The goddess of the Earth – Hou Tu – rules the earth alongside the Earth god, but is of greater cosmic significance. She is not an Earth Mother, but is probably a development out of the shamanic goddess of Tai Shan, who is believed in ancient myth to have helped create the whole of life on earth. She did not give birth to it; she created it. Her antecedents are as mysterious and ancient as that of the Queen Mother of the West and lie in the lost shamanic past of China. She rarely appears

119

except in the triad of the three cosmic women or as the female partner with the god of the Earth in the popular statues of the Parents – again reflecting the ancient Tai Shan story of them having created everything.

The Earth god Tu Ti is one of the most ancient gods of China, with roots well back into shamanic times. He originally started as the god of local areas, but as the cosmology of China grew towards the triad of Heaven, Earth and Humanity, he took up his place as the earthly equivalent of the Jade Emperor. He is to be found in two styles. Either as one of the triad of Heaven, Earth and Humanity or, more commonly, as the local earth god, deity of the very ground upon which the temple is constructed. As such he is quite often placed near the entrance to the temple, opposite the local area god (meaning the god of the administrative district) and together they are worshipped before entering the temple proper.

The Earth god is also considered a god of wealth and fortune and is sometimes depicted holding an old staff and a gold bar – looking like a little boat. In areas undisturbed by change, his shrine can be found outside many homes and shops such as in Macau and Hong Kong. On sacred mountains he always has his own temple or shrine.

Ancient Gods
Other ancient gods are Fu Xi, Shen Nong and the Kitchen god, Zao Jun. These gods again seem to go back to the shamanic past.

Fu Xi
Fu Xi is supposed to be the first of the Three August Ones, primordial rulers who were half human half animal. He and his sister Nu Gua are shown on ancient carvings as having human bodies and snake tails. Together, they are supposed to have fashioned human beings and assisted in the coming to life of the world. They also taught skills of civilization such as writing. Fu Xi is credited with discovering the Eight Trigrams (see below) on the back of a tortoise. He is depicted as a wild-looking man, clad in a grass skirt, and holding the Eight Trigrams before him.

120

This can mean he is quite easily confused with Pan Gu, the first Being on earth.

Shen Nong

Shen Nong is depicted with either an ox head or with two lumps on either side of his head. He is also clad in leaves, forming clothes from them and holds a sprouting plant. He is the original god of agriculture.

The Kitchen God

The Kitchen god is thought to be one of the very oldest deities. His usual place is in the home where, from the safety of his place beside the stove, he watches the goings on of the whole family. From there he goes every New Year's Eve to the Jade Emperor to report on the goings on in the family. He is often depicted with a cat on his shoulder or a dog beside him – domestic animals as befits the god of the home.

When Chinese New Year is about to fall, the family will gather to burn the slip of paper representing the Kitchen god. In order that he give as favourable a report on the family's affairs as possible, his lips are smeared with honey to sweeten his words. If that is not felt to be good enough, wine is poured over him so that he will be too drunk to make sense when he reports! I have always rather enjoyed the idea of a divine spy in the kitchen, given that this is where most family dramas are acted out. However, my delight in this ancient god was somewhat tarnished recently.

I met a delightful Chinese anthropologist called Dr Zeng while staying in a rather run down monastery at the foot of Tai Shan. One of my pet hates is cockroaches. It has always depressed me that according to accounts I read as a child, they would survive any nuclear holocaust on earth and would thus probably become the dominant species. This alone has struck me as a good reason for banning nuclear weapons. The old monastery dormitories were somewhat overrun with cockroaches and I commented upon this to Dr Zeng. He then informed me that the likely origin of the Kitchen god was that he was god of the cockroaches and was placated in order to keep some control on the wretched creatures. I've never been able to look at a Kitchen god in quite the same light since.

The Eight Immortals

The Immortals – Xian – are of immense importance in Daoism. The most common representation is the Eight Immortals, Ba Xian. These eight form one of the most delightful set of characters in Chinese religion, combining aspects of the hero, fool, conman, trickster, healer and fighter for justice for the poor. The Eight often feature in halls of their own, such as the one at the Bai Yun Guan – White Cloud Temple – in Beijing, or in temples of their own such as the Ba Xian Gong – Eight Immortals Temple – in Xian, or at the town most associated with them, Peng Lai in Shandong Province. Many of the Eight Immortals were actual historical figures.

Lu Dong Bin

Lu Dong Bin – the most popular of all the immortals, so popular he even appears in Buddhist temples. He is associated with medicine and healing and with exorcism – which in traditional thought are often one and the same thing. He is usually shown with a demon fighting sword hung over his back and a fly whisk in his hand to show he can fly through the air at will. When the eight are represented just by symbols – usually on the end of long wooden sticks – he is represented by a sword. Lu Dong Bin is especially venerated by the Quan Zhen school of Daoism (see page 37). Lu Dong Bin will often appear by himself, without the other seven immortals, so important is his role as a god of healing. His birthplace and the magnificent temples surrounding it are at Rui Cheng in Shanxi, at the Yong Le Gong monastery complex.

The story of Lu Dong Bin's conversion to Daoism and to the life of a hermit and thus to immortality is a classic Daoist tale.

Lu was a successful young official living during the Tang dynasty (618–907 AD). In front of him stretched the prospect of a highly successful career. One day, travelling from one city to another, he stopped to have a drink at a wayside inn. Without realizing it, he sat down opposite the immortal Han Zhong Li, and soon the two were deep in conversation. Han saw that the young man had the makings of an immortal, so he plied him with drink and soon Lu Dong Bin was fast asleep. As he slept, he dreamed. He dreamed that he rose swiftly through the ranks of the officials until at an early age he became Prime Minister. For 20 years he was the favourite of the Emperor and he and his family grew rich and famous. He had all that a mortal man could want. But then disaster struck. The Emperor was turned against him by rivals who sought to have his position as Prime Minister. Accused of treason, Lu was imprisoned and then exiled to the furthest, coldest part of northern China, but not before he saw his entire family, wives and children, executed before his eyes.

Lu Dong Bin awoke with a start from the dream. Simultaneously he realized the futility of his life as an official and that he was seated opposite an immortal. There and then he forsook his old world and devoted himself to Daoist studies, living as a true sage, on a mountain. In time, he became an expert in herbal elixirs and medicines and achieved immortality. He is worshipped in most Daoist temples for his skills in healing and his skills as an exorcist. Many Daoist temples sell herbal prescriptions based upon the Hundred Formulas of Lu Dong Bin.

While for the average Daoist, immortality is an unachievable goal, calling upon the great immortals for help is possible and can bring help, healing and even salvation.

Li Tie Guai

The second most popular of the immortals is a strange cripple called Li Tie Guai. He is again associated with medicine and his sign is an iron crutch or his gourd of medicine. His story is rather interesting. He was originally a handsome man, who gave up wealth and fortune to train as a Daoist and to seek immortality. After many years, he was able to fly about at will and to leave his body for up to a week. One day he asked his disciple to stay seated beside his body to protect it, while he went on an astral journey. He told his disciple that if he did not return within seven days, then he would have died, so he could burn his body. But until that time, the disciple was to watch over the body to keep it from being eaten by dogs or crows.

After six days, a messenger came for the disciple saying his mother was dying and that she desperately wanted to see him. Torn between conflicting loyalties, he decided that his master was probably dead, so he burnt the body and set off to see his mother. A few hours later, Li Tie Guai returned. He was furious to find his body burnt, for without a body, immortality is impossible. He had just one hour left to find a new body before his soul would expire, but it had to be a dead body, but not too long dead! Hunting around in desperation, he found the body of a crippled beggar who had just died. Into this decrepit body went the spirit of Li Tie Guai. As I said, Li Tie Guai had been very handsome. When he took a look at himself in a pool, he nearly died of horror! His face was misshapen and covered with warts; his back was humped and twisted; his legs were bandy and bent and his clothes were rags. And it is in this form that he now lives for ever.

Being in the body of a cripple and a beggar, he is especially concerned with the sick and the poor and there are countless stories of his fighting for justice for the poor.

Zhang Guo Lao

Next comes Zhang Guo Lao, who holds a strange looking musical instrument in his hands, long and thin with tubes appearing at the top. He is popular because it is believed he brings children to couples, especially boys. Pictures of him are still occasionally given to newlyweds. He is sometimes pictured riding backwards on his donkey. It is said that his donkey is a piece of paper which when Zhang takes it out and blows on it it turns into a donkey who can travel at amazing speed. However, the first time Zhang used it, the donkey set off at a cracking pace – but before Zhang had climbed on. Running after it, Zhang hurled himself onto the donkey's back, but at exactly that moment, the donkey changed direction 180 degrees, so Zhang ended up riding it backwards. Another tradition says that he could never bear to leave anywhere that was beautiful, so used to ride away backwards, in order to catch a glimpse of the beautiful view until the very last moment.

Zhang is sometimes worshipped alone, as with the previous two.

Cao Guo Jiu

Fourth is Cao Guo Jiu who seems to have no reason whatsoever to be in the Eight Immortals, or indeed, to be an immortal at all! He was a convicted murderer, a very nasty character and a member of a somewhat oppressive Imperial Court. Quite why he is a member of the Eight Immortals is unclear. His symbol is either a pair of castanets or an imperial tablet of office. He is sometimes shown wearing the winged headdress of a mandarin.

Han Xiang Zi

He is followed by Han Xiang Zi who is a popular immortal and can be found especially on mountains which were very much his home. His symbol is a jade flute and he is the patron of musicians. He prefers to be alone and is always the quiet one of the group, calming them with his music.

Han Li Quan

Next comes Han or Zhong Li Quan who lived during the Han dynasty (c. 210 BC–220 AD). He is renowned as an alchemist and was much adored by the External School of Immortality, for he is thought to have created the pill of immortality. His symbol is either a feathery fan with which he is able to control the sea, or the peach of immortality.

Lan Cai He

Seventh is Lan Cai He who is an hermaphrodite, capable of being a woman or a man at will. He is the odd one, the one 'touched by God' as would be said in the West. The lunatic, the madman. He/she is usually represented holding a basket of flowers and can either be pictured as a woman or man.

He Xian Gu

Finally there is He Xian Gu who is the only proper woman in the group. She became an immortal through the extraordinary ascetic practices which she developed. There are few such women in Daoist history, though there have always been Daoist nuns and, of course, certain scriptures were revealed by woman oracles. Her symbol is the lotus flower which she holds on a long stem.

The Eight Immortals are often represented as a group together, either floating across the sea or in the clouds, in a boat, or gathered around a bridge or drinking at a table. Peng Lai in Shandong Province is where they are supposed to have lived and the site is still venerated and visited for this reason.

It is perhaps one of the saddest things about the turmoil and upheavals of this century in China, that so many people have grown up not knowing their own myths and legends. This came home to me most forcibly when I first met a man who is now one of my colleagues in ICOREC (International Consultancy on Religion, Education and Culture) and who heads our China Projects office. Zhao Xiaomin grew up in the Cultural Revolution and comes from a devout Communist family. A brilliant student in English, he is also a true scholar of classical Chinese and of Chinese history and together we have roamed far and wide through China and through history in China. One day we were visiting the old mosque of Xian which is one of the loveliest and most peaceful places on God's earth. I mentioned to Xiaomin that I would like to try and visit the temple of the Eight Immortals which I had read had just been restored and reopened. Xiaomin had not heard of this and didn't know who the Eight Immortals are. My daughter Lizzie has grown up with stories of these wonderful characters and she was with me. A few years earlier my UK colleagues Man Ho Kwok and Joanne O'Brien and I had collected together some of the key stories of the Eight Immortals (published as *The Eight Immortals of Taoism* by Rider, London 1990) from the oral traditions of overseas Chinese, manuscripts and from story-tellers in Hong Kong and Macau.

Lizzie urged me to tell some of these Daoist stories and so I found myself in the great mosque of Xian, retelling these stories to my Chinese colleague while Lizzie made him act out all the more dramatic parts, leaping from rock to rock; prowling through the bushes or fighting off the evil ones in hand to hand combat beside the pagoda minaret! It was an extraordinary sight I am sure. The upshot of this is that we sent Xiaomin a copy of the book and he now regales visitors to China with these stories. So the tradition continues, perhaps with a little outside help.

To give you a flavour of these stories, let me just tell one, about my favourite, Li Tie Guai.

Each Immortal travelled the mountains and the plains of China and beyond. They often travelled in disguise, talking to villagers, observing the peasants, beggars, landowners, traders, sages and disciples. No story was ever forgotten, they were stored up to be retold at the Immortals' bridge.

The eight Immortals met regularly at the bridge, it was their private time and no human could hear or see what happened. But these meetings weren't usually marked out by feats of magic, they were relaxing times – a chance to gossip, play cards or entertain each other with stories of their travels.

One particular afternoon, the eight were gathered on the small, stone arched bridge singing songs in the bright, afternoon sunshine. As the sun sank lower they called for a story, something to entertain them in the evening. Zhang Guo Lao stood up and addressed the attentive Immortals with news of a dispute in a distant province.

A day's walk from Man Yo Street, there was a house surrounded by tall fir trees and in its main entrance was a finely carved alabaster door. The master of the house was Guang Zi Lian, a wealthy merchant and farmer. He owned ten thousand fertile fields, his clothes were sewn from the finest silk and in every room was an ivory chest encrusted with gold and silver. It would take twenty strong men just to carry these chests, but his wealth had been accumulated at the expense of the poor. The peasants who worked on his land were poorly fed and the labourers who build his houses underpaid. Zhang had heard that he would be 60 years old in a few days and planned to hold a party, even at that moment the servants were working from before dawn preparing the banquet. In order to prove that he was the most powerful man in the area he had filled the holes in the road with rice and laid a fine red woollen carpet over the rice to smooth the way.

The Eight Immortals who had encountered so much poverty on their journeys through the provinces were enraged at this waste. Li Tie Guai stood up:

'How dare he waste food and wool as though it were dirt to walk on when the peasants have so little they can barely survive. I will teach him a lesson that will not be forgotten by him or by the generations of the family that follow him.'

As he stood up from his place on the bridge the gourd hanging at his side changed to a begging bowl. Using his magical powers of flight he rose from the ground and within a few seconds had arrived at Guang Zi Lian's house. Layers of finely carved, brightly painted wooden beams formed a roof above the house and at the corner of each beam a golden painted dragon rose into the air. The most skilled craftsmen from the area had carved the stone into an array of animals and worked the wood into the most intricate shapes. The door had been fashioned in one piece from white alabaster and polished until the stone shone.

Servants were everywhere, carrying baskets and pots of food to the kitchen where the cooks had been preparing meals made with rare ingredients which the peasants had never tasted before. A train of servants were working their way down the red carpet, removing every speck of dust. Through the ornate hallways of the house, Li Tie Guai could see black and red lacquer tables arranged with delicate porcelain eating dishes. Nobody noticed the stranger in the midst of all this preparation.

As Li Tie Guai stepped forward he heard a crunching beneath his feet as the ground moved. He lifted the carpet to reveal a layer of rice as deep as a hand. The carpet stretched down through the garden and out of the arched gateway to the house. Word had spread through the villages and a crowd of beggars waited patiently around the gates of the house, their arms reaching out to the guests who began to filter through. In his torn trousers and jacket and carrying his begging bowl, Li Tie Guai walked up the wide stairs to the alabaster door. He was immediately held back by two servants and questioned by a guard:

'Who told you to enter this house? Get back beyond the gates where you belong.'

'My family hasn't eaten for days, I have only come to ask for leftover food and whatever you have they will eat', said Li Tie Guai as he raised his bowl to the guard.

One of the servants knocked the bowl from his hands while the others laughed to see the beggar so helpless. Then the guard struck Li Tie Guai across his face and head, vicious blows that sent him reeling down the stone steps, spattering blood on their clean surface. As he eased himself back to his feet, Li Tie Guai took a handful of rice from the floor but the guard gripped his wrist so tightly he was forced to drop it.

Meanwhile, guests were arriving at the house and to avoid them witnessing this commotion the servants pulled Li Tie Guai to one side. In a fierce hushed voice the guard spoke to him, 'We would rather feed our pigs than give you food. We would leave you here to rot only your sight and smell would offend our honoured guests.'

Li Tie Guai would not be quietened, 'The rice you have thrown on the floor for the rich to walk on would cost a thousand shi. All I want is enough to fill this bowl. You should beware of mistreating the poor and insulting beggars.'

The authority with which he spoke enraged his attackers who kicked him with such vicious strength he could not move. They turned their backs on him and returned to wait upon the party. While this attack was being made the beggars

129

surrounding the archway had crept into the gardens, concerned for this man who had spoken out for the poor. They begged him not to provoke the rich since the death of a beggar would mean nothing to them.

The sound of feasting and excited voices carried from the house into the gardens. The party had started and the servants continued to file through the hallways with trays of suckling pigs, glazed ducks and chickens, steaming crabs and prawns, aromatic fish and vegetables, and noodles and rice piled high in porcelain bowls. The wealthiest and most influential aristocrats, landowners and merchants sat with Guang Zi Lian and as they ate, their dishes were continuously filled by ever watchful servants. Suddenly, cries of pain broke through the laughter and echoed throughout the hallways. The porcelain dishes became as hot as a furnace and they fell from the blistered hands of the wealthy. The servants dropped their platters of food and those who reached for wine to soothe their mouths felt their fingers burn against the porcelain cups.

Slowly the food began to move as maggots emerged from the body of the suckling pig, from the mouth of the fish and from under the mounds of noodles. Before long there were thousands of maggots crawling across the table. Guang Zi Lian screamed for the head cook who ran to his side, and then his master hit him across the face.

'You have disgraced me in front of my guests and you'll pay for this trick. Clear this away, fill these tables with food again.'

The servants descended on the tables, clearing away, sweeping down the tables and calming the guests. Fresh bowls of rice and plates of poultry and sweet smelling pastries were hurriedly laid on the tables. Once more cries of disgust rose from the top table. The bowls of rice had turned to a mass of maggots and so many maggots wriggled under the skins of the ducks and chickens they looked ready to burst.

By now all the guests from the other hallways had gathered round the top table. Shocked by what they saw and insulted by this reception, they whispered to each other about Guang Zi Lian, 'How can he do this to us, his guests.' 'What an insult, this will never be forgotten.' 'What evil trick has Guang Zi Lian played?'

Guang Zi Lian was shamed in front of this influential company. At first he was silent and then he was struck by an idea. 'My guard told me of an evil beggar causing trouble outside my house. Some say they cast magic spells – this is his work!'

And so Guang Zi Lian was led outside to the crumpled form of Li Tie Guai. His servants pushed aside the beggars who had crowded round to protect him and dragged the immortal to their master's feet.

'Who are you? Where have you come from?' demanded Guang Zi Lian.

'I am only a beggar who heard of your banquet and came to beg for food. I am of no importance and only begged for leftovers that would be thrown to the pigs, and yet your guards beat me and left me lying in my own blood.'

Li Tie Guai's body shook violently, he vomited blood and then lay still before the rich man and the crowd of beggars and servants. Li Tie Guai was dead and the order was given to bury him. Guang Zi Lian returned to reassure his guests at the banquet but the beggars who had witnessed the murder of Li Tie Guai were not prepared to let him get away with it.

More than 30 beggars walked to the nearby town of Hunan to report the murder to the just police commissioner, Zhao Shen Qiao. They waited patiently in the walled yard of his office until Zhao Shen Qiao stood in the middle of them and heard their story. He stood attentively, nodding as each beggar added a new comment or piece of information.

After hearing their story he made a brief pronouncement, 'He is a wealthy man but this does not buy my protection. Bring me my sedan chair, we are paying him a visit.'

When they arrived at Guang Zi Lian's house a crowd of servants had gathered around the body which lay close to the alabaster door. Everyone had tried to lift the immortal's lifeless body, even five of the strongest guards had combined their strength to lift him but no-one could do so.

There was a cry from the back of the crowd, 'Make way for

the old gentleman of Hunan.'

The crowd pulled aside to make way for the respected magistrate who went straight to Li Tie Guai's body and knelt at his side. He called into the crowd for a Daoist teacher and an elderly man in a blue robe stepped forward.

'Please examine him, teacher', asked Zhao Shen Qiao, 'and tell me if there is anything unusual.'

The teacher walked slowly around the body and then examined the pockets in Li Tie Guai's torn jacket. He pulled out a crumpled piece of red paper and read out the words written on it for all to hear.

'Do not make Guang Zi Lian pay for this crime with his life. Make him sweep the roads leading from this house to every village and town in this province. He must learn that the rich cannot abuse the poor.'

The magistrate took the paper from the teacher and read the faded signature at the bottom. It was signed Li Tie Guai. He turned to his police escort, 'Arrest Guang Zi Lian, bring him to me.'

Guang Zi Lian was forced to kneel at the magistrate's feet. 'An immortal has been killed at your command. I hold you guilty. Are you going to pay with your money or with your life?'

'Take everything I have', replied Guang Zi Lian fearfully. 'I have gold, silver, jewels, my house, my servants. I will give it all for my life.'

'You have made your choice', answered Zhao Shen Qiao. 'Your remaining days will be spent as a road sweeper. You will never again have this power over the poor.'

Guang Zi Lian's arms were tied together and he was led away in chains through the jeering crowd. After he had gone the beggars tried to lift Li Tie Guai's body and were startled to find it was as light as a feather. His body was laid in the shade of a tree while orders were given for a coffin to be brought.

After permission had been given to bury the body on a nearby hillside the whole town turned out to pay respect to the immortal. But when the coffin was lifted it felt empty. The lid was opened but there was nothing inside.

A cry rose from the graveside, 'Someone has stolen our immortal. He was in our care. We will all be crossed by bad fortune.'

The anxious crowd surged forward to look into the coffin while a messenger ran to tell Zhao Shen Qiao what had happened. But the wise magistrate was not perturbed.

'Tell the people of the town they should not worry, they have done nothing wrong. Li Tie Guai's body may have gone but his spirit is always with us. When you need him, he will be there.'

The magistrate was right. Li Tie Guai had changed his body into smoke and risen far into the clouds. While the townspeople were mourning his death he had returned to the immortals' bridge where his friends were waiting to hear his story.

There are countless other immortals, many associated with specific places or even with particular temples. Usually a temple will house one or two such local immortals, who not infrequently turn out to be earlier gods or goddesses of shamanism, absorbed and rededicated as immortals.

The Princess of the Azure Clouds

One such reclaiming or rededicating, is the transformation of the goddess of Tai Shan into the Bi Xia Yuan Jun, the Primordial Princess of the Azure Clouds. She is the goddess of Tai Shan removed and somewhat sanitized as the goddess of childbirth. This continues an oblique reference to her role as the Mother of all creatures, meaning the one who made them, including human beings. She is sometimes represented as an Empress holding an official tablet. Other times she looks like an angel, floating freely with her garments streaming behind her. In the White Cloud Temple in Beijing, she and four other goddesses of childbirth are represented in a hall specially dedicated to them, and Bi Xia takes the central position. See under Tai Shan in chapter 7.

Guan Di

Guan Di or Guan Yu is the god of war, one of the gods of literature and the god of wealth, though usually temples to him are called Wu Sheng – meaning war. He was a historical figure who died in 219 AD, beheaded after a treacherous betrayal. He and his two friends, Lie Bei and Zhang Fei swore an oath together in the Peach Orchard of Zhang Fei, to defend the legitimate rulers of the fading Han dynasty. Lie Bei eventually became the ruler of one of the three kingdoms which resulted from the collapse of the Han Empire, the Shu kingdom covering much of present day Sichuan. He is buried in Chengdu at the Wu Hou Si – or Zhao Jue Temple, where another semi-deified hero of the wars is also buried along with his son.

Guan Di is usually shown stroking his long black beard and holding a halberd. He has standing behind him his son, who was executed at the same time as him, and his faithful assistant Zhou. He has become one of the most popular deities and his image is to be found in most Daoist temples and in many homes and shops. Two ancient and magnificent statues of the god can be seen in Shanxi Museum, Tai Yuan, Shanxi Province, taken from the two very different temples (one of which is known as the Old Guan Di temple) dedicated to the god.

Guan Di is supposedly buried in the Guan Lin temple near Luoyang. The temple has recently been restored and the tomb is a very popular place of pilgrimage and prayer, with many fine statues and carvings. In particular, there are the full set of standard models of Guan Di, ranging from the seated warrior with his two associates, to Guan Di reading, for he is supposed to have mastered the Annuls of Spring and Autumn by the time he was five and hence his title as god of literature.

The Ten Kings of Hell

The world of the dead is served, not just by the Dark Lord but by the Kings or Judges of the Ten Hells. These awesome figures of justice are sometimes portrayed together, with Yama, the head King of the Hells, seated in the middle. They are distinguished either by scenes of the specific tortures which take place in their hell, or by signs indicating which hell they judge. It is quite common to find the first and last kings have their symbols with them: the first is the mirror of souls into which each person looks and sees all those creatures whose lives have been taken to feed or satisfy the dead person when alive. The final scene is that of crossing the bridge from the after-world into a new birth. A full list and details of each of them is given in the section on Gods and Goddesses.

The Sixty Year Gods

Occasionally you will find a room with 60 gods in it. These are the year gods, for China has a 60-year cycle based on two correlated tables. These are the Heavenly stems and the Earth-ly branches. There are ten Heavenly stems and twelve Earthly branches. By repeating the ten Heavenly stems six times and the twelve Earthly branches five times, they form a complete cycle of 60. This is central to Chinese astrology and horoscopes and indeed to just about every aspect of Chinese divination and fortune telling. Traditionally the years were counted by giving the name of the Heavenly stem then the name of the Earthly branch and then the name of the Emperor. Thus, if you were born in the Xin You year of the Emperor Jia Qing, you would know this was the year 1801. As very few Emper-ors reigned for more than 60 years, this worked pretty well as a system.

The sixty gods are usually arranged in accordance with their place in the cycle and are dominated by a larger statue which stands for the god of the actual year you are in. Exam-ples of such halls are to be found in a number of the Daoist temples of Macau while a magnificent and vast hall in the Bai Yun Guan – White Cloud Temple – in Beijing has recently been restored. Visitors like to be photographed standing in front of their year god, so if you can find out your Heavenly stem and Earthly branch of the year you were born in, find your god!

Protector Gods

Zhang Dao Ling

Zhang Dao Ling is a popular figure in Daoist temples. He is very distinctive, with his thick black beard, fierce look and raised exorcism sword. He usually rides a tiger, or holds one of his charms in front of him. His image is also to be found on many charts or papers which can be bought as you enter Daoist temples, offering protection to you and your family against evil spirits.

Zhang Dao Ling is, after Lao Zi, the most important figure in popular Daoism. His story is a fascinating one and goes to the heart of contemporary Daoism.

Until around the 3rd century BC, the notion of personal salvation and meaning was virtually unknown. A person's identity came through being part of a much bigger unit – the family and the state. The Emperor undertook all ritual actions necessary other than basic ones such as birth ceremonies and funerals. Death led to nothing much other than life as an ancestor or existence in a shadowy underworld. But gradually the concept of individual salvation began to grow and the search was on for figures who could assist or give meaning to it. This is one of the reasons why Lao Zi was already deified as the divine/human link between Heaven and Earth and Humanity by the 3rd century BC.

Whatever the reasons, by the early-2nd century AD a new expression of religion had arisen, building upon the back of shamanism, drawing inspiration, imagery and even gods and goddesses from the philosophical writings of the likes of Lao Zi and Zhuang Zi. The origins of this religious development lie in the province of Sichuan where a remarkable man called Zhang Dao Ling was born at some point in the 1st century or early-2nd century AD. A deeply religious individual, his early life is lost in legend, but it is clear that he was a remarkable child. He is reputed to have mastered and understood the *Dao De Jing* by the age of seven. At some point he retreated from ordinary life to the sacred mountain of Qing Cheng Shan where he meditated for some three years or so and from which he sallied forth to begin his teaching.

Qing Cheng Shan is still a sacred mountain and his cave is still there. It is a place of quite remarkable peace and tranquillity, infused with a sense of the sacred which I found quite overpowering when I visited. It is a place where you know that you stand on holy ground and thus walk respectfully.

It was here that one day Zhang Dao Ling received a most extraordinary revelation. Sitting meditating, he suddenly found Lao Zi standing before him. The description of what Lao Zi commanded Zhang to do is fascinating:

> The Most High [Lao Zi] said: 'Men of the world do not respect the true and the orthodox, but honour only pernicious demons. That is why I have taken the name of the Old Lord Newly Appeared.' Then he installed Zhang as the Master of the Three Heavens, of the Orthodox One energy of Peace of the Great Mysterious Capital; he revealed to him the Way of the Covenant with the Powers of the Orthodox One. The order of the Old Lord Newly Appeared was to abolish things from the era of the [demoniacal] Six Heavens, and to install the orthodoxy of the Three Heavens, to banish the superficial and the flowery and to return to the simple and true.
>
> *(From the San Tian Nei Jie Jing of the Daoist Canon, translated by Kristofer Schipper in* The Taoist Body *page 61)*

This Covenant with the 'Newly Appeared' Lao Zi gave Zhang the authority to organize religious communities, to forgive faults and sins, to heal and, most important of all, to exorcize ghosts, demons and evil spirits. Lao Zi also gave Zhang a demon-slaying sword with which he could cause any demon to be trapped and defeated. Zhang is usually depicted holding his sword, of very ancient design as a badge of his authority. The date traditionally given for Zhang receiving this Covenant is 142 AD.

Zhang organized the first full-scale religious expression of

Daoism and his Five Bushels movement, named after the entry fee of five bushels or rice, soon spread across Sichuan and into neighbouring provinces. Zhang established his followers, whose fee entitled them to forgiveness of their sins and entry into the cosmic Covenant with Lao Zi, into parishes and diocese, very similar to that of the Christian Church in its Catholic or Anglican forms.

The tradition established by Zhang came to be known as the Celestial Masters' School, also known as the Orthodox Path Way – Zhengyi. It is still headed by a direct descendant of Zhang Dao Ling who lives in Taiwan. In China, members of the Zhang family are very involved in national Daoist affairs and a 68th descendant presented the Daoist declaration on Nature to HRH The Prince Philip at Windsor Castle in 1995, the first time such a leading dignitary of Daoism had ever visited England let alone met a member of the Royal Family.

The Celestial Masters' School still has its network of parishes with their local priests, though this was massively disrupted by the Cultural Revolution. Essentially Zhang's tradition provides the local, ordinary Daoist priests while the Quan Zhen tradition provides the monastic tradition.

Li Nuo Zha

A similar figure, evoked to defend you against evil spirits and in particular against forces which rise up to oppress you, is the striking statue of Li Nuo Zha, usually simply called Nuo Zha and termed the Third Son or Third Prince. His feet stand upon spinning wheels or circles and his hands grasp a flashing ring of metal and a long spear. His hair is also distinctive, being two bunches of hair on either side, like pony tails but shorter. He looks youthful and so he should. His story is one of the most popular in China for he fought a long and violent struggle against the water dragon kings, to clear his name. At the age of seven he was bathing in a river when he killed a dragon officer in a fit of pique using his golden ring. From this arose a whole series of incidents: the dragon king demanded the boy's life and when his father, the king of the country, refused, even

138

though he admitted his son has done a terrible crime, the dragon king threatened to destroy the kingdom. Nuo Zha gave his own life to save those of his parents and his kingdom.

He was however brought back to life by, some say, Lao Zi, and then returned for a long sequence of battles against his father. These were ended when Lao Zi in the form of the Primordial Nature of the Dao stopped Nuo Zha killing his father. Nuo Zha was tamed by flames leaping up around his feet – these are sometimes portrayed on statues or in paintings. Nuo Zha became a protector deity and his father, Li Zhang, became an immortal whose symbol is a golden pagoda which he carries and with which he defends the poor.

The God of Literature

The God of Literature, Wen Chang, who along with Guan Di is considered the patron of scholars, is one of the most complex of Chinese gods, for his origins lie far back in mythology. He is thought to have been the Thunder god of the Shu but he is more commonly traced from a variety of other sources, stretching back into history.

Venerated by Confucians and others alike, he is also known as the Emperor of Literature. His titles are Wen Chang Di Jun, Wen Chang or just Wen Di. The focus of scholars' devotion is Kong Fu Zi himself, but the legends of Wen Chang place him well before the sage was born, well before the 5th century BC. For Wen Chang is a god who comes to earth to bring wisdom and understanding to the people. According to the legends and accounts, he has come to earth seventeen times in different human forms. Wen Chang himself is a constellation of six stars in attendance upon the Great Bear. When Wen Chang perceives that learning and wisdom are weak upon the earth, he descends and takes human form.

Wen Chang has, for example, manifested himself as Zhang Ya Zi, known as the Spirit of Zi Dung – a mountain region in Sichuan. He appeared as Zhang Ya Zi around 300 AD and died after a violent fight, defending the Office of which he was in charge.

At other times he was revealed as a wise and just official who became the President of the Board of Ceremonies, and who was renowned for his wisdom and astuteness. For this manifestation he took the name Zhang Ya and was born during the Tang dynasty (618–907 AD). It was after this incarnation that he was given the Celestial Office of Keeper of the Registers of Titles. The Jade Emperor commissioned him to look out for those who were worthy of award and to bestow titles and honours upon those students and officials who deserved them. To him also falls responsibility for punishing those who betray their posts or offices and exploit the people.

One of his most dramatic interventions was in the year 1000 AD. He yet again appeared in Sichuan, this time at the capital of the province, Chengdu. At that time the rebel Wang Chun had seized the city and was using it as the base for his revolt against the Sung dynasty. The Emperor sent his loyal and devout general, Lei Yu Chong to retake the city. But try as they would, it held out against them and Wang Chun mocked their efforts. In an attempt to break their morale, General Lei Yu Chong fired arrows into the beleaguered town, carrying messages offering an amnesty to any who surrendered.

Then, suddenly and from nowhere, a man appeared who mounted a ladder and gesticulating towards the rebels shouted in a loud voice that he came bearing a message. He claimed that the spirit of Zi Dung (Wen Chang) had commanded him to say that the rebel city would fall into the hands of the Emperor's army on the twentieth day of the ninth month and that no-one would escape from the city alive.

Sure enough, on the twentieth day of the ninth month, General Lei attacked Chengdu and the city fell. Not a single rebel soldier escaped alive. To commemorate this event, the General repaired the temple of Zi Dung, originally built after his miraculous intervention to save the old kingdom of Shu.

Guai Xing
Wen Chang is not alone in his office as Bestower of Titles, Scholar Deity and Emperor of Literature. In particular he has

140

one very special colleague who usually stands either before or beside him. And he is a most odd-looking gentleman. He too comes from a constellation of stars in the Great Bear, the four which make up the chariot of the Great Bear and thus is to be found in the same part of the Heavens as the Wen Chang constellation.

The name of this deity constellation is Guai Xing and the story told of him is a very special one, as indeed is the form of his statue. Guai Xing is usually depicted standing upon the head of a sea monster. His left leg is raised behind him as if he is running. In his right hand he holds a writing brush, in his left, a seal of office. What is most striking however is his hideous face.

Long ago a son was born to a poor family in China. He was much loved by his family but he was hideously ugly. No matter how you looked at him, he was grotesque. But he was of delightful demeanour and exceptionally bright. The family, poor as they were, recognized that in his wisdom and knowledge they had a gem which if polished and perfected would bring honour and fortune to the whole family.

For years this child, Zhong Guai, studied. Night and day he learned to master the Classics of Kong Fu Zi. Year after year he took his exams and progressed rapidly, rising from town to city to county then to provincial examinations. At last he reached the peak, the apex of the imperial examination world. Travelling to the Imperial City, he entered the imperial examinations. To no-one's great surprise, he came first, clearly the best of a good group that year. An outstanding scholar, even if his visage was a terrible one.

It was the practice of the Emperor personally to meet the top scholar and to present him with a golden rose in commemoration of his success. Zhong Guai duly turned up at the Imperial Palace, and was eagerly admitted to the Imperial Presence. However, disaster struck. The Emperor, seeing Zhong Guai's terrible appearance, took fright and refused to have the scholar in his presence.

Zhong Guai, crushed and humiliated by this, rushed from

the Imperial Palace and, running to the sea, cast himself upon it, intent upon committing suicide. The gods, seeing this injustice, sent a giant fish or sea monster to rescue him. At the very moment when he was about to go under for the last time, Zhong Guai found himself being lifted up on the head of the creature. But he was not just rescued from the sea. The creature continued to rise, up through the clouds; up into the sky; up into the very firmaments themselves. The fish bore him to the Guai Constellation and there the gods gave him command over the fortunes of scholars. From there, along with his brother in Scholarship, Wen Chang, Guai Xing looks after the fortunes of scholars and officials.

Chu I

Wen Chang is accompanied by another god, Chu I, Red Gown as he is commonly known. He is very popular with students preparing for exams as he is known to help and to influence examiners if he feels a worthy student didn't do too well in the written paper!

The Dog Star

The Dog Star turns up in association with a protector and justice god, Er Lang, meaning second son. This denotes his origin as a reputed second son of a heroic king of the Sichuan area, who put his life on the line with Er Lang's assistance, in order to kill an evil river dragon. The temple to the two of them, built in the Tang dynasty, is still to be found in Guan Xian, Sichuan Province and is called the Temple of the Two Kings – Er Wang Miao. It stands at the site of the giant, 3rd century BC irrigation scheme of Du Jiang Yan. For the story of the struggle with the water dragon is actually a true story about controlling the massive rivers that flow through that area (Sichuan simply means Four Rivers). The statues of Li Bing the king and his son Er Lang are enormous and very modern, done in socialist art style, for this divinized pair are considered communist heroes because they controlled nature and saved the people. The temple complex is considerable and the view of the canalized and dammed river below, stunning. It is easy to see why the struggle with the 'water dragon' was so vital. Er Lang has since risen in position, out-flanking his father. Er Lang is the head of the troops of the Jade Emperor and is charged with fighting all those who threaten the stability of Heaven or Earth. His most famous and largely unsuccessful battle, is the one recounted in the *Journey to the West*, when Er Lang tried to control Monkey, Great Sage Equal to Heaven (see page 105).

Part of the Heavenly forces Er Lang has at his disposal are the two door gods of Daoist temples, Qing Long and Bai Hu – Blue Dragon and White Tiger. They are both gods of stars which go by these two names and which guard the entrance to all Daoist holy places. They are found in small shrines on either side of the gates into Daoist temples.

City Gods

The gods of the District, known as the city gods – Cheng Huang – were of great importance in the pre-Cultural Revolution days. Each city, each town, had its protective deity who acted as a sort of spiritual Mayor. Each city had its city god temple, but most have now disappeared as the whole edifice of Heavenly Bureaucracy has crumbled. The city god was usually someone associated with the city through history or through mythology. For example, in Shanghai, the city god temple – Cheng Huang Miao – still stands, though somewhat battered. There are two main deities of the city venerated here. One is Lao Zi, who was adopted by the city for reasons which are far from clear. The other is the hero General Huo Guang – he has a red face and the usual long beard of a general – who is associated with battles in the area.

One of the best preserved of all the city gods' temples is in Xian. The oldest known city god temple is in Wuhu, Anhui Province, dating back to 240 AD, but I have no idea what state it is in at present, or indeed if it has survived at all.

The most famous of all city god temples, even though he is no longer the city god, is that of Yue Fei in Hangzhou.

143

Yue Fei

By the great central lake of Hangzhou, nestling on the coast of Zhejiang province, stands a tomb and temple. It contains the beheaded body of Yue Fei, a famous general who was executed for treachery in 1142. Yet within a few decades, this disgraced, executed criminal was being worshipped as the city god of Hangzhou, to whom petitions and prayers were brought to avert plagues, siege or economic collapse. Within a hundred years or so of his death, stories were beginning to circulate that he was none other than the reincarnated phoenix who stands on perpetual guard by the side of the Buddha, ready to strike down any who would do harm to the Buddha. Under the Communists, Yue Fei has been elevated to the status of a patriotic hero and worshipped for his selflessness in the face of the enemy and his cry, 'Return our mountains and rivers'.

The stories around Yue Fei illustrate perfectly the way in which Chinese folk religion can absorb three completely different strands and produce a composite whole. First, the Confucian strand.

Yeu Fei was a loyal citizen of China. He was born in 1103 under the weak and feeble rule of the emperors of the Southern Song – so called because they had lost the north of China to invading tribes and had ended up making Hangzhou their capital, having been driven from their old capital.

Despite the fact that this was a weak dynasty, Yue Fei, as a good Confucian, was loyal to it. He was also loyal to his mother and to the virtues she impressed upon him. Literally impressed upon him, for when he went to join the army she tattooed the words, 'Loyal even unto death for my country', upon his back.

Over the years he rose in authority, taking on greater and greater commands until he became a general. In the year 1140, he led a vast peasant army north, and almost entirely on his own initiative, counter-attacked the invading Mongolians, inflicting a crushing defeat upon them. He was all for pressing further ahead, perhaps actually recapturing most of northern China, but he was betrayed. For back in the capital in Hangzhou, there was one, in a position of greatest trust, whose intention was betrayal. The feeble Emperor's prime minister Qin Hui and his wife were in regular contact with the enemy. They had no love of China itself. They feared the rallying cry of Yue Fei, 'Return our mountains and rivers', and saw in him a potential new emperor who would foil their own plans to rule.

They poisoned the mind of the Emperor and made him summon home Yue Fei. Once away from his loyal troops, the evil minister accused him of treachery and of planning to usurp the Throne – he the most loyal of the servants of the Emperor. Yue Fei sought to show his loyalty and removed his shirt to reveal the words of loyalty tattooed upon his back. But to no avail. The Emperor was weak and consented to the execution of Yue Fei and his son. Taken from the city, they were swiftly beheaded and their bodies cast into shallow graves.

Meanwhile, the prime minister and his wife, along with two other treacherous ministers, arranged a treaty with the invaders which virtually handed over the whole of China to them. Many years later, when the Chinese re-asserted themselves, the betrayal by the prime minister was reviled and Yue Fei honoured as a model of loyalty to the Emperor and to the Empire. A temple was built beside his tomb in 1221 and he was praised by poets and ministers alike in poetry, extolling him as a model Confucian scholar warrior. Ironically, it is as a model of national loyalty that he was also elevated by the Communists who have presented him as one of the greatest examples of a patriotic general.

So at one level, Yue Fei is venerated as a noble ancestor who exemplifies the true virtues of a Confucian – filial piety and loyalty.

Then there is the Daoist version. This follows much the same course as the historical tale set out above, except that Yue Fei in his fight against the invaders had the assistance of various Daoist gods – such as the war god, the god of Thunder – and the help of magicians who fought the evil spirits who accompanied the hordes of the enemy. Yue Fei became a fighter against evil both of this world and of the spirit world. His success was the victory of good over evil. His betrayal was the cost, the sacrificial cost, of such a struggle, for from his example comes the power to fight back. But it was after his death that he really came into his own. By popular acclaim, later confirmed by the ruling Emperors, Yue Fei was worshipped as the City god of Hangzhou. This meant that he was believed to now dwell in Heaven, in the court of the Daoist ruler of Heaven, the Jade Emperor. There, along with all the other gods of the cities of China, he cared for his city – ensuring that the prayers and entreaties of the faithful were heard and disasters either avoided or mitigated if possible. The temple surrounding his tomb was enlarged to make space for the hundreds of worshippers who brought their cares and tribulations to him and offered him food, incense and devotion. Yue Fei had become a god.

Finally there is the Buddhist story.

Once upon a time, the Buddha was meditating, protected by the phoenix, who never sleeps but who guards the Buddha night and day. Into the room flew a strange spirit of discord known as the Old White Bat, squeaking and flapping its wings. This disturbed the meditations of the Buddha and to protect him, the phoenix leapt upon the Old White Bat and tore it to pieces.

The Buddha was distressed and angered by the zeal of the phoenix and to punish him, sent him to be reborn upon earth in the form of a white eagle. This was a most demanding incarnation within which to work for salvation from his previous action, for the eagle is itself a violent creature, which lives by the kill. However, the phoenix knew he must live by the precept of taking no life. The phoenix sought to control his instincts in the hope of rebirth in a more favourable form. Sadly this was all to no avail. One day he espied a tortoise on a river bank. Overcome with the desire to kill he swept down, seized the poor tortoise and devoured it there and then.

Through the cycle of rebirth, the Buddha decided to provide another opportunity for his faithful servant the phoenix to redeem himself. So the phoenix/white eagle was reborn as Yue Fei the brave and patriotic general. Despite his valiant defence of his country and his model of loyalty, he was betrayed by the treachery of the Emperor's adviser, Qin Hui, who was none other than the poor tortoise the phoenix had killed in his previous life, and the even more treacherous wife of Qin Hui who was the reborn spirit of the Old White Bat.

The tortoise and the Old White Bat were out for revenge. They told the Emperor that Yue Fei was in communication with the enemy in order to betray the empire. In fact it was Qin Hui and his wife who were trying to betray the empire to the enemy and they feared that Yue Fei would find out.

The phoenix in the form of Yue Fei proved to have learned his lesson. Despite the most terrible provocations and the most dreadful betrayals by all around, he remained loyal to his oath of obedience. He could have raised his army as a rebel and overthrown the Emperor – but he did not. He could have attacked the evil minister Qin Hui and his wife – but he did not. He could have fled to safety – but he did not. He remained and took the punishment given him, always protesting his total loyalty and showing that on his own back his mother had tattooed, 'Loyal even unto death for my country'.

After his execution as a condemned criminal, he had to undergo the most awful punishments in the eighteen Buddhist Hells before at long last his countrymen recognized his real virtue and erected a temple over his tomb. When this happened, the Buddha was able to send a message to the Judges of Hell demanding that the soul of Yue Fei, the phoenix, be released and given back its phoenix form. The phoenix who never sleeps continues to guard the Lord Buddha day and night.

But Qin Hui and his wife had fallen prey to vengeance and violence. For them the cycle of dreadful rebirths has only just begun and they will turn in suffering for 80,000 rebirths each one as dreadful as the other until they have cleansed themselves of the crime against Yue Fei, the never sleeping phoenix.

The temple was rebuilt in 1979 to reflect a mixture of religious and nationalistic, even communist ideals. But at its heart there is still the same essence. A loyal citizen betrayed. People today still spit at the statues of the four betrayers, Qin Hui, his wife Wangshi, and Mo Qixie and Zhang Jun, generals who betrayed Yue Fei. Beside Yue Fei on the main altar are his faithful commanders Niu Gao and Zhang Xian. This is still a place to recall Confucian virtues of loyalty and honour, and as such it has made the transition from Confucian temple and shrine to Maoist temple and shrine with ease, and will undoubtedly make the transition back to quasi-religious shrine again when the times change.

The Iron Lady

The ability of China to create new gods and goddesses is without end. As I pointed out at the very start of the book, Mao Ze Dong has even been elevated. But perhaps the most alarming new addition to the pantheon of popular religion in China is a certain woman.

In 1991, I was in Guangdong province, near Mount Lofou, one of the main mountains in southern Guangdong, visiting a family of friends of mine from Hong Kong. The reason for the visit was a grand wedding. As is now usual in China, the wedding was an odd mixture of traditional Chinese with glossy magazine Western wedding. The bride wore a white dress then changed into a traditional dragon and phoenix dress. The ancestors were worshipped and a karaoke machine played throughout the whole celebration, throwing blurred images up onto the roof of the restaurant where the wedding feast was held.

At one point, however, we visited the local temple to make offerings to the earth god, village god, district god and various wealth, prosperity and pregnancy gods and goddesses. All was very familiar. There stood the traditional southern Chinese god of wealth in his big mandarin hat, holding a scroll with good luck sentiments upon it. There was a fat boy holding big carp and large peaches, symbols of fertility. There was the

148

smiling god of happiness. There was a picture of Mrs Thatcher smiling and waving! Never having been much of a fan of the Iron Lady, I enquired of my hosts what she was doing there. 'She is a very powerful lady', a view with which I did not demur. 'She will give lots of money to the happy couple', I was told. 'She will bring success to their business.' Yes, the worst fears of the Conservative Party have been fulfilled. Mrs Thatcher has become a goddess and is to be found being worshipped as a modern goddess of success and wealth in southern China.

Such is the diversity and fascination of visiting the gods and goddesses of sacred China.

PART THREE

THE SACRED LANDSCAPES AND BUILDINGS OF CHINA

TEMPLES AND MONASTERIES

Think of a classic Chinese landscape painting and you will almost certainly find a temple or shrine incorporated into the design somewhere. The temples, monasteries and shrines of China were one of the most all pervasive elements of sacred China. Even today, after nearly a hundred years of destruction and neglect, these wonderful buildings are still to be found in both rural and urban landscapes. In the countryside, especially in the hills and mountains, you can feel as if you have stepped back in time when confronted by a traditional Buddhist or Daoist temple on a mountainside. In the cities, often the only really beautiful buildings left are the temples, and not infrequently, where there are still trees and greenery, there will be a religious site.

In this chapter I want to quite literally take you inside some of my favourite buildings in China as well as provide you with keys which can unlock the significance of its sacred buildings. I hope that using this you can appreciate the design, motifs and purpose of these places, for they express not just the skill of the architect and the artists who made them but the theology of those who commissioned them. They are statements of the divine in layout and in stone.

To begin with, virtually all Confucian, Daoist and Buddhist temples are sited according to feng shui – wind, water –

meaning geomancy. Thus their axis is south to north and the temples almost always face south, the direction of the Emperor and of Heaven. All the statues face south.

Feng shui is the concept of sacred China at its most fundamental, for the art of feng shui is essentially the art of building, planning and even, indeed especially, burial in order to be in harmony with the flow of the Dao in a given area. Quintessentially, feng shui is about recognizing that the very land, the hills, the rivers and streams, are alive and that we must be a part of all that already exists, not stand apart from it. Zhong, the 5th century BC philosopher, put it rather nicely in his text Guan Zi:

> The earth is the origin of all things, the root and garden of all life; and the place where all things, the beautiful, the ugly, the good, the bad, the foolish and the clever, come into being. Now water is the blood and breath of the earth, flowing and communicating (within the body) as if in sinews and veins.

It is no accident that landscape gardening and landscape painting both originated in China. Feng shui is about ensuring that what humanity builds blends in with or emphasizes the best of nature. This is why landscape paintings so often include a temple, because the temple will have been built at the most auspicious and most enhancing part of the mountain or landscape. As the quote above indicates, traditional Chinese belief sees the very land and waters as being alive. Through picture language, terms such as dragons for hills and mountains and tigers for rivers, feng shui attempts to capture this sense of power and life in the very materials of the land. I would argue that those who look at the terms and see a literal belief in dragons and tigers being in the land are missing the point. Feng shui uses these terms as doorways to the imagination; to convey the sense that the shape of the land is imbued with meaning and significance; to try and make the point that human activity is but one activity amongst many on the land of China and that we should learn to know our place.

Feng shui was for many years mocked and derided by 'educated' Chinese and Westerners, who saw it as being superstitious. In recent years, however, we have come to appreciate its environmental importance. One of my colleagues, Man Ho Kwok, is the only properly trained feng shui master in the UK. With Man Ho, we have developed many feng shui programmes for our landscape, from working with the developers of London's Docklands to redesigning offices of major companies. This is not because people believe in dragons, but because Man Ho's approach to our own environment asks us to stop and think about scale, about colour, about tree planting, about direction, sunlight and wind and about what sort of living environment we actually find good to work within.

In China, the results of abandoning feng shui are all too clear to see. The old cities with their sacred directions – main streets running north/south and east/west – their auspicious coloured tiles and brickwork; their relationship between land and water and sense of scale and proportion, have been largely swept away. Instead, Socialist Realism and now market forces capitalism have come instead with their notion of functional, cheap, pack them in and build them high. The result is that China has some of the ugliest cities in the world, often swamping and obliterating cities which used to be renown for their beauty and their sense of being a part of the landscape.

To return to the topic of landscape paintings, this is to be clearly seen if you look at Communist inspired traditional landscape painting. For instead of graceful pagodas and temples nestling amongst the mountains, you have factories belching out smoke or high rise blocks dominating the landscape. Nothing could more clearly indicate the loss of proportion or the dramatic change in attitude to relationship with nature.

So to find a temple or monastery in the midst of this urban blight is to stumble upon an older, gentler world and to glimpse, perhaps only briefly, how different things can be.

Even before you enter a sacred building in China, there are signs which tell you this is special. To prevent evil spirits gaining entrance, there are three basic measures taken. The first is to have a false wall built in front of the main gate, for evil spirits can only travel in a straight line and thus when they rush the main gate, they are deflected by the false wall. Should this fail, then a second strategy is to build a pond or incorporate a stream into the front part of the temple, which is crossed by a bridge or series of bridges. Evil spirits cannot cross water, not even on a bridge, so this prevents any further entry. Good examples of this are the Confucian Temple in Qufu where a stream has been turned into a canal to run in front of the main halls, crossed by three bridges, and the Jin Si near Tai Yuan, Shanxi, where the diverted Jin river serves to aid agriculture and to defend the temple. Finally, most temples will have door gods (see page 72) who defend the site from attack. In Daoism these are usually Qing Long and Bai Hu, Blue Dragon and White Tiger. In Buddhist temples, they are the Four Heavenly Kings.

All temples and monasteries are walled with very clear and restricted entrances. This not only marks out the special nature of the place, but it also protects it from assault, both physical and spiritual. The walls of the temple grounds are usually covered with tiles, at the end of which are depicted grimacing faces and symbols of longevity such as bats or butterflies. The grimacing faces are there to scare away evil doers – in much the same way that gargoyles on European churches were designed to do. The symbols of longevity express this common and deeply held view and hope in China. The same designs cover the roofs of the temples as well.

The decision to site the temple at that precise place will have been in accord with strict feng shui rules. Where the site is in the countryside, or was until swallowed up by towns and cities, the feng shui master will have looked for a site which was either on the pulse of a dragon (hill) or in front of a dragon, stretching down to water. In cities, the temples are located on the grid plans of the city, which itself will have been drawn up by a feng shui master.

Most Buddhist temples follow a pattern established by use of the yin yang model which, so far as I know, is not repeated in Daoist temples. The first, third and fifth halls are dedicated to male deities, bodhisattvas, etc, as the odd numbers are yang, while the second, fourth and sixth halls are dedicated to female deities, as the even numbers are yin. This is very clearly to be seen in temples such as the Guan Yin temple in Macau – local dialect pronunciation, Kun Iam – and at the Wen Shu monastery in Chengdu.

On most temples will be seen elaborate figures at the ends of the roofs, on the ridges. In the oldest such temples, these will be guardian soldiers and deities, fierce in aspect, defending the temple from flying evil spirits. On more homely and more recent temples, these will be the strange sight of a man riding a chicken! It is believed that just as the chicken picks and eats gravel to help its digestion, thus it is able to pick and eat tough evil spirits.

Most temples will also have bell and drum towers. These stand just inside the main gate and have the practical purpose of calling the faithful to worship and of giving warning of attack.

So it is that even before you enter a hall or see a deity, you are in a magic, divine space. It has been consecrated by ensuring that it lies within the best aspects of the landscape and in accordance with the powers and forces that already exist in the land itself, in its river and hills. In a very real sense, the temples arise from the sense of the sacredness of the physical environment and seek to enhance it. Which, almost without exception, they do – especially when contrasted to the secular buildings which are rising all around them today. So enter the temple, aware that you tread on holy ground.

CONFUCIAN TEMPLES

The Confucian temples are no longer numerous, but they are a key expression of the formal culture of China, the imperial view of the divine if you like.

The greatest of the Confucian temples is of course the Temple of Heaven in Beijing and its sister, the much simpler Temple of the Earth. Their function was cosmic in the extreme, as the sacrifices by the Emperor at each of them, at the appropriate times (winter at the southern Temple of Heaven because it is the yang temple and the yang, male, hot force is at its weakest in winter; summer for the Temple of Earth in the north, because this is the yin direction and it is at its weakest in summer) kept the universe in order. All the buildings of the Temple of Heaven are circular, including the terraces where the sacrifices took place, while the Temple of Earth is square.

The function of a Confucian temple is to provide a palace for an official. Modelled upon the imperial bureaucratic system, the Confucian religious system simply elevated the whole imperial edifice into the spiritual realm. But this did not mean that you treated the gods as anything other than rather pernickety bureaucrats. Hence the title of many temples contains the word miao, meaning palace or residence.

Entrance is through a main gate, which would normally be protected by doors gods. The first courtyard will often contain fine steles with the names of those from the area who passed the imperial exams. The entrance gate, along with the other gates and halls of the temple complex, will reflect some combination of the titles given to Kong Fu Zi during the 2,000 years when emperors conferred titles upon him. To my mind, the most wonderful of all Confucian sites is the hometown of Confucius himself, Qufu. Here, in what I believe is the largest Confucian temple, you can see the whole gamut of Confucian ideas and values, laid out in architecture. For Confucian temples were built to embody the moral and hierarchical values of both Confucian teachings and practice, and of the Empire. To give you some idea, these are the titles of the major gates and halls in the Confucian temple, Qufu:

1 Archway of the striking of Gongs and the Musical Stones (see below).
2 Gateway of the Ling Xing star of Literature (part of Great Bear constellation).

3 Gateway of the Original Ether of Supreme Harmony.
4 Temple archway of the Exalted Sage.
5 Gate of the Timelessness of the Sage.
6 Gate of Esteeming the Lofty.
7 Gate of Augmenting the Truth.
8 Gate of the Great Mean.
9 Temple of the Constellation of Scholars.
10 Gate of the Search After Purity.
11 Gate of the Spectacle of the Virtues.
12 Gate of the Succession of the Sage.
13 Gate of Great Achievements.
14 Hall of Silk and Metal – meaning stringed and percussion instruments.
15 Hall of Great Achievements.
16 Temple for Honouring the Sage.

It may seem an odd point to raise about someone whose temples we are currently discussing, but it has to be asked, was Kong Fu Zi in any sense religious? He is supposed to have replied when asked about the world of spirits and gods, that he found it quite enough work trying to sort out this world, never mind any other! He also put the issue of the importance of the other world into a rather nice perspective:

> Ji Lu [one of his followers] asked how the spirits of the dead and the gods should be served. The Master said, 'You are not able even to serve humanity. How can you serve the spirits?'
> When the unfortunate Ji Lu asked about death, Confucius replied in similar vein:
> 'You do not understand even life. How can you understand death?'
> (Analects, *Book XI, 12. Adapted from the translation by D.C. Lau*)

The values of scholarly integrity are to be found in the many steles in Confucian temples. For ren – benevolence – was no empty concept. Many scholars took real risks. For example, one major festival, Dragon Boat Festival, celebrates just such an incident. Chu Yuan was a local magistrate who ruled his district with compassion and largess. He loved the people and the people loved him. Unfortunately, the Emperor of the time was not a good Emperor. He oppressed the people with taxes and military levees. Chu Yuan tried to be a loyal citizen but he increasingly found it difficult to obey the orders that came from the corrupt Emperor.

One day it all proved too much and, taking up his pen, Chu Yuan penned a Memorial to the Throne, taking the Emperor to task for his corruption, avarice and lack of benevolence.

The Emperor was bound by tradition to read all such Memorials, but he paid no attention and simply laughed at the complaints of the magistrate. Driven to despair by this, Chu Yuan decided that he must try and bring the Emperor to his senses by some last dramatic gesture. He climbed to the top of the local hill overlooking the lake of the city and threw himself in, having left a suicide note explaining that the corruption of the Emperor left him no other recourse. The local people saw his suicide dive and took to their boats to try and rescue him. As they drew near they saw evil dragon spirits rising from the depths to consume his body. To divert these dragons, the people threw balls of rice into the water and as the dragons were diverted, the boats were able to reach Chu Yuan's body and bring it back to the city for burial.

Needless to say, the Emperor was shocked out of his abuse of power and became a model ruler. And to this day, on the fifth day of the fifth month of the Chinese calendar, the Dragon Boat Festival takes place to commemorate this brave man.

Unfortunately, not all such stories have happy endings. Often, courageous officials who sought to remind the Emperor of the importance of ren, were executed as traitors or sent into exile. But still Confucian scholars would continue to send in Memorials to the Throne, despite the risk to their own lives. Ren was not just a nice idea. It was central to good government.

Confucian temples reflect the cardinal elements of Confucian belief very clearly in their names for the different areas and in the rituals which used to be carried out within them. Some combination of the titles used in the Qufu temple will form the succession of gates and halls in a Confucian temple such as the one in Yixing, Jiangsu Province, which is renowned for its statues.

In the Confucian temple in Beijing, for example, the succession of gates and halls goes as follows:

1 Ancient Teacher Gate.
2 Great Achievement Gate.
3 Great Achievement Hall.
4 Temple for Honouring the Sage.

At Qufu there is a particularly lovely reminder to the descendants of Kong about the proper hierarchy and about Dao, ren, de and li. In the Mansion of Kong, the great family or clan houses of his descendants, there is a simple yet beautiful painting of a qi-lin. This creature, which has features of the unicorn, lion, dragon and deer, is often associated with legends of Confucius. But it is placed here because one trait of the qi-lin is that it goes too far and is destroyed. For example, it can fly but will try and fly to the sun and is thus burnt up. It can fight well, but will choose to go on against odds that are overwhelming and thus perishes. The Kong family, honoured and revered even by Emperors, needed a reminder that they might lose it all if they went too far – if they reached out for the Imperial Throne for example. They never did, and perhaps the fact that to leave their Mansion they had to pass the painting of the qi-lin, kept them mindful of their place in the order of life!

Often present in a Confucian temple are stone and metal chimes. For example, the Confucian temple of Heaven has a magnificent set. These chimes, consisting of stone or metal bars in a sort of fat boomerang shape, are again reminders of the cosmic nature of Chinese tradition. The tones were established in antiquity and Kong Fu Zi comments on their having been perfectly tuned and pitched in the past, in accordance with Nature, with the Dao. One of the signs of the decline of culture

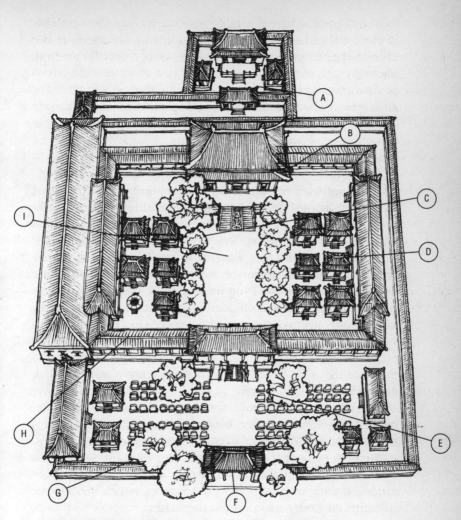

Figure 1: Kong Miao or Wen Miao – Confucius Temple. Beijing

A Temple for Honouring the Sage

B Da Cheng Dian – Great Achievement Hall. Tablet inscribed to Kong Fu Zi in the centre of main altar

C Tree for Humbling Officials

D Halls covering Steles concerning the honours accorded Kong Fu Zi by various Emperors

E Da Cheng Meng – Great Achievement Gate

F Ancient Teacher Gate

G Steles commemorating famous Confucian scholars

H Well

I Imperial walk way, only used by Emperors

in Kong's book is that the tones, the chimes, have become disjointed, out of harmony, literally, with the universe. It is the role of the Emperor to ensure they are correctly pitched. Hence in every major administrative city, the Confucian temple would have had such chimes to ensure the right pitch for all ceremonial music. These now hang oddly silent, as if being in harmony with the universe was either no longer desirable or no longer possible. Hence the Gate of Striking Gongs and Musical Stones and the Hall of Silk and Metal in Qufu.

Inscriptions, often by the hand of an emperor, are important in Confucian temples as signs of the imperial investment in Confucian rites and beliefs. Statues are not as common in Confucian shrines as in other temples and very few survived the purges of the Cultural Revolution, nor indeed the purges that when on before this. Essentially, Confucian temples have been out of favour since the Revolution in 1911, when the imperial dynasty of the Qing was ended in all significant ways (they hung on in the Forbidden City, performing their rituals until 1924). From 1911 onwards, many Confucian temples, no longer needed for official rituals and not greatly used by the ordinary people, became schools, libraries or museums – roles many of them have today which is why few can be visited, even where they do survive.

The statues which would have existed and still do, as at Yixing in Jiangsu Province, or as a few in Beijing, are of worthies such as Kong Fu Zi himself of course and famous disciples such as Meng Zi or later teachers such as Zhu Xi (1130 – 1200 AD) whose synthesis of Confucian, Daoist and Buddhist thought produced what is called neo-Confucianism, which became the standard for Confucian thought thereafter.

Inside the main hall where sacrifices would have been offered at the appropriate times of year, there is usually a statue of Kong plus, on either side, rows of the most important disciples – the number of which differs from place to place, but most commonly there are twelve of them. This mirrors the eighteen lohans concept of Buddhism and is obviously a straight borrowing from Buddhism.

Today, the few remaining Confucian temples not in use for other purposes, are quiet places of trees and old buildings. The sense that their time is past is overpowering, for there is no conceivable way that they will ever serve again the imperial, cosmic and bureaucratic role they once served for over 2,000 years. Here, one feels, is a belief system which time has left stranded. Yet perhaps for precisely this reason, I find them places of great peace; places where one reflects almost instinctively about the passing of greatness, as in Shelley's 'Ozymandias':

I met a traveller from an antique land
Who said: 'Two vast and trunkless legs of stone
Stand in the desert. Near them, on the sand,
Half sunk, a shattered visage lies, whose frown,
And wrinkled lip, and sneer of cold command,
Tell that its sculptor well those passions read
Which yet survive, stamped on these lifeless things,
The hand that mocked them and the heart that fed.
And on the pedestal these words appear –
"My name is Ozymandias, king of kings:
Look on my works, ye Mighty, and despair!"
Nothing beside remains. Round the decay
Of that colossal wreck, boundless and bare
The lone and level sands stretch far away.'

BUDDHIST TEMPLES

The title for a Buddhist temple or monastery is si – meaning hall. The term indicates the primary function of such buildings, which is to provide a meeting place, a hall where the Dharma, the teachings of the Buddha, can be expounded by the Sangha, the community of the monks. This reflects the Three Jewels of Buddhism, namely the Buddha, the Dharma and the Sangha. Buddhist temples are unique in China amongst the three main faiths in being designed for teaching as much as for worship. In all the major temples, you will find that while the main halls running down the centre of the south/north axis are for worship, along the sides are teaching halls. Increasingly today it is possible to be in a Buddhist temple and to hear the chanting of sutras or the sound of the teaching monks echoing through the compound.

I love staying in Buddhist monasteries. Once the visitors have gone and the monks are settling down for the night, a great peace descends. I find the final prayers of the day, often performed as dusk comes upon you, are as lovely and as meditative as attending Evensong in some great English cathedral. The worries of the day; the concerns of life; the hassles and tribulations, fall away as you journey with the prayers and chants of the monks into another realm. The sonorous chime of the bronze bell or the clack of the wooden bell seem to awaken you from the unreality of ordinary life into the reality of the transcendent. I really do find it hard to express the sense of being at one with all around which comes to me at such times. For I am not a Buddhist, but a Christian, perhaps a somewhat unorthodox one. Yet here, in the quiet prayers before darkness falls, none of that is of the slightest concern.

To attend such prayers on one of my beloved sacred mountains adds to the joy, but I can just as happily be staying in an urban monastery. After the prayers, in halls and shrines now barely distinguishable by the feeble lights which suffice for the simple needs of the monks and guests, we repair to the dining hall for a simple vegetarian meal. Again, there is something quite wonderful in being looked after by monks and fed with the same food they eat. I find this to be so whether it is in Daoist or Buddhist monasteries. For a brief while, you become part of the flow and rhythm of the monastery; a rhythm which puts all else in perspective.

Lights go out soon after darkness falls, for the morning starts very early indeed. When I first stayed at a Buddhist monastery in China, I and my colleague thought we would be able to get a lot of translation work done. We knew we would have to be in bed by 8.00pm and so we imagined we would

The Imperial Walkway, Forbidden City, Beijing, showing the yang
Dragon and the yin Phoenix

The Buddha at Leshan

A Daoist chanting, part of the daily ritual of the temple

A Family tomb from the Sichuan province

Votive candles offered at a Daoist temple

The Jade Emperor, ruler of the Daoist deities

The Bodhisattva of Compassion, Guan Yin, in the temple of
Ten Thousand Buddhas, Shatin, Hong Kong

Bodhidharma crossing the sea

One of the Ten Courts of Hell

Detail of bell covered with One Thousand Buddhas

The Immortal Lu Tung Pin

God of the Dead who summons the souls to judgement

The Tortoise of Longevity, in Chengdu

Worshippers at a Buddhist temple gate

A Buddhist archway in Puto Shan

Temple roofs of Yong Quan, at Gushan, Fuzhou

A Nestorian cross from the 12th/13th century, from the Museum of Overseas Communication, Quanzhou, Fujian

The Daoist Suspended Temple at Heng Shan, a Sacred Mountain

work until about 10.00pm and then go to sleep. But this does-n't work in such surroundings. All is so peaceful that you feel as if you are violating some ancient sacred ritual if you work on. We strolled outside and looked at the stars, but were both in bed and fast asleep by 8.30. Such is the calming and cen-tring effect of these places.

Nowadays, the monks in both Buddhist and Daoists monas-teries rise even earlier for they not only have their religious duties, but must also staff the monasteries to deal with visitors. Life at such places is hard, but if the Government would lift its very restrictive limit on the number of monks or nuns that temples and monasteries could have, the applicants would run into the tens of thousands.

Perhaps part of this sense of being at one comes from the fact that all Buddhist temples conform to the feng shui princi-ples set out above and many have, as mentioned earlier, the yin and yang arrangement of halls.

The temple will be surrounded by walls and protected as described above, but the doorway will be guarded by the four Heavenly kings rather than by the two doors gods common in Daoist and Confucian temples.

What so often strikes me on entering a temple is the com-mon sight of the fat, laughing Buddha of the Future, Mi Lo Fo, who is almost always seated right in the first gateway. There may also be a statue of Sakyamuni, the historical Buddha, whose teachings are for this era, and who heralds the salvation of the Future Buddha. Theologically, this is not without signif-icance. Here you encounter the four kings of the four direc-tions who guard against evil influences. But the purpose of their guarding is to help the coming of the Future Era of Mi Lo Fo. This messianic age is greatly wished for by devout Bud-dhists for it will mean an end to suffering and the beginning of peace and happiness for all. Thus, on entering the temple, you are re-minded that this world will pass away and a better one will come if you are devout.

Once inside the first main courtyard, it is the incense burn-ers which tend to dominate the scene. Usually there are three

165

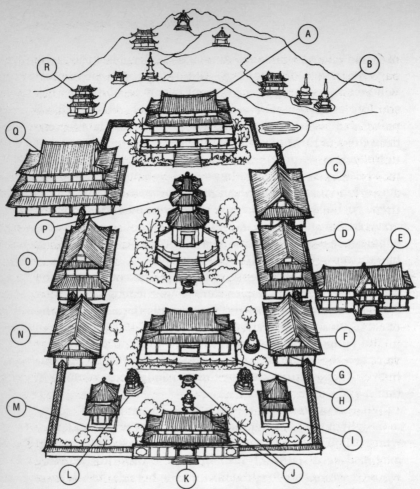

Figure 2 : Nan Pu Tuo Si – Southern Pu Tuo Monastery. Buddhist. Xiamen, Fujian Province.

A Hall of Sacred Scriptures
B Stupas
C Guests Hall
D Vegetarian Restaurant
E Teaching Hall
F 9 Lohans
G Gong
H Da Xiong Bao Great Treasure Hall –
   3 main statues; Guan Yin; Sakya-
   muni; Wen Shu
I Bell Tower
J Incense Burners

K Tian Wang Hall, Hall of the Four
   Heavenly Kings. Central statue
   is Mi Lo Fa, the Future Buddha
L Pagoda
M Drum Tower
N 9 Lohans
O Library
P Da Bei Hall - Hall of Great
   Mercy. 4 statues of Guan Yin
Q Abbots Hall
R Meditation Hall

of them, and at least one will be circular, rising like a mini pagoda and representing the circle of Heaven, while the others will be square or rectangular. These are, in one way, the reason for the temple existing at all. Here is where the gods are propitiated; where offerings are made to the ancestors and the dead in general. The incense burners are almost always wonderfully decorated. Usually cast in bronze they are mini-masterpieces of art, curling with dragons, alive with symbols, a veritable living expression of traditional folk religion. For these are the gifts of local villages or districts of the town and are jealously guarded by such groups.

The first main hall, in fact counted usually as the second hall as the covered gatehouse counts as the first, contains Guan Yin the Bodhisattva of Compassion in her female form and sundry assistants, both male and female. Having encountered the cosmic salvation promised by the Coming of the Age of Mi Lo Fo, the worshipper is now confronted with the beginnings of a personal salvationary drama. Here is the bodhisattva of compassion who will hear your cries and come to offer help and release from suffering and especially from rebirth. If it is not Guan Yin here, then it will be one of the other bodhisattvas who offer rescue from Hell and from rebirth.

The third hall usually contains either one of the sets of three Buddhas, past, present and future, or Buddha nature, Buddha revealed and Buddha incarnate, or it contains one of the major salvationary Buddhas. The most popular of these are Amitabha Buddha who saves souls and carries them to his Western Paradise, or Manjushri – Wen Shu. The main hall is almost always marked out by having the eighteen lohans in it, ranked on the east and west walls in rows of nine each side.

Finally, for it is unusual for temples to have more than four halls unless they are very major centres, there will be a fourth hall which contains a mixture of female and male bodhisattvas, often centred upon one of the sets of Three Buddhas.

The arrangements differ from temple to temple, but the progression is essentially the same. You enter to an expression of hope in the future. You pass by the bodhisattvas of compassion and you end with the Three Buddhas who offer you both personal and cosmic salvation in a continuum of past, present and future.

En route you may well encounter the Ten Gods of Hell or various other bodhisattvas who in their own way spell out a cosmic vision or drama. The whole temple complex is a drama and you a player in it, who through the incense burners becomes part of the flow of enlightenment and salvation.

One of the most lovely and important of Buddhist temples, and reputedly the first, is that of the White Horse in Luoyang – the Bai Ma Si.

According to tradition, Buddhism arrived in China as a result of a dream. In the year 64 AD, the Han dynasty Emperor Ming (58–75 AD) had a dream one night. In his dream he saw a golden deity flying before his palace. The next morning he asked his advisers what this could mean. One of them, Fu Yi, said he had heard that in India there was a sage who had achieved Buddhahood, who could fly at will and whose body was golden. Hearing this, the Emperor despatched envoys to India to bring back the teachings and statues of this deity. The envoys returned some years later, bearing with them upon the backs of two white horses, statues and the text of the Forty Two Article Sutra.

The capital city of that time was Luoyang in Henan Province. Today the Temple built on imperial orders to house the statues and the sutras still stands. It is called the White Horse or White Horses Temple – Bai Ma Si – in commemoration of this story.

It is highly unlikely that the above story has any serious element of fact in it. What is clear is that by the time of Emperor Ming, Buddhism was beginning to enter China via missionaries and traders from present day Afghanistan, India and lands between. It is also clear that the White Horse Temple at Luo-yang is one of the oldest if not the oldest extant Buddhist temple in China. Outside stand two fine stone statues of the horses. Inside, the layout, whether based on an historically verifiable accounts or not, illustrates the realities of how

168

Buddhism came to China. Immediately inside the gateway, to the left and right are two tombs. In these tombs are interred two foreign missionary monks – Buddhists from Afghanistan, which was then a Buddhist country. It is even possible that they were Greeks, for the Greek kingdoms established by Alexander the Great in that area *c.* 320 BC became major centres of Buddhism from about 100 BC onwards. Indeed it was the Greeks who first started making statues of the Buddha, based upon the sun god Apollo (see page 77).

The two foreign missionaries were called Matanga and Zhu Fa Lan. Throughout the early history of Buddhism in China – from the 1st to the 6th century AD, Chinese Buddhism relied upon foreign missionaries to bring texts and traditions to China. This brings us to the second feature of the Temple of the White Horse. The final major building of the temple is the Cool Terrace, built it is said by the Emperor as the place where the sutras could be translated. This is significant, for whenever new texts arrived from the West, it was necessary to have wealthy sponsors who would fund their translation.

In these two features – tombs of foreign missionaries and a translation centre, we can see the origins of Chinese Buddhism. For Buddhism is still to this day described by the Chinese as a foreign religion, in marked contrast to Daoism and Confucianism which are valued for being truly Chinese.

Whether the White Horse Temple in Luoyang really is the earliest Buddhist temple in China is uncertain. What is certain is that it is the oldest temple which can trace its line of descent back to the 1st century AD. Buddhism may have started arriving in the 1st century but it was not until the end of the 3rd and beginning of the 4th century that Buddhism began to have any really significant presence. It needed the emergence of scholars who could be fluent in both Sanskrit and Chinese before Buddhism could really expand and that didn't really happen until the 5th century.

One feature which is distinctive of Buddhist sites is the pagoda and the stupa. The pagoda first appears in China in the 5th century AD and the oldest extant one is at the Song *first pagoda*

Yue Si on Song Shan in Henan, one of the Daoist sacred mountains. This pagoda, twelve sides and fifteen stories high, made in brick with delicate relief, is outstandingly beautiful and was built in 520 AD. Pagodas are to be seen all over China, many of them now bereft of their temples because of the wastage of wars and of turmoil. The detail on them always rewards close attention. From leaping animals, mythological beasts, floating deities, or tens of thousands of mouldings of the Buddha in miniature, they are visible lessons in Buddhism and Chinese culture.

Their function was primarily as a library or store house. For example, the enormous pagoda at the Great Maternal Grace Temple in Xian, known as the Great Goose Pagoda, was built to house the collection of sutras brought back from India by Xuan Zang (see page 282). But their role as educational aids is very important. They are the equivalent in many cases of the old paintings on church walls in medieval Europe. To a largely illiterate peasantry, they offered picture illustrations of the heart of Buddhism. Thus the pagoda of the 7th century at the Qi Xia Si, Qi Xia Shan, Jiangsu, has scenes from the life of the Buddha at its base, illustrating his personal journey to enlightenment and teaching, while the pagoda of the Wen Shu temple in Chengdu has panels showing Xuan Zang's journey to the West, accompanied by his four odd assistants, a sort of everyman's journey to enlightenment. Interestingly, not far from Qi Xia Si is the failed Ling Gu pagoda. This was commissioned in 1929 by Chiang Kai Shek, the leader of the Kuomingtang – the ruling party of post-1911 China until the Communist takeover in 1949. It was intended to portray the success of the Revolution and to celebrate it in the same way the life of the Buddha or Xuan Zang is celebrated. However, perhaps appropriately, it was never finished.

Occasionally you will find a stupa. While pagodas are based upon the stupa, the stupa itself is very distinct. These breast-shaped mounds with their centre rising into a small tower, house relics of the Buddha or of holy men and women. The best such stupas are to be found in the grounds of Tibetan

170

(known as Lama) temples in China. Of these the best examples are at places such as the Ta Er Si, at Lu Sha Er, 25 miles from Xi Ning in Qing Hai Province, where a particularly fine example rests over the burial place of the placenta of the great Teacher of Tibetan Buddhism, Tsong Kha-pa (in Tibetan the stupas are known as dagobas); an indoor one covers the bones of the Third Dalai Lama (1543–88); at Wu Tai Shan Mongolian/ Tibetan architecture has existed side by side with Chinese for centuries because this mountain is sacred to Manjushri, especially revered in Tibetan/Mongolian Buddhism. For example, the Zu Shi stupa at the Fo Guang Si (temple of the Buddha's Glory) contains the bones of the 5th-century founder monk.

Buddhism today is strongest in the north of China and is still focused upon the old main centres such as the sacred mountains or the great metropolitan monasteries such as those in Beijing, Xian or Yangzhou. It is still organized into the two main traditions, Chan or Pure Land. As this book does not cover Tibet, I am not including details of Tibetan Buddhism today.

Estimates of the number of Buddhists in China vary greatly, but it is somewhere between 70 and 120 million. There are some 9,000 to 10,000 temples and about 40,000 monks and 50,000 nuns.

Many Buddhist temples have been able to restart as monasteries again. They are engaged in recreating their old statues, carving new ones, painting frescoes and printing the sutras. They are restoring their old function as school, library, worship centres and soteriological image.

DAOIST TEMPLES

I have to confess that I enjoy visiting Daoist temples most of all. They often have about them an air of gentle decrepitude and a sense of not really minding what happens. In those temples relatively undisturbed by time – places like Macau, or a few of the temples on sacred mountains such as Qing Cheng Shan or occasionally in rural temples – the dirt and dust of decades or even centuries of accumulated burnt incense provide an over-all patina of black and a heady smell which is distinctively 'religious'! Even in newer or renewed temples, such as the Eight Immortals in Xian, the piles of deities and the waft of incense gives a very distinctive feel to the temples.

One feature which I like in old temples is the multitudinous layers of deities. In each hall there will be a main deity such as Zhang Dao Ling or Lu Dong Bin, surrounded by scores of smaller statues – a veritable pot pourri of the divine. On either side, but at ground level, there will be small niches cut into the wall, with deities, often of the dead, Hells or some form of afterlife, accompanied by earth gods and other local deities. Just by looking at such a hall one can sense the hierarchies of the divine in Daoism.

There is a general air of nonchalance in Daoist priests and monks for, except in certain schools and temples, discipline is fairly relaxed. While similar hours to a Buddhist temple are observed, it is far more common to find a Daoist monk fast asleep by the altar than a Buddhist monk! I rather like this for it seems to betoken an acceptance that life, the Dao, just goes on whether we are aware of it or not.

The term for a Daoist monastery or temple of any size is guan, meaning to look or to see. It is the same character as the first character in the title of the bodhisattva who is known as the One who Regards the Cries of the World. The reason why Daoist temples are called Regarding or Looking is not clear, though there is a story told that is used by some to explain this. It is said that when Lao Zi went West, he met the gatekeeper of the West who had been waiting for him. The gatekeeper had been told that a sage would leave China via his pass over the mountains and he built a small grass hut to keep a lookout. Here it was, so legend tells, that Lao Zi wrote, in one night, the classic *Dao De Jing*, and then went on West. It is from this look out that, so some claim, the title guan for Daoist temples originated. Whatever the reason, it is an odd title.

Everything that has been said earlier about how temples

were aligned and their basic protective design applies to Daoist temples as well. With a Daoist temple, the sense of walking through a cosmic drama is not so often present as in Buddhist temples, though there are exceptions, such as the Yong Le Gong near Rui Cheng in Shanxi province. Usually the Daoist temple is more a series of separate halls which cluster around the central one, almost always featuring the Three Pure Ones as manifestations of the Ultimate Dao, the realized Dao and the incarnate Dao. But the sense of journeying towards the Three Pure Ones as one would with the Three Buddha natures, is not there in the same degree in a Daoist temple. For in the compound will be found any number of side halls and altars, each of which has its own theme. Very often there will be a hall of the Eight Immortals, worshipped both collectively and for the important members of the group such as Lu Dong Bin – the medicine immortal. Yet Lu Dong Bin will probably have a hall or certainly an altar dedicated just to him elsewhere as well. The Three Agents – Heaven, Earth and Water – will possibly have a side hall, as will goddesses of fertility, of sons and of childbirth. Local deities, many pre-dating Daoism as a system, will have a shrine or a minor hall somewhere in the grounds.

On the central axis of south to north will fall the main halls, housing the Three Pure Ones at the north end, preceded by halls to deities such as the Jade Emperor or the Queen Mother of the West or in port areas, the local sea goddess such as Tian Hou in Fujian Province in towns such as Xiamen or Qangzhou. Lao Zi himself, or the founder of the particular school, such as Lu Dong Bin or Zhang Dao Ling, will have a central hall and these change according to the region and the school. Suffice it to say that if you find three large statues in a main hall, these will be the Three Pure Ones.

What is fascinating about Daoist temples are the side halls. These take the place filled by the teaching halls in Buddhist monasteries, but they are more scattered and idiosyncratic, often not achieving the symmetry of Buddhist temples and giving a sense of having evolved rather than been planned.

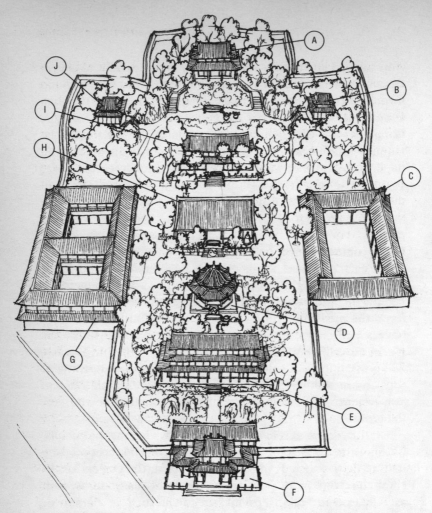

Figure 3: Qing Yang Gong – Green Sheep Palace. Daoist. Chengdu, Sichuan Province

A Emperors' Accomodation Hall.
B Holy Mother of Lao Zi.
C Library of wood blocks for printing the Daoist Canon
D Ba Gua Pavillion – 8 Trigrams (Yi Jing). Central statue, Lao Zi
E Central statue of temple founder Zhang San Feng. At the back is Guan Yin
F Entrance Hall. Central statue – Thunder God. On reverse,ch. 42 of Dao De Jing, (yin/yang symbol).

G Yi Jing Study Centre
H San Qing Dian - Hall of 3 Pure Ones – Great, Jade and Supreme Ones. At back, Wang Yi Zu, Lu Dong Bin and Zhang Dao Ling
I Doumi Hall. Hall of the Mother of the Bushel (Central statue) On right, Queen Mother of the west; left, rumler of the Earth. 7 star gods either side.
J Lao Zi Temple; visitors pray here for a 'new life'.

And this is exactly what has happened in Daoism. Whereas Buddhism is a foreign missionary faith which has taken root in China and brought its own world view and theology to bear, Daoism has emerged from the many strata of ancient China, collecting and amalgamating all sorts of bits and pieces en route and from this making a functional whole which is at its strongest in its various parts! Daoist temples often seem to have grown organically from the local surroundings. Buddhist temples seem more to have been imposed upon their surroundings.

Given the organic, sometimes peasant origins of most Daoist temples, childbearing features strongly as does concern with wealth, evil spirits, healing and divination. Of lesser interest is the question of salvation, though this does play its part, but only a part. The Daoist temple is a market of divinity. The Buddhist temple is a story of salvation.

Key to the salvationary theology of a Daoist temple are the immortals, the Jade Emperor and a teacher figure, be that Lao Zi, Zhang Dao Ling or Qin Chan Chun. These, together with salvationary deities such as the god of the north, the Dark Lord Pai Kai, hold the centre in the salvationary story, for they express the quest for immortality or at the least longevity. The sense of order in a ruthless world is represented by the Jade Emperor; and the power of great teachers to help you now through charms and exorcism or through plucking you from the Hells is represented by Lao Zi, Zhang Dao Ling and saviour gods such as the god of the north or Er Lang.

Small Daoist temples have a similar function but are often more coherent in their expressed layout. For example, in southern China, Daoist temples, like Buddhist ones, consist of three main halls running south to north, flanked by two minor halls on either side, and again three deep running to the east and west but up the same south/north axis. Here the main gods are to be found in the central halls, though usually with a powerful local deity in the final hall, while in the side halls are the functioning rooms to deal with divination, the year gods, funerals and other such basic needs, all with small altars and shrines.

Northern temples tend to have the main axis of central halls and then a mixture of different halls in different places.

A good example of a Daoist temple expressing a diversity of models and meeting a range of needs, is the Jin Si temple near Tai Yuan in Shanxi Province. It is called a si because its origin is as an ancestor temple, built to commemorate the prince Tang Shu Yu of the Zhou dynasty who is supposed to have lived c. 1000 BC. However, the focus of the temple today, and for the last thousand years, is the Hall or temple of the Holy Mother – Sheng Mu. This vast and stunning hall, almost complete in its original Song dynasty statues, is a masterpiece. It is the focus for the women devotees who throng the place.

But the complex also houses local gods of great antiquity, quite apart from the memory of the Zhou dynasty prince. The temple to Tai Tai, for example, celebrates a hero who tamed the floods around this area before even Yu the Great – thus putting him supposedly into the period of c. 3000 BC. Another local deified inhabitant is celebrated in the Shui Mu lou or Water Mother temple. There are temples to ancestors, to the local river and so forth. It is, in effect, an expression in stone of the mythology of the area as it has grown over the last 5,000 years right up to the present day, for it has a collection of engraved steles bearing poems by Mao Ze Dong! While the temple or hall to the Holy Mother dominates the complex, it is by no means the only major centre in the compound.

Daoism is the traditional Chinese sense of the sacred and mythology in a collective form. The temples express this perfectly.

SACRED MOUNTAINS

7

The sacred mountains of China are numerous. Almost every region has its own quite apart from the nine major ones, the Five Daoist Mountains and the Four Buddhist Mountains.

Mountains have dropped from being sacred over the centuries, indeed millennia of Chinese civilization. Qi Shan, 150 kilometres west of Xian in Shaanxi Province, was the sacred mountain of the Zhou tribes. Here they consulted their oracle and from that oracle sprang the I Ching of centuries later. When the Zhou conquered the Shang dynasty and moved the focus of their life to the heart of ancient China, the old ancestral sacred mountain of Qi Shan was still worshipped each year in a big ceremony but its real power had already started to slip. By the time the Zhou fell *c.* 770 BC, the mountain had passed from the central life of its people. Until recently rediscovered as the mountain of the original I Ching texts, it had no place in the catalogues of sacred mountains of China. However, in the area around Qi Shan, its power had never diminished and fortune tellers who grew up on the yang, sunny side of Qi Shan are reputed to be the most successful and powerful in the whole region. Echoes of its sacredness continued.

Of the scores of sacred mountains that Qin Shi Huang Di, the first Emperor of China (*d.* 210 BC) climbed in the pursuit of immortality, only a handful have been identified from the current sacred mountains. Yet through this long period, some mountains have retained their sacredness in an unbroken line. Of these, the greatest is Tai Shan, considered the greatest of all the nine formal Sacred Mountains of the Daoists and Buddhists.

In devoting a whole chapter to the Sacred Mountains I want to illustrate their importance to any real understanding of the sacred in China. I began the whole book with the ascent of Hua Shan as a vehicle for introducing the way the different religions all interact around a greater theme or for a wider purpose. This is what is so fascinating about the Sacred Mountains. They are Daoist and Buddhist; shamanic and Confucian. They are all this and more and they offer some of the most beautiful and numinous experiences travel in China can afford. As pilgrim centres for over 4,000 years, they offer the modern pilgrim, the tourist searching for the soul of a country, the perfect journey. That in making these journeys, you will be in the company of thousands of Chinese, just shows the central importance of these pillars to Heaven.

To give a flavour for these extraordinary places, I have decided to take you up four of them, all four being very different. For those visiting China or interested in further details about the other five mountains, please consult the appendix on Sacred Mountains where you will find quite detailed itineraries and descriptions.

I have already described Hua Shan which I love because it was the first I ever climbed. But the four given here are places of very special significance to me. In telling their stories I have tried to capture some of the rich web of mystery and legend which is associated with each place, for they are all microcosms of Chinese religion, history and, most important, of the sacred in China.

DAOIST SACRED MOUNTAINS

Tai Shan

This mountain, the foremost of all the sacred mountains of China, rises in Shandong Province, the only significant mountain range in eastern China. Around it, either to the right or left of this great block, has flowed the Yellow River since time immemorial. It is easy to see how this one vast massif, standing alone on the east of China, should have gained its reputation as not just a sacred mountain but, in ancient folklore, as the very place from which life descended in its myriad forms upon earth. For Tai Shan is the mountain of creation or, to be more accurate, the Origin of Origins. It was also believed to be the place to which the dead souls returned – Origin and End. Here ruled male and female deities, shamanic gods and goddesses, who still linger on today as the God of Tai Shan and the Princess of the Azure Clouds.

Shamanism was undoubtedly practised at all the nine main sacred mountains of China. At some, such as Tai Shan, the traditions have been diluted and at times deliberately distorted, but still the shamanic deities can be discerned beneath the accumulated centuries of history. Of the shamanic mountains, it appears that Tai Shan was the greatest.

Tai Shan has an influence that no other sacred mountain can match. All over China, and in Japan as well, you will find small shrines inscribed to Tai Shan. A stone from the mountain, or even just a shrine inscription mentioning the stone of Tai Shan is considered to be a charm against evil and a harbinger of good fortune. Tai Shan shrines are everywhere, even at the other sacred mountains. For this is no ordinary sacred mountain, if such a thing can exist. This is the Emperor of Sacred Mountains; this is the home of the Dao, long before the Dao became a religion.

Yet it is neither the tallest mountain nor the biggest. It is neither the most spectacular nor the most dangerous or dramatic. But it is the most special and the holiest and this imprints itself upon you from the moment you begin the climb.

One thing I have observed in climbing the sacred mountains of China is the very real difference between Daoist and Buddhist mountains. On a Daoist mountain, the pathway is itself the sacred journey. It is redolent with mythology and symbolism. It winds and weaves its way through the mythology, beliefs and hopes of the people and of spirituality. The Path up the mountain is a part of the Path of the Dao. The temples and shrines en route are but enlarged presences of the divine – though sometimes the greatest sense of the divine comes from an old, hallowed cave or a great rock resting high above the path. On Buddhist mountains, the feeling is the reverse. The focal point of the mountain is the monasteries, great centres of architectural splendour. The pathway up is simply the most convenient way of getting from monastery A to monastery B. There is little of the sense of mystery and of the divine that a Daoist mountain path has. Indeed, the language about the two kinds of mountains is different.

On Buddhist mountains, the emphasis is on the views, on the beauty of nature, on spectacular vistas. The pilgrim there is an observer, outside nature, looking in. On Daoist mountains, the pilgrim is part of nature and caught up in the story of the place. The emphasis there is on meditation and on wonder, not so much at nature but at what has happened here before. Time and space collide on Daoist mountains and carry the pilgrim with them.

Tai Shan is very heavily visited. On a summer's day, the crowds can be enormous. But if climbed out of season, or early in the morning before dawn, or even late in the afternoon so the descent takes place in darkness, the mountain owns you and enfolds you in a most special way.

The journey begins in the pilgrim town of Tai An. Here pilgrims have gathered for at least 3,000 years. Here the Emperor came to worship his celestial equivalent, the Emperor of the Eastern Peak. This great god controls the destiny of millions, and rules either as the regent of the Jade Emperor or in some cases is seen as being the same as the Jade Emperor.

Tai An is full of fascinating temples and shrines, but the

central masterpiece is the Temple of Tai Shan – Dai Miao. This Daoist temple covers a very large site and used to constitute one quarter of the entire town of Tai An.

In front of the main gate is a small temple compound which is called the Yao Can Ting meaning the Pavilion for Greetings from Far Away. This became the temple of the Princess of the Azure Clouds, who is the original Mother goddess of the mountain. It is a small compact temple compound built in the Ming dynasty and restored many times since. Before it, close to the road, stands the Arch of Greetings from Far Away.

Behind the Yao Can Ting stands the elegant Arc of the Eastern Peak, for Tai Shan is in the cosmology of China, the Eastern peak, of which the other four Daoist mountains form the West, South, North and Centre – as will be explained at each mountain. The arch dates from 1672 and is a masterpiece of this type of arch, known as a pailou.

The entrance to the temple compound is via three gates set into the wall in a quite unusual manner for temples. They look more like fortification gates. The central one is called The Great Yang gate, or gate of the Origin South. Yang as a term in Chinese cosmology means the sunny or south side of a mountain. Hence the gate's title. Beside it, to the left, is the Seeing Greatness Gate and to the right, Admiring Scale Gate.

There has been a temple here for at least 2,000 years. The first recorded visit of an Emperor was in 219 BC and I would hazard a guess that some form of temple stood here before that as all the mythological evidence points to the mountain having an even more pivotal role in the religion and culture of Shang and Zhou China. Be that as it may, what we have today is the Tang dynasty plan, much adapted and rebuilt, not to mention reduced from the reputed 813 buildings it was recorded as having in 1122.

Entering the temple compound, you walk into a very large garden courtyard in which there are many steles set about the place. Two major ones dominate to left and right. The one to the left dates from 1013 and celebrates the elevation of the god of Tai Shan to the status of Emperor 'equal to Heaven, good and Divine'. This commemorates the edict passed by the Song emperor Zhen Zong. To the right is a stele from 1124 recording the restoration of the temple with just four great characters calling upon all future generations to observe what has been done.

The gate/hall temple in the centre of the courtyard is dedicated to Tai Shan's role as the pillar linking Heaven and Earth. It is called the Pei Tian Men, meaning the Uniting with Heaven Gate. This harks back to its role in shamanic culture and its role in imperial rituals when the Emperors came to offer special sacrifices to their Mother, the Mother of Heaven, the goddess of Tai Shan.

To the right of the gate is a side courtyard full of fascinating steles and six very ancient evergreens supposedly planted by the Emperor Wu in 110 BC. They are certainly old. Moving north again, but staying within the side courtyards, you come to the temple of Dong Yu Zuo. The interest here is a small glass-covered fragment of stele. This is all that remains of the oldest stele on Tai Shan which stood in the temple of the Princess of the Azure Clouds until the fire of 1740 destroyed it. It has ten characters inscribed and dates from 209 BC. It is an invocation for help from a minister of the Qin dynasty, just before it collapsed into ruin.

Returning to the main courtyard and passing through the Pei Tian Men, and then through the next gate, the Gate of Benevolent Harmony, you enter another gardened courtyard. Here was the court of Tai Shan as God of Hell – his name is still given to the king of the seventh Hell (see Gods and Goddesses). Here were seats for the 75 judges of Hell who, it was believed, judged each soul. This harks back to the old role of Tai Shan as the place where the dead returned at death. The courtyard is full of magnificent and historic steles, ranging from a Tang dynasty Buddhist sutra pillar to imperial edicts and poems.

The main hall of the complex is before you. The Tian Kuang Dian – temple of the Celestial Gift. This stunning building houses the greatest treasure of Dai Miao, the giant fresco of the god of Tai Shan as an Emperor, visiting the mountain peak itself, accompanied by a vast array of deities. First painted in the Song dynasty (960–1280 AD) but subsequently repainted many times, it is a major art treasure of China and ranks alongside the Yong Le Gong paintings as a picture of Daoist concepts of deity at the time. Indeed, not just Daoist but Confucian as well. The frescoes range to left and right of the main statue which is of course of the god of Tai Shan, dressed like an emperor. The only other statues you will see wearing the strange flat hat with the strings of pearls hanging down in front, are the Jade Emperor and the Emperor of the Eastern Peak – who is of course Tai Shan himself.

The frescoes show Tai Shan leaving his palace – the Dai Miao – and being seen off by sundry deities. His journey up the mountain is beautifully portrayed, with gods and goddesses, divine bureaucrats and administrators accompanying or welcoming him at different stages. The scene of his arrival on the top is a feast of colour, deities and vibrancy. His return is a gentle descent, with the local gods in attendance. It is a magnificent picture of how the pilgrims of old saw their journey up Tai Shan. They felt, indeed many still feel, surrounded by deities who greet them at every bend of the path, at every shrine, and who journey with them to the summit. As I climbed, I could not help but feel their presence, a presence both rumbustious and divine!

In front of the statue of Tai Shan the Emperor are five ritual vessels, each one symbolizing one of the five sacred mountains of Daoism. They date from the Ming and Qing dynasty and were used in the imperial sacrifices which took place here right up until the end of the last dynasty.

Behind the Tian Kuang Dian stands a small temple dedicated to the wife of the Tai Shan emperor, known as the Zhing Qin Gong – temple of the bedroom. Here she sits with her husband and her attendants. A nice piece of Confucian remoulding! The earliest myths talk of the god and goddess of Tai Shan as being equals – shamanic figures who together create and fashion life. On the mountain she still holds her position as a very special and powerful goddess and indeed some imperial ritual acknowledged this. But Confucian rewriting of mythology often made the old myths conform to the new (*c.* 220 BC) orthodoxy that women served men in the ordained hierarchy of life. Hence this bedroom of the goddess.

Finally one reaches the gate which leads to the pilgrim path – the Pan Lu, the Broad Road to Heaven – and the ascent of Tai Shan can begin, all 7,000 steps of it, albeit that for the first few miles you have to endure modern Tai An, karaoke bars and all.

Leaving the Dai Miao, the first sign of being on the pilgrim path is the great arch Dai Zong Fang, not wonderfully restored in 1956 but originally built in this version in 1730. The area around this arch contains over ten temples, some in ruins or in other use. One of the key temples, away to the right, is the Lao Jun Tang – the Hall of Lao Jun which is one of the titles of Lao Zi. His being here is no accident. As Daoism took over from shamanism, it was important to authenticate the site in Daoist terms. Having a temple of Lao Zi at the very beginning was one way of doing so. It is said that one of the two followers beside him in the main hall is Guan Yin the gatekeeper of the Western Pass, to whom Lao Zi gave the Dao De Jing. This is not the same person as Guan Yin the bodhisattva. If this is indeed Guan Yin, it is one of the very few statues of him I have ever seen in any temple in China.

From here, the path takes you through a journey whose roots lie back in the ancient shamanism of the mountain which draws in just about every major Daoist and a few Buddhist deities. For example, further east from the path lies a complex of building dedicated to the best loved of all the Eight Immortals, Lu Dong Bin. This includes a cave in which he is supposed to have lived and a cave of one of his companions, the hornless dragon – Qiu Xian Dong – whom Lu Dong Bin endowed with a horn through magic.

To the right of the start of the path is the Wang Mu Chi – Pool of the Queen Mother. This is the Queen Mother of the West, the most powerful goddess in Daoism and a worthy successor, or more likely, contemporary, to the Goddess of Tai

184

Shan, now called the Princess of the Azure Clouds. The Queen Mother of the West is a shamanic deity who has the same ancient role in Heaven as did the goddess of Tai Shan (see page 287). The site is a small nunnery which appears to go back to the 3rd to 4th century AD. This would be very early indeed for a Daoist monastery and may have actually been a group of women shamans.

Further up the path, but before the First Heavenly Gate, is the temple to Guan Di the god of War and Wealth.

Just beyond the First Heavenly Gate – Yi Tian Men – is a stone inscribed with five characters which say, 'Here Kong began to climb the mountain'. This refers to Kong Fu Zi who climbed the mountain and exclaimed how he found that not only the kingdom of Lu (the surrounding kingdom in his time) looked small, but also, from the top, the whole empire looked small. This seems to be an attempt to say that even Kong found the physical world to be put into perspective by the spiritual world as experienced on Tai Shan. It reflects the shamanic two worlds view rather neatly, though any good Confucian would have been horrified to hear that!

Just up from there are two temples either side of the path. On one side is the Raiment Changing Hall where officials slipped into something a little more comfortable for actually ascending the mountain, having had to wear formal ceremonial garb for the rituals lower down the mountain. On the other is a classic example of how religions in China run side by side. In the Hong Men Gong, Palace of the Red Gate, the Princess of the Azure Clouds is worshipped alongside Amitabha Buddha, the Buddha of the Western Paradise. A classic example of a shamanic deity turned Daoist, sanitized by the Confucians and worshipped alongside the main salvationary Buddha. Every aspect of Chinese religion in a single temple!

Up again through another arch to the Bai Luo Zhong – the tomb of the White Mule – said to have carried the Tang Emperor Xuan Zong up the mountain and down again in the year 726 AD. Having fulfilled its task, it died at this spot on the way back. The Emperor immediately elevated it to the status of a general (something Emperors tend to do to natural objects and animals on sacred mountains – see further on up Tai Shan) and then ordered it be given a formal funeral worthy of a general. Just above this is a strange tower rising up over the path, for all the world like a pagoda. This is the tower of the Myriad Spirits – Wan Xian Lou – built in 1620. Here we begin to see what will be a constant feature of the path from now on, poems set into walls and carved in the rock, along with two, three, four or more sentences thought to capture the essence of a spot or call to mind an incident there.

Next is a socialist realism sculpture to the martyrs of the fight for liberation. This is the Communist addition to the mountain up which Mao Ze Dong climbed, observed the sunrise as others have for millennia, and made the somewhat obvious observation that at dawn the East is Red. This, taken as a statement of great profundity, became the title of one of the most famous Cultural Revolution songs.

Next comes the sadly empty nunnery of Dau Mu Gong – the Palace of the Goddess of the Bushel (see page 119). This great cosmic goddess of Daoism, mother of the Jade Emperor and herself goddess of a constellation within the Great Bear, is one of the ancient goddesses of China. The temple was rebuilt in the 1530s and has recently been restored. The second hall is used to house the Mother and her attendant stars and deities (such as the Queen Mother of the West and the Earth goddess). In the third hall the Princess of the Azure Clouds was worshipped. Thus in this one temple the three great goddesses of shamanism came together in their own right, under the protective supervision of Daoist nuns.

From the Dau Mu Gong you can take a path to the right, which winds down into the valley and then rises again to bring you to an extraordinary rock carving. The whole text of the Diamond Sutra (admittedly not a very long sutra) is carved on the side of the mountain. The inscription dates from c. 580 AD but has been added to and re-engraved many times since. To make sure Buddhism didn't think itself too important, a Confucian scholar of the Ming dynasty (1368–1644 AD) has added

a quote from the Confucian classic, the Great Mean, beneath it.
Buddhism and Confucianism did not get on well. The Confucians distrusted the Buddhists because they were foreigners
and because they taught monasticism. This means leaving your
parents, having no children and becoming part of a different
kind of family. All this was anathema to Confucians. They also
mocked the Buddhist notion of reincarnation. Reincarnation
was unknown in China until the Buddhists came. Before that
Daoism and Confucianism taught that the ancestors continued
to exist in a sort of shadow world. When Daoism and Confucianism could overcome their own hostility to each other, they
would gang up as true Chinese religions against the foreigner
religions of Buddhism, Manichaeism and Christianity. But it
was Buddhism they both disliked and feared most. Yet ironically, much of what is now present day Daoist practice can be
traced back to Buddhist influences – monasticism, scriptures
and even rituals – while Chan Buddhism owes more to Daoist
thought and practice than to conventional Buddhism.

Next comes the San Guan Miao. This is the temple to the
Three Agents, Heaven, Earth and Water. But originally it was
built to venerate Qin Shi Huang Di after his ascent. It must
have been built very soon after he came, as his dynasty collapsed only three years after his death and he was not greatly
loved! An ancient site, but a more recent temple.

Next comes the rock called Hui Ma Ling – Where Horses
Turn Back. At this point you might sympathize with them! The
horses referred to are either the horses which took the Emperor Xuan Zong (ruled 713–56 AD) or the Emperor Zhen Zong
(ruled 998–1023 AD) up the hill. The archway over the road
also commemorates this.

Above this, up a very steep part of the path, comes the
Zhong Tian Men – the Second Heavenly Gate – and here you
know you are over halfway, but the toughest part is yet to
come. As if to make up for this, there is a small temple here
called Zeng Fu Miao – The Happiness Temple – where one of
Tai Shan's assistants, responsible for bringing joy into peoples
lives, is thought to dwell.

On all the sacred mountains, natural features which look like carvings are greatly prized and around them any number of legends cluster. Near the Second Heavenly Gate is a rock which looks like a tiger, due to the colouring patterns on the stone. The single character for tiger was engraved upon it in the 18th century by the famous calligrapher Wu Da Hui. A little further on is the Sinuous Dragon Bridge and the rock known as 'the Sword that cuts the Clouds'.

From here a good view can be had of the massive carved poems of the Emperor Qian Long (ruled 1736–96 AD) which cover the face of the mountain rock opposite. The poems extol Tai Shan and the emperor himself in remarkably similar style! Even though the characters are three feet across, it is still not easy to read the poems from anywhere on the path unless your eyesight is very good.

Crossing over the Yun Bu Qiao – the Bridge over the Clouds – you come to one of those delightful stories of which the sacred mountains are full. Here is the Wu Song Ting – the Five Pines Pavilion – somewhat heavy-handedly restored in 1956. Beyond, somewhat confusingly, stand three pines and the actual story refers to one pine! For it was here that the First Emperor Qin Shi Huang Di stopped on his ascent of Tai Shan in 219 BC. He was anxious to receive the blessing of Tai Shan as confirmation of his title as Son of Heaven and as part of his pursuit of immortality. A tremendous thunderstorm broke out as he climbed – taken ever after to be a sign of the disapproval of the god and goddess of Tai Shan – and he had to take shelter under a large pine tree. Obviously grateful, he dubbed the helpful pine as a fifth level official in his government. This meant that the tree had to be treated with immense respect. Some confusion over the last 2200 years has led the title of the site to be changed from the fifth level pine to five pines. This is a favourite spot for people to sit and rest beneath the pines.

Near the Five Pines is a strange cave shrine. Set just beside the main path it is dedicated to the Grandmother of Tai Shan, the original goddess of the mountain. The shrine is inside a vast boulder where a small worship area has been hollowed.

There are just a couple of very old stone statues, so covered by centuries of incense smoke as to be without clear features. Here women come to pray for help from this ancient goddess. It is a powerful reminder that Daoism is but a recent comer to this mountain and that older traditions which flowed into Daoism still have the power to exist and to exert influence to this day.

The next site, the Southern Heavenly Gate, heralds that the end is nigh, with its three statues immediately inside. The three are not without significance. In the central shrine is Tai Shan the god. To his right is Guan Yin the Bodhisattva of Compassion. To his left is Tai Shan the goddess, here known by titles such as the Grandmother of Tai Shan and the Princess of the Azure Clouds. An interesting trinity in that the women outnumber the men. Again one is forcibly reminded that the mountain has long been a centre where goddesses and gods have been worshipped, with the emphasis being more towards the goddesses, despite over two millennia of Confucian paternalism.

Rising up from the triad of deities, I was taken aback by Heavenly Street – quite literally a Qing dynasty, 17th century Chinese commercial street, stuck 8,000 feet up on a sacred mountain! It's a bit like finding some half-timbered houses forming a street on the top of Snowdon or a row of Georgetown Georgian houses on top of the Rockies!

Walking on beyond Heavenly Street, with its shops, restaurants and bars, you come to the White Cloud Cave – Bai Yun Dong – from which, it is said, the rain bearing clouds of China come. In fact, clouds do seem to come out of the mouth of the cave, a natural phenomenon due to variations in temperature and the angle and shape of the clouds. Confucian commentaries of the 3rd century BC first comment upon this.

Beside this is the peak from which Wu can be seen (Wu Guan Feng). This relates to yet another story about Kong Fu Zi and his ascent of Tai Shan. It is said that Kong spotted a white horse tied to the gate of the capital city of the state of Wu – some 500 miles away at least! He asked his disciple Yan Yuan whether he could see it too. Yan Yuan said he thought he saw some silk flapping beside the gate. Kong touched his eyes and the disciple could see clearly. However, the effort proved too much and as they descended the mountain Yan Yuan's hair turned grey, his teeth fell out and he expired soon after. Quite what the point of this story is, no-one seems to know, nor care! But to this day, you will find people staring off into the distance from this point.

The main temple is dedicated to The Original or Primal Princess of the Azure Clouds. This beautiful Daoist temple complex, small, compact and walled, is a gem and provides a peaceful and meditative place on arrival at the summit. This is where the pilgrims go first, and where they linger longest, not to the top temple on the actual highest point itself, the Jade Emperor's temple. The Princess's temple dates from the early Qing in its present state but is very ancient. Legend tells that when the third Song Emperor Zhen Zong (ruled 997–1022 AD) visited the temple, a stone statue of the goddess was found in a well, where it had been lost 1,000 years before. This is an ancient site indeed.

From the beautiful temple of the Princess, you rise up past the Stele with no Words – so old all the lettering has worn off. Legend says this was erected by Qin Shi Huang Di in 219 BC. This could be so, and archaeological studies have certainly placed it in the Eastern Han (*c.* 23–187 AD) if not earlier. This rather squashes another story about this stele which I was told by a somewhat disreputable looking 'guide', namely that the poet who had it brought up so he could inscribe his inspired thoughts was so overcome by the beauty of the site that he was speechless and thus left the stele uncut.

Above the stele rises the rather severe temple of the Jade Emperor – Yu Huang Ding – and inside the temple is the actual summit of the mountain, engraved with the two characters Supreme Summit just in case you weren't sure. The statue of the Jade Emperor is a magnificent one showing him in full regalia.

Just below the Temple of the Primal Princess of the Azure Clouds is a small temple to Confucius, though it seems to have earlier been a Daoist temple, taken over in the 17th century by the Confucians. Here is the terrace from which observations of the stars were made – see the earliest observatories on Song Shan.

The temple and deities now have to share the mountain peak with the army and with various weather stations. Yet a workable balance seems to have been struck between the Daoist monks and the army. Because of their strategic significance, many sacred mountains are now also military sites. The Daoists are not happy about this. They resent the intrusion of the army and the violence that is implicit. But as they no longer control the land around their temples, they are currently powerless to do anything but grin and bear it.

Finally, the most popular place for many visitors who toil up overnight is the dramatic rock from which you can watch the sunrise. This was where the emperors offered the feng sacrifice, a very rarefied version of the annual sacrifice to Heaven offered at the imperial capital's Temple of Heaven (the one in Beijing being but the most recent in the most recent capital).

Returning to Tai An, it is appropriate to visit the last great temple complex in the area, the Temple of the Bronze Pavilion or the Temple of Divine Fulfilment. Just to the southwest of the main part of town, this temple is on Hao Li Shan, which is where the dead were supposed to return after death, the entrance to the afterlife. The temple is dominated by a vast statue of the Princess of the Azure Clouds and is dedicated to her. Here again is an echo of the old tradition that she made all human beings, created from earth and to her they return. The temple as it stands was built in 1611 and is being repaired currently. The hill is where the shan sacrifice took place to the Earth, the complement of the feng sacrifice on the summit. These very special rituals took place very rarely. For example, the shan took place in 104 BC, 666 AD, 725 AD and 1008 AD.

The nearby Sen Luo Dian celebrates the kings of Hell and the Great Recorder. Here is enacted the full drama of what awaits the sinner in the afterlife.

Song Shan

Song Shan is the mountain of the Centre in Chinese cosmology. Situated in Henan Province, it was pretty much in the centre of ancient China for the oldest capitals, Anyang, Kaifeng and Luoyang lie not too far away. Rising to only 5,000 feet, Song Shan is a much more laid back mountain, sprawling rather than soaring, though at its heart it is a place of swirling clouds and jagged peaks.

Song Shan is the highest point on the Funiu mountain range and this name alone tells much of the antiquity of this site. Funiu means Taming the Ox and is one of the names of Fu Zi, the half-snake, half-human shamanic figure at the start of legendary Chinese history, who with his sister is supposed to have made all life on earth. Echoes here of the same kind of myth as that of Tai Shan being the place where life began.

The mountain, being sprawling rather than soaring has many, many different peaks, over 70 all told, but two dominate, the Tai Shi and the Shao Shi peaks. The names mean Great Hall and Small Hall, referring to the temples associated with them. But they have more romantic names, being also known as Hei Feng – Black Peak – and Yu Tai Shan – Jade Girdle Mountain. The poet Fu Mei of the Ming dynasty described them thus:

> Tai Shi is like a dragon asleep,
> Shao Shi resembles a phoenix dancing.

The area around Song Shan is as significant as the places on Song Shan, for here, as the old tradition puts it, the three religions coexist in a very special way. There is an old saying that:

> Buddhism, Daoism and Confucianism, the three coexist
> on Song Shan and ten thousand virtues melt into one.

The whole area around Song Shan has been so pivotal to ancient Chinese history that one is overwhelmed by the variety. For example, the great pyramid tomb mound of the son of the first Tang emperor (c. 630 AD) rises by the town of Gong Ling en route from Gong Xian to the mountain.

Deng Feng, where most visitors start their tour, means the place where the feng sacrifice was offered. This sacrifice, only undertaken by emperors, was undertaken here by China's only ever female ruler, the Empress Wu (the Dowager Empress of the 19th century ruled in the name of her various sons and grandsons, not in her own name). The Empress Wu came here to offer feng in 695 AD and the town took its name from that.

To the north-west of Deng Feng is the famous Shao Lin Si, site of the monastery founded by Bodhidharma, the monk who introduced Chan (Zen) Buddhism to China. The monastery also houses, as you will be relentlessly reminded as you approach, the famous Shao Lin boxing and fighting school. The Buddhist monks of Shao Lin were expert fighters and developed much of what we today think of as Chinese martial arts. There are now a number of schools offering this kind of training in the vicinity of the monastery and the monks in this thriving monastic centre still train in martial arts (see page 103).

Close to Shao Lin and on the other side of the Forest of Stupas are some 230 burial mounds and stupas for monks of the monastery, dating from the Tang dynasty (609 AD) onwards, and a very ancient temple. It is in fact the oldest wooden building in Henan and dates from 1125 AD. The temple is called the Chu Zu An – The First Ancestor's Monastery. The mention of First Ancestor reminds us that Song Shan is associated with just about every single mythological and historical figure in ancient Chinese history. The First Ancestor here seems to be Fu Zi, the bringer of Civilization. However, it is also used sometimes to describe the Yellow Emperor – Huang Di – the first of the Five August Rulers, semi-mythological figures who reigned in the third millennium BC. For to this mountain, in all the historic and legendary accounts of their lives, came the great and the good of ancient China.

Huang Di is supposed to have toured the area in his great

peregrinations around China. The next August Ruler, Yao died while visiting Song Shan and is buried in Yang Cheng. Perhaps this site marks the spot where the next Emperor Shun ordered Yu the Great to build an ancestral hall and to offer homage at Song Shan. There is no reason to think it shouldn't be for Yu is very much associated with this area, having had to cleave the mountains apart near here to allow the Yellow River to flow freely to the sea. If so, this site is one of the oldest religious sites in China, but there seems no way of telling, except to note the very unusual dedication of First Ancestor Monastery.

North of Deng Feng is Hui Shan Si – a major 5th century AD Buddhist monastery and thus an early one. The pagoda is especially beautiful as are the two steles, covered with bodhisattvas.

To the east of Deng Feng is the famous Song Yang Academy – Song Yang Shu Yuan. The title means the Yang, or sunny South, side of Song Shan Academy. This boasts a fascinating story of how the three religions have interacted on this mountain. The Academy began life as a Buddhist temple in 484 AD, built by the northern Wei Emperor Xiaowen, a great supporter of Buddhism. At some time around 610 AD it was changed into a Daoist temple and then a Daoist monastery. In 683 the Emperor made it his temporary residence and called it the Palace of Obeying the Heavenly Mandate. Then around 955 AD, it was made into a Confucian Academy for the training of scholars and administrators for the Empire and named Tai Yi Academy. Finally in 1035 it was called the Song Yang Academy and rose to be one of the four great Academies of Confucian China, the others being Yue Lu Academy, Hunan; Bailudong Academy, Jiangxi and the Suiyang Academy in Henan.

The Academy had its greatest days during the late-17th century when it trained 200 students at a time. Its library was renowned, as were its teachers. This truly is one of the great shrines of Confucianism – now silent and empty and just a shadow of its former self.

Today the Academy is visited primarily to see two generals who have been living here since the visit of the Emperor Wu who came in the year 110 BC. The two generals – there used to be three but one has died – are enormous cypress trees of tremendous size, girth and vitality. The famous Tang dynasty stele of 774 AD, inscribed with a strange tale of a Daoist monk trying to make the elixir of life for the Emperor of that time, was written by an infamous traitor called Li Linfu. The grounds also abound in steles to the former students here, as one would expect to find in a Confucian temple.

Southeast of Deng Feng, at the start proper of the route up the mountain, stands one of the greatest Daoist temples, the Zhong Yue Miao – Middle or Central Peak Temple. It is claimed that the temple was first built *c.* 215 BC during the Qing dynasty. This is not an impossibility for the oldest parts of the temple are the two que or pillars which stand just to the south of the temple proper. They were built in 118 AD and formed the entrance to a temple. Thus we can safely say that a temple existed here then, but to whom and run by whom it is impossible to say – though presumably this was a shamanic based temple of some sort, albeit that by then the shamans had simply become court priests. The que are covered with fascinating carvings of early legendary characters, deities and animal devices. The inscription, from which we know the exact date, is still quite legible in places. This is one of the most important artistic objects in China and a vital source of information about beliefs and design at the time. There are two other sets of Han dynasty, indeed of second century AD, que – one set a mile and a half north of Deng Feng and another on the slopes of Shao Shi, not far from Shao Lin monastery. The ones north of Deng Feng stood before a temple to the Mother of Qi, the second king of the Xia dynasty (*c.* 2200 BC) and describes the activities of Yu the Great's father, Gun, the grandfather of Qi, who tried unsuccessfully to stem the floods which his son, Yu, eventually managed. Apart from the mythological interest, the Chinese also claim that it shows the earliest carving ever of a game of football (123 AD).

The set of que on Shao Shi mountain were also built in 123 AD and stood before the temple of the Younger Daughter, a goddess worshipped locally as the younger sister of the goddess of Song Shan, who in turn was the wife of Yu the Great. The temple has long since gone. However, a particular rock formation nearby commemorates another exploit of the famous Yu. The rock looks like the face of a woman and it is called Qi Mu stone – the Mother of Qi. The story goes that Yu, being a shaman, could change himself into a bear at will. One day he was fishing in the form of a bear when his wife, who knew nothing of this power, and who was pregnant to boot, came to bring him has lunch. Rounding a corner she saw the giant bear. Highly alarmed, she screamed and ran off down the mountain. Yu was very distressed at having upset her and set off after her. Unfortunately, he forgot to change back into a human being. The poor woman ran as fast as possible but when she reached this spot on the mountain, she turned to stone, so great was her fear.

Yu sat and mourned her for a number of days. Then he rose and addressed the stone, telling it to split and deliver his child. The rock did so and that was how Qi, the first Emperor of the Xia dynasty, was born.

Returning to Zhong Yue Miao and its long history, the temple was one of the key places visited by the emperors who came to venerate Song Shan. As such a straight continuation from the shamanic priests who were at the mountain and the Daoists as they arose is easy to imagine.

The last major redesign of the temple was in 735 AD and the temple remains a faithful copy of that Tang design. This vast complex is one of the largest Daoist temples still in existence, with its twelve courtyards and its host of ancient trees, some going back to the Han dynasty. It is essentially designed as a Tang Imperial Palace.

Most famous of its artifacts are the four vast iron figures standing in the first main courtyard, and the stele engraved with the symbols of the five mountains. The somewhat battered figures are the four guardian deities of the Four Quarters, Daoist versions of the Four Heavenly Kings, which they were cast in 1064 AD. The stele of the five mountains was carved in 1604 AD and shows the five Daoist sacred mountains, using their ritual symbols. In the central Hall sits the enormous statue of the God of Song Shan. The temple is a thriving Daoist centre with many monks.

The route from Zhing Yue Miao leads up to Hei Feng or Tai Shi Shan.

Other routes from Deng Feng lead to Hei Feng's base and allow you to take in the cave of Lao Zi – Lao Jun Dong – and then walk on along the ridge to view two ancient pagodas. The first one lies in the lower folds of the mountain range and is called the Fa Wang monastery. The site is stunningly beautiful and so are the claims made for this place. This monastery claims to have been founded in 71 AD, just three years after the White Horse Temple in Luoyang. Fa Wang means King Law or Chief Law, the law being the teaching of the Buddha. Here are two lovely pagodas dating from the 7th to 10th centuries. If this temple is as old as it says, it is probably the second oldest Buddhist temple in China.

Further up the mountain range lies the oldest pagoda in China – dating from 520 AD and sited in the small monastery of Song Yue. The one remaining pagoda is all that survives of the reputed 15 built by the Emperor Xuan Wu in 520, when he used the monastery as a base for his excursions to Song Shan.

Song Shan is still a major place for shamans and usually a little enquiry will reveal where they are currently operating. Not favoured by the Government, they nevertheless have a steady following, especially amongst the women who come to worship at Song Shan and visit the many small shrines to the goddess of Song Shan and to the Mother figures of Qi and others who still haunt this ancient place.

BUDDHIST SACRED MOUNTAINS

Buddhism, not to be outdone by the traditional Daoist/Confucian sacred mountains, has created four of its own. Indeed, created is perhaps too gentle a word. In some case it has physically

197

expelled Daoist communities from the mountains and then converted them into Buddhist mountains, for example, at Emei Shan in Sichuan. This was once one of the 36 Caves of Heaven, and indeed ranked as seventh in the ancient order of Daoist sites. Lao Zi is supposed to have lived there in his mythic incarnation as the teacher of the Yellow Emperor. But by the Ming dynasty (1368–1644) the Buddhists were so powerful and had so much support, that the Daoists formally left the mountain complaining of bad treatment and harassment. The situation has much improved since then but this is indicative of the struggles which have taken place for mastership, albeit that now they work side by side.

The Buddhists also have four direction mountains, guarded by the Four Heavenly Kings. In my journeying up sacred mountains, I want to especially introduce you to two, to match the two Daoist ones given earlier. Those Buddhist sacred mountains not covered here are given in the end section on Sacred Mountains.

Pu Tuo Shan

This island mountain is the smallest of all the nine sacred mountains and the only one dedicated to a female deity. It is the home of Guan Yin and is the Eastern mountain of Buddhism. As I have a particular devotion to Guan Yin, I want to take you to her very special home.

The name Pu Tuo comes from the legend that Guan Yin was visited on her mountain by the Buddha. This mountain is called the Potala in Sanskrit and this is where the name Pu Tuo comes from. It is the same derivation as the Potala Palace in Lhasa, Tibet, for the Dalai Lama is thought to be a reincarnation of the male form of Guan Yin.

Guan Yin is the most important deity of all China, and is as revered by Daoists as by Buddhists. Her island has been a place of pilgrimage to her for nearly 1,000 years ever since she appeared miraculously walking upon the raging waters in a storm and saved the Chinese ambassador to Korea from certain drowning. This took place in 1080 AD and the fame of the

198

island has grown ever since.

The approach to the island is of course by boat which allows the full beauty of the place to greet you before you set foot on it. The island is a delight, set in deep waters, and with the twin peaks rising dramatically from the sea. Despite the ravages of time and ideology, it is still a green place, looking from a distance as it must have looked to centuries of pilgrims as they neared their chosen destination.

The main centre of devotion on Pu Tuo Shan has always been the Chao Yin cave – where in the spray and mist caused by the sea's pounding, the image of Guan Yin can be seen by the devout. Today, old ladies there will assure you that if you look with sufficient devotion and proper intent, you will espy the goddess, drifting in the gentle light at the back of the cave. I love this image. Recently I was fortunate enough to find and buy a beautiful 18th century carving of Guan Yin sitting on her sacred island – the name Pu Tuo Shan is engraved with characters across the top of the carving. She sits in her special cave, holding a child in one hand, for she is the giver of children, while her other hand rests on a pile of scriptures. Beneath her feet swirl the dangerous deep waters of the sea and her pet dragon rises up to greet her. It is a carving of great beauty and holiness and it faces me now, seated on a desk by the window where the light can play across the statue at the centre, making her appearance change as the sunlight moves. I find her a vision of great peace and loveliness. It is this which, despite the changes to Pu Tuo Shan, makes the place so special.

The main monastery of the island is Pu Ji Si – Monastery of Universal Salvation – but better known as the Southern Monastery – Nan Si. Here in the main hall can be seen Guan Yin's 32 incarnations or manifestations, 16 to a side, flanking her main statue. The monastery itself dates from 1080 but has been added to over the centuries to make the vast site it is now. There are 7 temples, 12 pavilions and a score of other buildings such as libraries. If one bears in mind that Pu Tuo Shan used to have over 200 temples and monasteries, one begins to wonder how they fitted them all on, given the size of the site.

The island has two peaks, north and south. The northern peak is called the Fo Feng – Buddha's peak – as this is supposed to be where the Buddha alighted when he came to visit Guan Yin on Potala. The southern peak is called Tao Hua Shan – Peach Blossom Peak – and this refers to a legend which predates Buddhism on the island. An immortal, An Chi Sheng, lived here in the 1st century BC who one night got very drunk. In his ecstatic state, he painted peach blossom on the cliff face of the mountain peak. Hence its name, and hence the claim that if you look hard enough, you can still see the traces of this painting!

The island has been a sacred place for at least 2,000 years, for it was originally a Daoist sacred mountain, and one of its other names, lasting through most of the Tang dynasty until the fame of Guan Yin overcame it, was Mei Tsen Shan. It was named after a famous 1st century BC Taoist alchemist Mei Fu who retreated to the island to practise his alchemical skills. To this day, the tallest mountain peak at the southern end of the island is still called Mei Tsen Feng.

By the 1st century BC, the island was famous as yet another of the places where the pill of immortality had been created. One traveller in 113 BC reported even meeting An Chi Sheng alive on the island – which would have made him about 150 years old.

The northern peak has its monastery to balance the southern monastery. This northern monastery is called Fa Yu Chan – Law of the Rain Monastery. This refers to the image of the rain sweeping away the clouds of ignorance and leaving the world fresh for the Law of the Buddha to take affect. The monastery dates from 1580 when the then Emperor and his mother patronized the cult of Guan Yin across the whole of China. They paid special attention to Pu Tuo Shan and many of the buildings date from this period of immense activity and renovation, which came after nearly 150 years of decline due to piracy. The main hall is dominated by the enormous statue of Guan Yin whose faithful friend the sea dragon has a hall of his own behind hers.

On the summit is the Hui Ji temple – Favour and Compassion – which is one of the most recent additions to the island, having been completed only in 1907. Hidden away down below the north peak is a temple to the Daoist female deities, welcomed here as companions in arms! It is called the Mu Xi Wang temple – Queen Mother of the West – and here she is enthroned with the Three sisters: the Black Lady; the White Lady and the Princess of the Grey Cloud, wife of the Jade Emperor.

The island is devoted to the divine feminine in all its forms, so it is sad to see prostitution taking place quite openly here, especially around the main monastery of Pu Ji.

Two other caves are of interest. Near the northern peak is the Cave of Brahma's Voice – Fan Yin – this bearing witness to the belief that the Hindu deities worshipped the Buddha. The other cave is Sudhana's cave, also called the Dragon Prince's cave. This cave recalls the story told in the Buddhavatamsaka Sutra.

The Buddhavatamsaka Sutra describes the wanderings of a young man, Sudhana, who was advised by the Bodhisattva Manjushri to travel the world seeking true friends who would help him to enlightenment. This he did, encountering 53 different spiritual masters from as diverse a bag of characters as you could imagine. It has been described as the *Pilgrim's Progress* of Buddhism.

The 28th such true friend that Sudhana encountered was the bodhisattva Guan Yin who lived on an island at an 'isolated place at the end of the ocean'. The name of this island was Potalaka. The popularity of this book in the 9th to 12th centuries in particular was one of the major stimuli for the worship of Guan Yin, and the 'identification' of Pu Tuo with Potalaka was one of the major reasons for the island becoming a sacred site of the goddess. Alongside this very popular text another, somewhat less well-known text also fed into the tradition of an island called Potalaka associated with Guan Yin. However, this tradition also claimed that the Buddha had visited there.

The snappily titled Sutra of the Thousand Hand and Thousand Eyed Guan Yin of the Great Compassionate Heart (Qian Shou, Qian Yan Guan Shi Yin Pusa ta pei xin duo le ni Jing) was translated at the beginning of the 8th century and depicts Sakyamuni Buddha teaching within the palace of Guan Yin on Potalaka island. Interestingly enough, both these texts depict Guan Yin in male form, yet it is the female Guan Yin who reigns supreme on the actual island of Pu Tuo. The influence of these tales is shown in the names of places on Pu Tuo. The highest mountain, the majestic peak to the north of the island, is called Buddha Peak in 'memory' of his having taught there. Meanwhile, down on the seashore in one of the caves which are a feature of the southern end of the island, there is Sudhana's cave where he is supposed to have met Guan Yin and to have sought his/her advice.

The beauty of this island holds on by a thread. It used to be renowned as a place where humanity and nature coexisted in harmony. This now looks to be threatened. It would be wonderful if Pu Tuo Shan could recover this and again be an island of the Blessed.

Emei Shan

This is the Western mountain and is dedicated to Pu Sa – in Sanskrit, the bodhisattva Samantabhadra (see page 86).

When my colleagues and I came here, we stayed in a very pleasant but basic Chinese hotel. It was also staffed by that extraordinary breed of Chinese who are able to totally ignore your existence. This would have been all right if it wasn't for the fact that for some obscure reason, there was only one set of keys to the rooms. To get into your room, you had to first find the lady with the keys and then persuade her that your desire to enter your room was not some childish fancy which would go away. It all makes for an exciting time, especially as there were very few people in the hotel (I wonder why!) and thus the few staff felt quite at liberty to either disappear into the hidden areas of the hotel, defying any search, or go home – still clutching the one set of keys.

Eventually we got the key to our room and collapsed with relief. It was then that we found the most wonderful bedside console I have ever seen. It was made in China, a fact which it proudly boasted – and I would guess it was made *c.* 1958. Somewhat ominously it was named 'Spy – 33'. It had the usual buttons for the bedside light – which would have been great had there been a bulb; for the main light, which didn't work; for the night light which took its name very seriously and thus didn't shine at all so as not to disturb the night, and finally it had a button to press if you didn't want to be disturbed. At least that is what it said in Chinese, for each button had a Chinese sentence and then below it some English. In Chinese it said very politely, 'Please do not disturb my rest'. I liked that. But it was the English which completed the whole experience of the hotel. Indeed to some degree it could be seen as a statement about a lot of travel in China. It simply said, 'Don't Bother'.

Having discovered as it were the credal statement of much of tourism in China, we set out the next day to scale Emei Shan.

Emei Shan is a very ancient site, revered locally for millennia, and rises 11,000 feet from the Sichuan plains, dominating the area. The name is capable of many interpretations, from Lofty Eyebrow Mountain to a corruption of the opening sounds of the invocation of the salvationary Buddha – O Mei To Fo. Local legend has it that the character has altered and that it should really mean younger daughter in memory of a local farmer whose daughters became the mountains.

The mountain is vast and the distance from base to summit is 50 kilometres. Many parts of this vast massif are still wild and untrammelled, so enormous is the area.

Entrance to the mountain is usually from Emei Shan town via the gate inscribed Most Famous Mountain Under Heaven. The broad road leads swiftly to the first temple, and one of the greatest, Bao Gue Si – Loyalty to the Country Monastery. This was founded in the 16th century, but on a different part of the hill. It has in part been described earlier. The temple

203

is unusual in having a hall with seven Buddhas in it – the only other temple with such a number is Fenguo temple, Yi County, Liaoling Province. The seven Buddhas are, from left to right, Vipasyin, Sikhin, Visvabhu, Sakyamuni, Krakucchanda, Kanakamuni and Kasyapa. These are the three Buddhas of the past aeon and the four of the present aeon.

The temple was originally built by a Daoist as a place where all three religions could be together. It was transferred to this site in the 17th century. The complex is one of the best examples of classic Buddhist architecture there is and all the major deities are represented – as well as some Daoist ones.

The next temple is Fu Hu temple, meaning crouching tiger or taming tiger, and was built to control tigers on the mountain, both real and spiritual in terms of evil forces counter to good feng shui. The use of temples to influence feng shui is most clearly seen at Leshan where the giant Buddha was carved to control the convergence of the two rivers. It is said that if the waters of the rivers ever rise above the feet of the giant Buddha at Leshan, all China will be destroyed.

The Fu Hu temple as it stands dates from the early Qing. The temple has been greatly enhanced in recent years, not least by the addition of the Hua Yan pagoda pavilion. Here the six metre high copper pagoda is housed. Made in 1585 it has over 4700 images of Buddhas and bodhissatvas and the complete text of the Avatansaka Sutra – all 195,048 characters of it. The Avatansaka Sutra means the Garland Sutra and it formed the basis for one of the most important of Chinese Buddhist schools, the Hua Yan school. The Sutra is a highly complex cosmological and soteriological text and the Hua Yan masters of the school were renowned philosophers. The tradition was founded in the early-7th century and its greatest exponent was the monk Fa Zang. Like so many of the key figures of Chinese Buddhism, he was not Chinese. His family came from Sogdia, although he was born in China. He worked in Xian with Xuan Zang the great translator and pilgrim and it is from him that the great translations of the key Hua Yan texts come. His successor, Cheng Guan (738–838 AD), is seen as an

204

incarnation of Manjushri. The tradition of Masters of the School continued until the Great Persecution, but it never recovered from the Great Persecution of 841–5 and became a minor tradition.

The path winds its way past small temples until it reaches the Qingyin Pavilion built as a scenic spot, for here the Black Dragon river and the White Dragon river come together in a beautiful location.

Up the hill one comes to the temple of the Ten Thousand Years – Wannian Si. Note on the path up, the remains of old tombstones and steles which were destroyed during the Cultural Revolution and have been used to make the flagstones of the path. Some contain Daoist iconography.

The Wannian Temple contains the extraordinary brick hall housing the enormous copper and bronze statue of Pusa on his elephant, eight metres high and made originally in 980 AD. The brick hall looks like a small Byzantine church, and is unique in Chinese architecture. It is the most popular place on the mountain for visitors and one can see why.

Hong Chun Ping temple – Ages Old Tree temple – lives up to its name, being surrounded by ancient trees.

Xian Feng – Immortal Peak temple – was built in 1328 but as it stands now dates from the Qing. This is almost entirely a Daoist area, with the god of wealth enthroned in the temple and nearby is the Tian Huang – Heavenly Emperor terrace. Not far away is the largest set of caves on Emei Shan, called the Nine Old One's Cave, meaning the Nine Immortals Cave – Jiulao. There are 67 chambers here and it is very deep indeed.

On up, past another temple to immortals until you reach the Elephant Bathing Pool temple – Xi Xiang Chi. Here Pusa brings his six-tusked elephant for a wash when he passes by. The three great figures in the main hall are of Guan Yin, Amitabha Buddha and Mahasthamaprapta, the bodhisattva of great strength and the incarnation of one of Sakyamuni's disciples. In the Chu Hall can be seen a statue of Pu, an old man who is credited with building the first temple here. Chu means first.

From here it is a long climb to Golden Summit – Jin Dang. There used to be many temples here but weather and turmoil have reduced them. Until recently only one temple survived intact, the Woyun nunnery. However, in 1986 the provincial government decided to rebuild the Hua Zhang temple and the Tong Hall. These are now complete and the Tong Hall gleams bright gold from its bronze tiles and gold paint, giving the summit its golden appearance.

It is here that people come to watch for the Buddha's aura. This phenomenon of light and clouds does have the appearance of a halo but is not always possible to see as it depends upon the weather, which can be pretty foul at this height.

Returning to the base, look up and try to see the mountain take the shape of Pusa's elephant. Good eyesight and a certain degree of imagination will help.

OTHER SACRED MOUNTAINS

There are countless others ranging from small hills in cities such as Wuhan, which are considered sacred, to massive mountains which have not been designated as special sacred mountains – such as Huang Shan not far from Jui Hua Shan – see below. In the gazetteer I have listed the main ones.

To climb a sacred mountain in China is to travel through the religious and numinous life of China from earliest days to today. These are places where past, present and future collapse into one another. They are, in a very real sense, the spiritual backbone of China.

BUDDHIST CAVES AND GROTTOES

8

The most distinctive contribution of China to Buddhist art are the many Buddhist cave carvings. These are not unique to China – Afghanistan had them first – but in China they reached a scale and beauty beyond anything that can be seen anywhere else. There are nearly 60 cave sculpture sites and in many places, small carved rock faces can be found which are not included in that list. The caves are usually hollowed out niches in rock faces, though some, such as those at Long Men, are in large natural caves.

The earliest caves are those at Dun Huang in Gansu Province, though the earliest actual carvings – as opposed to paintings – are at Yungang, Datong, Shanxi Province. Dun Huang was begun in the 4th century AD as the first major site in China on the old Silk Route down which the notion of such sculpture passed. The fashion for making such caves had died out by the time the Great Persecution of 841–5 took place. The bulk of the figures therefore are from this 400 year period.

The caves are of interest at many levels, but not least because they show outside influences arriving in China and then gradually being adapted to Chinese style and taste. Thus the earliest statues of the Buddha reflect the Greek influence (see page 210) in the toga and in the nimbus – halo. Gradually the Buddha shifts into a more Chinese style and this is especially pronounced when the carving of bodhisattvas as the main figures begins in the 7th century.

The apsaras are an interesting case in point. These angel-like devotees of the Buddha and especially of the bodhisattvas have excited many Western scholars. They see in them the final eastern journey of an idea which began in ancient Persia and went east and west. Zoroastrianism is usually credited with inventing angels, which appear in Zoroastrian scriptures and carvings. Travelling west with the Jews who were taken into captivity in Babylon at the fall of Jerusalem in 587 BC and who returned to their lands c. 530 BC, the angel entered late Jewish texts and iconography. From Judaism it passed into Christianity and hence the angels of Christian art.

Travelling east, the Zoroastrians had temples well into China by the 3rd century AD. Mani, the founder of Man-ichaeism, also adopted the angels and the faith was well estab-lished down the Silk Route. Finally, Nestorian Christianity in China (c. 600–1300 AD) also had angels – beautiful examples of this can be seen at Quanzhou.

The angel creatures in the Buddhist rock carvings are there-fore traced to this original Zoroastrian influence. However, it is also possible that the Chinese had created angels of their own volition for the Daoists talked of feathered immortals at an early stage in the growth of their faith. Whichever way it went, the interaction between Chinese artists and the Western influences coming via Persia, Afghanistan and the Turkish tribes was considerable. In some of the paintings around Dun Huang and at Yungang, Byzantine and Persian style pillars, Western style clothing and faces and artistic mouldings of the capitals shows that Greek and Persian art designs were bor-rowed and adapted.

The caves are now largely silent in terms of worship. Occa-sional altars exist where incense can be offered and the great Buddhas or bodhisattva statues will have offerings placed before them. But spirituality, as places of worship they are dead, unlike the many temples or most of the sacred moun-tains. However, in terms of their message of salvation and enlightenment, they remain places of inspiration. As monuments to the devotion and skills of these early Buddhists, they are without rival. And in the quiet which can sometimes be found in them, they do bring you close to an encounter with the numinous, which undoubtedly was at least part of the reason for their creation.

I am only going to cover three sites in some detail here – Dun Huang, Long Men and Datong. These three sum up the scale and diversity of the caves, and what can be said about them can be said for virtually all the other caves. I will not be detailing the caves – most guide books give such details. Instead I want to look at the religious dimension of the caves. In terms of identifying the various Buddhas and bodhisattvas I refer you to the chapters on the gods and goddesses – chapter 4 in particular.

Dun Huang

The whole area around Dun Huang is one of the most important regions for Buddhism in its earliest days in China. Here was a meeting place between cultures – Chinese Daoism, Mongolian Shamanism, Turkish and Mongolian Christian and Manichaean tribes, and the Buddhism of Central Asia, Afghanistan, Gandhara and other areas north of present day Tibet – for at this time Tibet was not Buddhist.

The most important site at Dun Huang are the Mo Gao caves – named after the region in which they are situated, or the Qian Fo Dong – Thousand Buddha Caves. These were begun in 366 AD and the last dated materials found within them are from 1004 AD. The remarkable thing about these caves is that for nearly 1,000 years they were unknown. Some time in the 11th century, they were filled with a vast treasure of ancient manuscripts and sealed. Until 1900, no-one entered them or even knew they were there.

Opened by accident in 1900, the Qing dynasty failed to appreciate their significance and took no measures to protect probably the greatest single collection of ancient manuscripts ever discovered anywhere in the world. Some 50,000 scrolls were interred here. While the vast majority are Buddhist, some are Nestorian Christian and some Manichaean. Over the next few years, Western explorers took many, but many were lost. Dun Huang manuscripts are to be found in great museums around the world with the British Museum having a particularly fine series. Few of these manuscripts still exist at Dun Huang itself. What does exist are the priceless frescoes and carvings, many still in pristine condition and protected. There are 492 caves at Dun Huang containing 45,000 painted figures and 2415 statues carved from the rock and painted.

Being the earliest, these caves show evidence of the original forms of Buddha statues which arose from the Greek sculptors of Gandhara (see page 207). But within a short period of time, the Chinese artists had begun to develop the distinctive style of the caves for themselves.

Most of the caves follow a similar pattern of a main chamber, at the end of which is an apse which contains a statue of either a Buddha or a bodhisattva. The changing interests of the Buddhist monks and lay people is reflected here as elsewhere by the dates and types of Buddhas and bodhisattvas. Starting with the major figures of Sakyamuni, as the carvings move into the 7th, 8th and 9th centuries, he falls off in popularity to be replaced by salvationary bodhisattvas and Buddhas such as Amitabha, Guan Yin and Manjushri.

In terms of paintings, the favourite early subject matter is the life of Sakyamuni and then increasingly the Jataka stories. These are stories told of the previous lives of the Buddha during which he worked his way towards a state to achieve enlightenment in his last life. The most popular stories are ones such as when he was born as the Monkey King and sacrificed his life to save his troops from a hunter human king, and his incarnation as an elephant and as a deer. The Jataka stories are beautifully portrayed.

The Buddha lying on his side, which occurs here quite often, is called Parinibbana – meaning Just Before Nirvana. This shows the Buddha at the age of 80, lying on his side to give his last sermon to his followers before he ended his last physical life and entered nirvana.

In the Tang dynasty caves – which form nearly half of those still in existence, the bodhisattva has taken centre stage from the Buddha. Usually the bodhisattva is shown alone and the fresco paintings now tell the stories of their incarnations or manifestations rather than the Jataka stories or the story of the life of Sakyamuni. The art of the bodhisattvas also develops, so that the earliest portrayals of Guan Yin with many arms is found here. This is not surprising for it is almost certainly from the interaction between cultures in this area of northwest China that the transformation of Guan Yin from a male bodhisattva to a female one took place – this can be charted on the walls of Mo Gao. Here also begin to appear the mandalas which were to become such an important part of Tibetan and Mongolian Buddhism. These are circles within circles, depicting small scenes such as the seven stages of life, the temptations which destroy, or various bodhisattvas of the directions. They were used for meditation and represent both the cosmic pattern and the microcosm of the universe which is the human being.

It is assumed that the caves were used by individual monks as meditation halls, with the communal life lived in the monastery below.

Long Men Caves – Luoyang, Henan

These are the best known of the Buddhist caves, possibly because they are more easily accessible than Dun Huang or Datong, though the Datong ones are in better condition. The statues suffered badly this century when antique hunters cut off the carved heads; the Sino-Japanese war raged furiously around them and then in the 1950s farmers used some of the caves as winter shelter and lit fires in them. Now they are well protected by the Government and considered one of its greatest treasures.

There are 1350 caves, 750 niche and 100,000 statues ranging from a tiny 2cm statue to the giant Buddha of 17.4 metres in the Ju Xian cave. Over 2800 inscriptions survive, providing a fascinating glimpse into the Buddhist world of the period. The first carvings were started in 493 AD and the last were carved during the early-12th century. However, the bulk were carved between 493 and 755.

The name Long Men refers to the Dragon Gate, being a narrow gorge through which the river Yi flows. The title Dragon Gate is a common one for dramatic gorges on rivers. The gorge produced a wall of rock 600 metres long and this is where the majority of the caves have been created.

What is so striking is the sheer detail. Quite apart from the main statues, the backgrounds are covered in detailed scenes from the lives of the Buddha or the bodhisattvas. The halos of the main statues contain exquisite figures and the inscriptions are some of the most finely carved calligraphy – prized in their own right.

The genesis of the whole place came with the move of the northern Wei dynasty's capital from Datong where it had sponsored the Datong-Yungang caves, to Louyang in 493 AD. Within a few months of the move, a new site for Buddhist caves had been sought and found at Long Men, and the artists of Datong began again.

The Japanese scholar Tsukamoto Zenryu undertook a systematic study of the different Buddhas and bodhisattvas in order to ascertain which were most popular. This chart records the following, surveying only those with inscriptions:

Amitabha is first with 222 statues and dedications. Next comes Guan Yin with 197. This is followed by Sakyamuni with 94, Maitreya with 62, Ksitagarbha with 33, Bhaishajyaguru (the Medical Buddha) with 15 and Mahasthamaprapta with 5.

He then looked at when they were carved and at what this shows about changing beliefs and attitudes and found that in 530 AD Sakyamuni has most statues carved (11), followed by Guan Yin with 10. Maitreya had 8 and Amitabha 1 in 690 AD, Amitabha was top with 15, Guan Yin next with 8, Maitreya had 1 but there were none of Sakyamuni. No clearer testimony could be given to the shift towards bodhisattva and salvationary Buddhism.

Interestingly, there are a few Daoist carvings in amongst the Buddhists. One cave has the Eight Immortals, according to guidebooks, but there are actually eleven figures and the Eight Immortals emerged as a group much later than these carvings.

Yungang Caves – Datong, Shanxi

These are the earliest carved figures – in contrast to the paintings at Dun Huang. The complex was begun in 453 AD under the very pro-Buddhist, but in Chinese terms, 'barbarian' dynasty of the northern Wei. The Wei moved their capital from Datong in 493 when they then began the caves at Long Men close to their new capital at Luoyang. Thus the peak of activity here lasts but forty years, though carvings continued until the early-6th century.

Thus one has, in one of the most extraordinary galleries imaginable, a massive concentration of art over a very short period. Largely ignored for centuries, the caves were only really rediscovered and their importance recognized in 1903. Thereafter, Western antique hunters committed many acts of desecration and destruction during the 1920s–40s. Despite this, however, they have survived in far better condition than their later companions at Long Men, though wind erosion has begun to threaten them. The Government is, however, taking strenuous steps to protect them.

The northern Wei became very devout Buddhists and began a tradition within Buddhism which owes far more to Daoism or shamanism than to classical Buddhism. It began to see its own Emperors as living reincarnations of the Buddha. Thus many of the Buddha statues at Yungang have the faces of one of the five Emperors of the northern Wei. In these carvings, the Western and Indian influences are very clear indeed – at times you could be looking at a Hindu temple or a Greek shrine or church. Yet at the same time, the Chinese artists were taking basic ideas and expanding them. For example, the halos around the Buddhas and bodhisattvas. In Greek Buddhist art, they are plain. In Chinese art they begin at Yungang to be filled with exquisite little Buddhas, apsaras, scenes of life and so forth. The idea of the Buddhas being the Emperors meant that they began to see the figures as being human rather than divine and a loosening up began which started to appear most strongly in the bodhisattvas.

The scenes of the Buddha's life found here are the best in China and combine reverence with a lively local style which brings these stories to life.

The temples here reflect a continuing worship which is absent from the other two sites.

All over China, but especially along the Silk Route from the old capitals at Luoyang and Xian westwards, caves are to be found with similar carvings. It is probable that there are over two million carved figures in the major caves. This represents an immense labour of love. Yet in almost all cases, these artistic masterpieces have been left to quietly moulder and have not been major centres for pilgrimage or for worship. Today they are centres of pilgrimage for those interested in art and for many Chinese who come to marvel at what the working classes of China achieved – to use the classic Marxist reasoning – not without some justification. To visit the sacred mountains and the Buddhist caves is to enter two very different worlds of the sacred in China. Both are so distinctively different and yet, through them all runs the continuous sense of the sacred within China and of the action of the sacred upon China.

MINOR DEITIES

The following lists, according to faith, the minor statues of gods, goddesses and Buddhas, and complements chapters 3 to 5.

Three Buddha Statues

Apart from the three sets of Buddha figures outlined in chapter 4, there are other combinations of three, which are the Three Bodies of the Buddha.

The Three Bodies of the Buddha constitute another set of three. These show the various Buddhas who have been known as Manushis – in their three forms:

1 Manifest in human form on earth as a mortal
   and ascetic who has achieved enlightenment
   (for example, for this era's Buddha is Sakyamuni).
2 In Nirvana, as the embodiment of supreme purity
   or as the supreme Law of Buddhahood.
3 In the state of total inner enlightenment – the
   spiritual state.

These can also be classified as the essential nature of the Buddha; the body of bliss which is his own particular body, and his body of transformation by which he can manifest himself as he wishes.

The three forms emanate from each other. Thus the spiritual state, the inner enlightenment also known as the Dharma body, is foremost. From it proceed the bodhisattvas who manifest the Buddha nature in their existence and in their compassion which spans time. They represent the Sangha – the teaching community which according to Mahayana teachings is eternal. Finally there is the actual manifestation in a given time of the Buddha nature in human form for a limited period. This is the historical Buddha and his predecessors or those who will come in the future. This represents the Buddha.

Thus the three bodies of the Buddha can be broken down into five main collections of these three forms, each of which has an animal symbol attached which makes for easier identification. Going from dharma body, through bodhisattva body to historical Buddha body we have:

1 Vairocana, Samantabhadra, Krakucchanda – lion.
2 Akshobhya, Vajrapani, Kanakamuni – elephant.
3 Ratnasambhava, Ratnapani, Kasyapa – horse.
4 Amitabha, Avalokitesvara, Sakyamuni – goose or peacock.
5 Amoghasiddhi, Visvapani, Maitreya – the Hindu bird creature, Garuda.

Another threesome is Sakyamuni with his two closest disciples, Kasyapa and Ananda. These are easily identified as the two disciples are dressed as monks and obviously in attendance upon the historical Buddha.

The Eighteen Lohans
The following lists the titles and major symbols of the eighteen lohans.

1 Bin Du Lo Bo Lo Duo She – Pindola the Bharradvaja – he is shown as either a hairy, skinny old man holding a book and begging bowl, or seated beside a table with a gong on it, with a boy assistant, while

the lohan holds a book.

2 Jia Nuo Jia Fa Cuo – Kanaka Vatsa – he is sometimes shown floating in clouds and holds a fly whisk in his right hand.

3 Jia Nuo Jia Bo Li To She – Kanaka the Bharadbvaja – very hairy eyebrows and often seated on a rock holding a book in one hand and a fly whisk in the other.

4 Su Pin Te – Subhinda – shown as a wandering sage with a scroll, alms bowl and incense vase, often apparently clicking his fingers, to show that he found enlightenment that quickly! Can be accompanied by a goat.

5 Nuo Chu Lo – Nakula – he is accompanied by a mongoose looking creature, or occasionally, a three-legged toad, while he holds a rosary.

6 Bo Tuo Lo – Bhadra – a cousin of the historical Buddha, accompanied by a tiger.

7 Jia Li Jia – Kalika – wears a hooded cloak while reading a scroll, or wears gold earrings or holds them in each hand.

8 Fa She Lo Fu Duo Lo – Vajraputra – shown as very thin and hairy.

9 Shu Bo Jia – Supaka – he is accompanied by a sage and holds either a fan or a book.

10 Ban Tuo Jia – Panthaka – he is one of a pair of twins (see 16) born while their mother was travelling and thus stand as symbols of the pilgrim's journey. He sits beneath a tree, accompanied by a dragon. Can be shown with a feather fan over his head of holding a bell.

11 Lo Hu Lo – Rahula – the son of the historical Buddha, he seems to be disappearing into clouds, holding his crown (he renounced his father's kingdom) or with a halo held by an attendant and with a scroll before him as he makes his abdication.

12 Jia Xi Na – Nagasena – can be shown seated with an

alms bowl in both hands from which water is spurting, or holding a vase in his right hand and a ringed stick in his left, or sometimes a pyramid of jewels instead of the vase.

13 Yin Jie Tuo – Angaja – a manifestation of Maitreya Buddha, he is either an old man with legs bound together, and exceptionally long eyebrows, or a fat jolly person holding an umbrella.

14 Fa Na Po Si – Vanavasa – one of the five ascetics who were with the Buddha in the forest, he either has a vase with a dropping branch of willow in it or a firepan.

15 A Shi Duo – Ajita – he is shown as an old, bent man either leaning on a staff with a vase of peonies beside him, or sitting meditating cross-legged.

16 Zhu Cha Ban Tuo Jia – Chota Panthaka – twin brother of the 10th lohan, he either sits with his back turned towards the viewer, head thrown back and looking upwards, or holding a rosary with two deer beside him, or on a mat holding a staff with a deer's head on it.

17 Do Mo Duo Lo – Dharmatrata – he has long hair and either holds a vase and fly whisk while carrying a bundle of books on his back, while adoring a statue of Amitabha, or he sits under an umbrella with a fly whisk, beside a tiger.

18 Bu Te – Upadhyaya – he resembles Mi Lo Fa, the Future Buddha, and is believed to be the last reincarnation of Maitreya. He holds a rosary and a peach and frequently has children running over him.

The Apsaras

Often carved flying above bodhisattvas and Buddhas are the apsaras, Tian Nu. They look like angels, with garments streaming out behind them. They are believed to be beautiful women who live in the Western Paradise of Amitabha, and they frequently carry musical instruments. They are very elegant and beautiful.

The Great Disciples
The ten Great Disciples are usually shown with shaved heads, in monastic garb and with halos. They are:

1 Sariputra, who holds a long handled fan.
2 Maudgalyayana, who holds three lotus stalks in a vase.
3 Kasyapa, holding a jingle stick resting on the ground.
4 Aniruddha, whose hands are pressed together, pointing upwards.
5 Subhuti, who holds a sceptre, resting its base on his left hand.
6 Purna, who holds a long handled censer.
7 Katyayana, whose hands are in a position of prayer and held against his chest.
8 Upali, his index fingers touching tip to tip and pointing upwards, while the rest of his fingers point downwards.
9 Rahula, who holds a fly whisk over his shoulder and a scroll.
10 Ananda, hands pressed together praying.

The Twelve Deva Kings
The twelve Deva Kings represent directions and elements of nature. They are:

1 Prithivi, the Earth deva, holding a bowl of fruit, her left hand held upwards.
2 Vaisravana, the deva of the North, a man in full armour, with a long beard, holding a sceptre in one hand and a pagoda in the other. Sometimes he holds a sword, spear or halberd instead of a sceptre, but he always has the pagoda.

219

3 Varuna, the deva of water and of the West, who has five snakes coming from his head and holds a large sword in one hand and a cobra hood raised in the other. Sometimes he holds two snakes and a cup and can be seated upon a crocodile type creature or a tortoise.

4 Soma, the deva of the moon and of the Northeast, who holds a disc of the moon in one hand while the other hand is held palm out at chest level.

5 Vaya, the deva of the winds and of the Northwest, who is bearded and holds a banner floating out from him in one hand and a wind-catching bag under his arm.

6 Nacriti, whose hair is stiff and his right hand holds a sword, while his left hand is at shoulder level, palm out but with the thumb and little finger touching.

7 Brahma, deva of the Centre, feminine in form with three heads each of which has three eyes, above which are two heads with two eyes each. She has four arms, the top right one holding a trident, the top left a lotus, the bottom right is empty but turned outwards and the bottom left holds a vase.

8 Isana, a dramatic looking deva with three eyes, holding a trident and a covered bowl.

9 Agni, the deva of fire and of the Southeast, who is a bearded old man with a flaming halo. He has four arms, the top right holding a rosary, the top left a staff which seems to be sprouting, the bottom right a triangular fire symbol, the bottom left a bottle, while he wears around his middle a tiger skin.

10 Surya, the deva of the sun and the Southwest, who is female. She holds a lotus in one hand on which the sun is marked while the left holds the base of the lotus.

11 Indra, deva of the East, has three eyes, a thunderbolt in one hand and in the other a bowl.

12 Yama, deva of the Hells, and King of all of them, and

of the South. He has three eyes, and in his left hand a staff with a bodhisattva head on top, the right hand stretching out. He usually wears a crown with the character for king.

Xu Kong Zang – Akasagarbha

This is the Essence of the Void, one of the bodhisattvas, and can be either male or female. His/her special sign is the sun, which is shown resting on a lotus rising above the right shoulder. In some statues the left hand holds a lotus from which springs a sword, while a long thin scarf is wrapped loosely around the body.

Ma Ni Li – Marici

Known in China as the Queen of Heaven and the Mother of the Dipper. She is a cosmic ruler, associated with the sun as well as with the stars of the Great Bear. Although a woman, she is fierce and often male in appearance. She has eight or sixteen arms and three heads, with three eyes in each. In her arms she holds some combination of the following – the sun, the moon, a bow and arrow, spear, sword, thunderbolt, hook, fan, needle and thread. She is often mounted upon a charging pig, or in a lotus or chariot drawn by seven pigs. One of her three faces is sometimes that of a pig. The pigs are supposed to be the dray animals which pull her across the sky in her form as the sun.

Gods of the Five Elements

The Gods of the Five Elements do not appear very often in temples. They are also linked to the five planets of traditional Chinese astrology, and to the five directions. The linking of certain deities, colours and directions goes way back into ancient Chinese mythology, giving the following combinations:

The Metal star is linked to Venus and the direction West and autumn. He is also called the White Emperor and is usually dressed in White. He can sometimes be represented by the most ancient of symbols for the West, the White Tiger.

The Wood star is linked to Jupiter, the East and spring. He is considered a dangerous deity and his colour is Green. He is sometimes represented by the ancient symbol for the East, the Green Dragon.

The Water star is linked to Mercury, the North and winter. His colour is Black. Of all the gods of the directions, he is the one, along with the Yellow Emperor, who has survived and come to have a role independent of the others. He is known as the Dark Ruler, Emperor of the North and Great Yin, as north is the direction of the male force in the universe. North is also the direction of death, making him the ruler of the dead. Thus, one can clearly see why such a deity continues to exercise power.

He is very distinctive looking, for his hair is smoothed back from his face and brow, and hangs down the back of his head as a full head of hair. He is almost always shown either standing upon or seated above a snake and tortoise. These illustrate the great antiquity of this god, for in the earliest records and myths, the north is ruled by a Dark Warrior, a giant black tortoise. He may be attended by his servant, who carries a black standard.

The Fire star is linked to Mars, to the South and summer. His colour is Red. Sometimes he is represented by the ancient symbol for the South, the Red Bird.

The Earth star's direction is the centre and colour is Yellow. Hence the Yellow Emperor is the Earth star god (see above).

Legends of the earliest times depict great struggles between the various deities of the directions and colours, in what might best be described as a primal struggle for supremacy out of chaos. Today, only the Yellow Emperor and the North Emperor still hold any real place in the popular pantheon of Daoism.

The Ten Kings of Hell

1 Qin Guang Wang – whose Hell is actually the court of judgement where souls are brought at death. He is

often accompanied by the officers who fetch the souls at death. They are very distinctive in that one has the face of a horse, the other the face of an ox, while the third is deadly white, has a pointed hat and a red tongue hanging out, while the fourth has a black face.

The ox-headed and horse-headed deities – Niu Tou and Ma Mian respectively – are people who ate and sold horse and ox meat in their lifetimes, and who are given these posts as punishment. When they have expiated their sins, they are released and another two take their place.

The White Master and the Black Master – Bai Lao Ye and Hei Lao Ye – are also known as Yang Wu Chang and Yin Wu Chang – meaning the male principle Impermanent being and the female principle Impermanent being. They are also referred to as the Wu Chang ghosts. Their roles are to bring in the souls according to age. Thus Yang Wu Chang fetches those who die before they are fifty, while Yin Wu Chang collects those who die after fifty. As such, White Face or White Master is the most feared and in temples, he is the one who is worshipped most, to try and persuade him not to come for those who are young. The reason his tongue sticks out is that he is believed to be a suicide. Suicides are greatly feared in traditional China because they haunt the area of their death seeking to trap others into doing the same.

On White Master's conical hat there are four characters which seem rather odd. They read One Look Great Fortune. This has led him to be worshipped in some areas as a god of wealth! He and Black Master are usually dressed in white, the colour of mourning, and in rough, sack cloth type material. They are usually surrounded by piles of Bank of Hell notes as bribes. The temples of Macau are especially fine for such figures.

2 Chu Jiang Wang is the King of the second Court of Hell and his specialities are torturing dishonest marriage brokers, bad doctors and those who harm animals. His symbols include two prison cages – one hot, one cold – a scorching pillar and an icepool.

3 Song Di Wang rules the third Hell and deals with bad tempered women and slaves who disobey. Flaying and being ground down by hammers are his speciality.

4 Wu Guan Wang is in the fourth Hell and he deals with those who are mean or swindlers. Being forced onto spikes or being buried under rocks are his symbols.

5 This is where the King of the Kings of Hell resides, King Yama, also called Yan Le Wang. Here stock is taken and the dead are usually seen looking back at their old lives to see how badly their children now behave or how friends have forgotten them.

6 Bian Cheng Wang rules and punishes those who blasphemed or insulted the gods, desecrated the temples or harmed any of the religions. His instruments of torture are the roller, the two planks to crush and the post at which the dead are flayed alive – if you follow my meaning!

7 The King of the seventh Hell is also the god of the Eastern Peak, Tai Shan Jun Wang, though this is no longer considered by most believers to be a real incarnation of that deity. In the Han dynasty, it was believed that all souls went to Tai Shan at death, reflecting the notion that all human beings were created by the god and goddess of Tai Shan. But that link no longer exists for most people. Here come those who damaged tombs, practised cannibalism or who were cruel to those beneath them. His signs are a boiling cauldron, being gnawed by animals or having the stomach ripped open.

8 The King of the eighth court is Ping Deng Wang

and this is the destination of those who lacked filial piety. Chariot wheels as crushing implements, tongues torn out and being cut into ten thousand pieces are the specialities of this hell.

9 Du Shi Wang is King of the worst of all the hells. Here come those who commit suicide, abortionists and writers of pornographic books. Here is the City of Suicide, where those who commit suicide re-enact their deaths endlessly.

10 Zhuan Lun Wang sends the souls out again in a new body, but not before they have been made to drink the Potion which Forgets. This is administered to them by an old woman and means that no soul can recall any details of a previous life. Once they are ready, the souls are sent out across the bridge linking both worlds.

The Sun and the Moon

The god and goddess most associated with the sun and moon are Shen Yi and Cheng E. Shen Yi is the famous Yi the Archer, who is supposed to have lived at the time of the Emperor Yao, c. 2500 BC, and whose skills were such that when nine false suns rose burning the land dry, he despatched them one by one with his arrows, shooting the black raven that was at the heart of each out of the sky. This is why the sun is sometimes represented by a raven. However, he began to get imperial ambitions and his wife, Cheng E, was worried by this. One day Shen Yi undertook special services for the Queen Mother of the West and in return was given a magic potion for immortality. Cheng E found the potion and fearful that her husband, once immortal, would become powerful and evil, she swallowed the pill. At that moment Shen Yi burst into their room. Cheng E found she had the power of flight and flew out of the window, with Shen Yi pursuing her on his cloud. The gods took pity on Cheng E and took her to the moon where she lives to this day making pills of immortality and endowing the moon with its yin quality. Shen Yi was taken by the gods and placed in the sun, where his yang energy created the force of the sun.

Each usually holds a plaque with either a raven or a rabbit (the symbol of the moon) or the characters for sun and moon. Shen Yi is shown with his arrows.

Wind and Weather

Feng Bo is the god of the Winds and is easily recognized by his long white beard, yellow coat and a hat made of red and white strips. In his hands are a sack from which he despatches the winds.

Near him is often the god of Thunder. Lei Gong is a very ancient deity indeed, stretching back to shamanic times. He is fierce to look at, always scowling and menacing and often standing with his foot on a whirling disc which represents lightning. He may also have drums beside him from which thunder echoes out. Sometimes he has a monkey's face, bat's wings and an eagle's beak. In his hands he may carry a hammer and chisel.

Patron Deities

In local Daoist shrines, patron deities are often found, for example, the various sea goddesses of sailors, like A-Ma in Macau. One of the most widespread is Lu Ban the carpenter's god. He is usually seated, with two assistants, and is easily recognized in that he and his assistants carry various woodworking tools such as the square, axe and plane.

Gods of Medicine

While Lu Dong Bin is consulted by the ordinary people, the god of doctors is Yao Wang. He learnt much of his skill as a doctor from the Dragon King of the Waters, which is why he is often depicted with a dragon apparently whispering into his left ear. He is supposed to have lived during the 7th century AD and to have treated the Tang emperors of his time. He is usually shown in mandarin's dress to denote his high status when alive and has two assistants who carry either boxes of medicine or a gourd and a leaf.

Popular with women seeking a child is the god of Children, Zhang Xian, who appears as an old man with the customary long beard, with a child or two beside him. He draws back a bow and arrow pointed, strangely, at a dog in the sky. This is the Dog Star whose influence is adverse for those wishing to fall pregnant. Zhang Xian is thus defending the woman from this bad influence.

Heavenly Bureaucracy

In old books on Chinese gods, there were pages devoted to the numerous bureaus of Heaven. Bureaus to deal with everything from city drains to smallpox; from rain to ceremonial wear, each with its chief god and countless minions. All this reflected point for point the Imperial administration on earth. With the total destruction of that system, these gods and their administrative bureaus have largely gone. Never taken too seriously by the ordinary people who have always had a healthy disregard for any officials, divine or human, they have withered on the vine as the root of Imperial culture has been broken off. Today only a few, such as the god of Thunder and the Jade Emperor himself, have survived. It is unlikely that they will be revived.

Local Deities

As stated earlier, there are numerous local deities who have no role outside certain geographical or ethnographical regions. It is impossible to describe all these deities, but you will often find that local guidebooks or leaflets will give at least a basic outline of the most significant local deity. One example is the vast Wong Tai Sin temple in Hong Kong. He is a Daoist immortal to whom immense powers of divination are ascribed. Yet outside Hong Kong and the Pearl River estuary, he is not known at all.

Another example is one of the biggest temples and certainly one of the most popular, in Chengdu, Sichuan: the Zhaojue Miao. Here is enthroned a loyal general who served the famous Liu Bei, one of the Three of the Peach Orchard – see Guan Di above – who are recalled so vividly in the Romance of the Three Kingdoms, covering the period of the 3rd century AD. While Liu Bei, as the former king of the area, is recalled in his tomb and by a temple at the start of the complex, the heart of the shrine is the hall and altars to Zhuge Liang, Zhuge Zhan and Zhuge Shang. These three, grandfather, father and son, all served the state of Shu, Zhoge Liang being one of Liu Bei's most faithful servants while his son and grandson died in battle defending the state against its enemies. These three are only worshipped in Chengdu. You will not find their statues anywhere else that I know of in China, and yet they are very dear to the people of Chengdu. There is an old saying there that Zhuge is more revered than Liu Bei – meaning, the people prefer the loyal servant more than the egotistical ruler!

GAZETTEER OF SACRED MOUNTAINS

DAOIST MOUNTAINS[1]

Hua Shan

The Mountain of the West, Hua Shan, means Flower mountain. I have already given a partial tour up this mountain, so this section will cover what was not covered in the opening chapter (see pages 5–8).

Hua Shan is the steepest and most dangerous of the sacred mountains and should not even be contemplated by those who find heights, crowds and alarmingly steep rockfaces with precarious handholds, disturbing! That said, the first few miles of the route are quite gentle, so the more cautious can at least do this part! Hua Shan rises 7986 feet and is a dramatic series of three peaks, which arise at the end of steep and thin ridges.

This mountain has been a centre for religious activity for millennia. Legend, perhaps more than just legend, tells that in 1766 BC, the founder of the Shang dynasty (1766–1122), Tang the Victorious, came here to offer sacrifices in celebration. When the Shang fell in a welter of corruption and scandal to the victorious armies of the Zhou around 1100 BC, the victorious king Wu, long associated with the I Ching, came and made similar sacrifices.

The start of any pilgrimage is at the Xiyue – Great Western

– temple where imperial sacrifices have been offered since its foundation in 212 AD, if not earlier. One of the highlights of the temple are the four stone arches dating from the late Ming–17th century.

Entrance to the mountain is along a ceremonial pathway leading to the first temple, the gate to which is called the Pavilion of Going to Heaven. The pathway you follow was cut during the Ming and Qing dynasties and the temples along the way all date from then – but mostly from the Qing. In recent years, after a tragic flash flood killed scores of pilgrims, the Government has radically improved parts of the path, but without destroying the beauty and the challenge of the higher sections.

The earlier part of the path I have covered already. I suggest that you look out for the caves and shrines of the hermits, now mostly deserted. They are to be found in the most inaccessible places and often it takes some looking. Enjoy also the vast array of calligraphy en route: poems, sayings, exclamations of the famous and not so famous are to be found at almost every step of the way, as they are on so many of the sacred mountains.

The first gate reached on the ascent is some six or seven kilometres from the base and is called Yun Meng, or Gate of Clouds, and leads to a small, flatter area where two Daoist temples, called East and West stand, though they seem to function more as tea houses than temples today. Inside the East temple is the statue of the Maiden of the Nine Heavens, a local deity of the mountain of whom little is known. The term Nine Heavens, however, comes from Han dynasty beliefs about the layers of Heaven and the King of the Nine Heavens is an early version of the Jade Emperor. Nearby is the Big Dipper or North Dipper basin. The term Dipper, referring to the seven stars in the Great Bear and the centre of the Mother of the Bushel/Dipper cult, is again a reminder that ancient female Heavenly deities have always been a part of Daoism.

Near here are the ruins of the great Tong Xian Guan – the temple of the Tong Immortal. This was a vast Daoist academy

230

with a major library, built in 1549. Its passing is a sad commentary on the decline over the last few centuries of Daoism, hopefully now being changed.

Moving on, two rock formations come into view. One is supposed to look like a phoenix, though I have to say a lot of imagination is required! The other has two rocks sticking up which look like two people sitting close together. This is the Two Immortals playing Chess.

Next comes the rock for turning back. While this might sound like a sensible suggestion, it actually refers to an old legend. A Daoist monk had two assistants whom he worked hard but fairly. Together they cut 71 caves for hermits and cleared the scrub on the mountainside. But the two assistants became very fed up because the monk would never let them just rest in one of the caves. So they decided to kill him. One day as he was hanging on a rope over a steep fall, they cut the rope and set off down the mountain. To their considerable surprise, when they reached this point in the descent, there was the monk, fit and well. He simply said: 'Whatever you learn and whatever you do, always do it in honesty and steadfastly. If you are not honest, all that you do will come to nothing.'

The two assistants realized their folly and turned back from their descent and from their false understanding. This is why it is called the Rock of Turning Back.

A series of very steep and dangerous steps now go ahead, called the Thousand Foot Precipice and then followed by the Hundred Foot Gorge. Crossing the Two Immortals Bridge, you come to Quan Xian Guan – Temple of the Group of Immortals. Here it is possible to imagine one is an immortal, high on the mountain in the clouds. Near here is the famous Earth god cave in which there is a jar too big to have even gone through the entrance.

Beyond this temple you enter the Furrow of Lao Zi or to use the name used here Lao Jun – which means the Old Noble One. Lao Zi is said to have been moved by the struggles of people to make their way to the top so he hitched up his ox and ploughed this helpful furrow.

The terrace and temple next encountered is another place where the immortals are said to gather, and here the path divides. North Peak, the lowest of the three, juts out here, with passes so small they seem to close in on you. At the end are the scattered buildings of the North Peak monastery. Back on the main route, comes the journey along the infamous Black Dragon Ridge – Bei Long – which is so steep on either side it is said even the King of Hell is frightened here.

This leads to a slight depression called the Gold Lock Pass – Jin Suo. From here can be seen the Sleeping Immortal. This rock formation is supposed to be Ma Zhen Yi, a Daoist who sought immortality and so came to Hua Shan. He so loved the views here that he spent more and more time just lying down looking at the scenery. Eventually he achieved immortality but he had also by then become part of the rock!

Here the path heads off to either the East Peak or the Middle, South and West peaks. Taking the East Peak first, a dangerous, almost vertical path brings you to the Bo Terrace or Chess Pavilion. The story goes that the first emperor of the Northern Song dynasty, *c.* 970, played an expensive game of chess with a Daoist monk, the stake being Hua Shan itself. The emperor lost and Hua Shan has been Daoist ever since. The story makes little sense, but at this altitude, after that climb, who cares! This is where the imprint of the hand of the immortal who helped control the floods can be seen (see page 20).

The Middle Peak is quite a civilized climb. It is also known as the Jade Woman's Peak. The Jade Woman was the daughter of a king who lived in the 7th century BC. A sage was invited to play his flute at the court and the effect was such that the very dragons and phoenixes on the carvings got up and danced. As a reward he was given the hand of Princess Nongyu which means Jade – and together, assisted by the dragons, they were brought to live on this peak.

The South Peak is the highest peak and comes next. Here there once stood the Gold Heaven Palace – Jin Tian – and here can still be seen the ruins of what is claimed to be Lao Zi's furnace in which he made the pills of immortality and in which he once famously tried to burn to death Monkey – if the anti-Daoist novel *Journey to the West* is to be believed! Here there is another place where immortals used to gather and possibly the most extraordinary place of all on Hua Shan. The cave of He Lao which can only be reached by walking along thin planks held by ropes to the sheer mountain face and with a thousand foot drop below. This hermit cave sums up the spirit of complete withdrawal from society that the sages sought on the sacred mountains.

The West Peak looks like a vast lotus flower and hence its other name of Lotus Flower Peak. Here is the lovely Zhen Yue temple with its impressive statue of the Jade Emperor. Further on one comes to the giant axe which is such an integral part of this peak. For here is where a loyal son split the mountain in order to free his mother. The story goes that a scholar, one Liu Yan Chang, met a goddess and the two of them fell in love. They married and had a son, Cheng Xiang. But their marriage was illegal in the eyes of the gods. They determined to punish her for her crime of marrying a mortal. So her eldest brother was told to pick up a vast mountain and to drop it on her. This is how Hua Shan came to be where it is.

The mountain was duly dropped and the poor goddess crushed and trapped beneath it. But her son determined that when he grew up he would free his mother. Sure enough, when he came to maturity, he was able to obtain divine assistance and in particular the magic axe. Lifting this high, he brought it crashing down on West Peak and split the mountain. His mother leapt out, free at last, and they all lived happily ever after. The axe mark and the axe itself are still to be seen today. In the Cui Yub temple near the peak can be seen a statue of the goddess, uncrushed. Here too is the weather station. It must take some dedication to work there in winter.

Hua Shan was one of the sites where immortality mushrooms grew which, if picked at the right time, would ensure eternal life. This is why it has so many sites associated with immortals. It is today a busy Daoist mountain in that monks live and work all along the path, though they have to do so in cooperation with the tourist authorities who have set up hostels and restaurants in the temples. But to some extent this is simply continuing the old monastic tradition.

No account of Hua Shan is now complete without the Communist story. In summer 1949, the People's Liberation Army were en route to total victory, forcing Chiang Kai Shek's troops towards their eventual departure in autumn 1949 for Taiwan and the then declaration by Mao of the Chinese People's Republic. But using the difficult terrain of Hua Shan a group of Kuomingtang soldiers hid out up here and conducted guerrilla operations. There was no way a conventional attack up the path would be successful. So one night in June 1949, a group of seven PLA men, led by a local woodcutter, scaled the eastern face of Hua Shan, something no one had ever done before. They surprised the enemy and overwhelmed the superior force by sheer surprise. Taking Hua Shan by strategy has become a favourite theme for plays, films and even opera.

So Hua Shan continues to keep its hold on the imagination and affections of China.

Heng Shan – Shanxi

There are two Heng Shans, both Daoist sacred mountains. One is the Northern Mountain in Shanxi, the other is the Southern mountain in Hunan. This is about the northern mountain.

The pilgrimage route starts in the ancient city of Hun Yuan, with its almost perfect ancient houses and courtyards. Here the main sites of religious interest are the Yong An Si – The Eternal Peace Temple, a vast Buddhist monastery first built in the early-12th century and then enlarged in the 14th century and representing, as do so many of the buildings around Heng Shan, a fusion of architectural styles. For this is a part of China where the influences of the Mongolians and through them of the West, have had some impact. The beautiful temple contains within the main hall some excellent frescoes showing popular Buddhist (and Daoist) deities from the 14th century. The Yuan Jue Temple contains a fine pagoda built in 1118 AD.

Heng Shan is associated with three great figures from

Confucian and Daoist belief. The oldest figure is the August Emperor Shun, a model of filial piety who, despite three attempts by his father, stepmother and step-brother to murder him, was always a model of politeness and filial obedience. In the end the three realized the error of their ways and became models themselves. Shun was appointed Emperor because of these virtues. He is supposed to have visited Heng Shan in the third millennium BC. The two most popular figures here are two of the Eight Immortals. Lu Dong Bin is worshipped here and medicinal herbs are still gathered here for use in his prescriptions. But it is Zhang Guo Lao who is best remembered here for you can still see the hoof print of his donkey when he rode on it backwards and the tree with exposed roots, supposedly pulled from the ground by the same donkey in alarm at Zhang's riding techniques! (See page 122).

Many of the temples owe their foundation to the patronage of dynasties which ruled this area of northern China during the times when the great dynasties had broken up into warring states. In particular, many were founded during the Northern Wei, Qi and Zhou dynasties (386–590 AD) and especially during the Jin dynasty (1115–1240 AD). Repaired and extended under yet another Mongolian dynasty, the Qing (1644–1911), the area has been extensively repaired since 1979 as a tourist centre.

The mountain is 7280 feet high and has two major routes onto it known as the front and back routes. I will follow the front route. Before starting on the climb proper, Heng Shan's most famous site comes into spectacular view, the famous Suspended Temple, Xuan Kong Si, a Daoist temple built, so local legend has it by 'feathered monks' – flying monks, which picks up on the notion that immortals can fly. The temple itself only functions as a formal religious centre once a year when Daoists are permitted to hold services here, but it is well preserved. The temple was founded in the early-5th century AD and expanded many times, especially under Mongol patronage by the famous leader of the Quan Zhen school, Lu Chongyang. Reflecting the tradition of the Mongols which was to respect all the major faiths, the main hall contains statues of the Buddha, Lao Zi and Kong Fu Zi. In the other main halls are a famous statue of the Thousand Armed Guan Yin and an unusual collection of Five Buddhas, representing the past, present and future as well as the two main saviour Buddhas of Amitabha and Manjushri.

The main deity of the mountain is the god of Heng Shan, Cui Yang, the great grandson of the Yellow Emperor, who ruled this area of China in the last years of the second millennium BC according to Chinese mythology. He probably did exist as a powerful local ruler with the usual shamanic powers as legend records. His elevation to godhood is classic of traditional folk religion in China. His statue, dressed as an Emperor with the flat hat and beaded strings hanging down, can be found in many places.

Moving out of the river gorge over which the temple hangs, you pass the gate to Heng Shan with its Ming dynasty carved lions. To your right is the temple of the Three Origins, one of many small temples dotted along this path. Stunning views appear around every corner and the various rock carvings of poems and sayings warrant attention by their sheer diversity.

The Heng Zong rock – rock of the God of Heng Shan – is the first tourist stop. Here imperial edicts were read out to the god on ascribed days. The temple of Zhen Wu was where the rituals took place. The giant characters carved into the rock say the words Heng Zong and are 13 metres high each – the largest characters on Heng Shan. Here also you can see the pine tree that Zhang Guo Lao's donkey pulled up and nearby is a ridge where the immortal is said to have liked to sit and think.

The next major temple is the exquisitely coloured Ma Shen temple – temple of the Horse Spirits. Here are two statues of horses which are the favourite horses of Heng Zong. Down a side path you come to the Ten Kings Temple; they are of course the Ten Kings of Hell. Nearby are the bitter and set wells. From one comes delicious water; from the other rank water which can make you sick! Further off and a bit of a scrabble, lie the caves of the Three Mao brothers, a trio of immortals who are said to live here. At the end of this detour you come to the flying stone which is supposed to have landed at the feet of the August Emperor Shun when he visited, and then the Sleeping Palace which lies inside a cave grotto. This extraordinary site, created to resemble an imperial palace, was constructed in the Northern Wei (5th century AD) and this is considered to be the bedroom of Heng Zong.

Returning to the Ma Shen temple, proceed up again via the Memorial Arch, to the Lu Dong Bin temple. This is a popular temple where Lu Dong Bin, the famous medical doctor of the Eight Immortals, is venerated.

Beyond lies the Jiu Tian temple, the temple of the Nine Heavens, which is most popular and interesting. The Nine Heavens refers to a very ancient Daoist cosmology of the Heavens and indicates that the temple is almost certainly pre-Daoist in origin – i.e. before the 1st century AD. The central deities here are three goddesses all associated with childbirth and accompanied by the god of children, Zhang Xian. The goddesses are known as the Three Sisters and appear to be local deities. Around the hall are other gods such as the god who guards against smallpox, the god who guards against childhood illness and the god who ensures a safe delivery. The most intriguing of all is the god at the left of the entrance to whom one prays for an intelligent child!

This temple sums up for many the purpose of making the pilgrimage. It is a shrine to motherhood and to parental concerns and undoubtedly stretches far back in time. As indeed do other temples clustered around here such as the Temple of the Mother of the Dipper behind the Jiu Tian temple and the pavilion of the star god Kui Xing who accompanies the god of literature Wen Zhang (see page 139–40). The temple en route to the Kui Xing pavilion is dedicated to the Jade Emperor – Yu Huang – while next to that is a temple dedicated to the Princess of the Azure Clouds, the ancient deity of Tai Shan.

From the Jiu Tian temple, the main temple is reached. The Heng Zong temple is dedicated to the god of the mountain and here he sits in splendour. In the same hall is a rarely noticed inscription to the god of agriculture, Shen-nung, one of the Three August Rulers. This prayer was recently erected in the late-19th century as an imperial thank you for an end to a famine. He is associated with having introduced agriculture. The approach to the temple up the 103 steps is a dramatic vista.

On again to the Gathering of the Immortals Temple. This is the highest point of the mountain and here the immortals were supposed to gather to party. In the temple there are the three gods of happiness, fortune and longevity (see page 117), while carvings of the Eight Immortals are to be found beside them.

Finally, on the way down the back route look out for the Hall of the White Dragon and the temple of the Three Pure Ones – San Qing – the Daoist temple expressing the notion of universal Dao, revealed Dao and incarnate Dao (see pages 109–15) and a lovely peaceful place. Cross over the Bridge of the Eight Immortals and head for Hun Yuan again.

Heng Shan – Hunan

Rising 4,500 feet, this is the southern Daoist mountain, hence its alternative name, Nan Yue – Southern Mountain. It is said that the Emperor Shun, in his peregrinations, came here and offered sacrifices. However, uniquely for any of the five great sacred mountains, around 110 BC the Emperor Wu decided that the Southern Mountain should be Huo Shan in Anhui, which was much closer to the ancient capitals. This lasted until early-7th century AD, when Heng Shan was reinstated.

The mountain has always been a mixture of Daoist and Buddhist communities and continues to be so to this day. Temples here date from the Tang onwards, with major rebuilding during the Qing.

The entrance to the mountain is through a very elaborate but recent archway and past a shrine to the star god of literature Kui Xing in the town of Nanyue Zhen. Here are two magnificent temples, the Zhu Sheng Si – Temple of Consecration – and the Nan Yue Da Miao – Great Temple of the Southern Mountain. The Zhu Sheng Si was built in 1714 AD to be a palace for the Qing Emperor in his travels south. Its major feature, apart from its size and imperial splendour, is the Jian Jing Tang – the Hall of the Classics, with its statues of the five hundred lohans. It is very unusual to see them all together like this. The main hall houses the Great Buddha. Nearby the Medicine Buddha has a hall to himself.

The Nan Yue Da Miao was first built in 725 and has been constantly rebuilt and expanded since. The elaborate 72 pillars denote the 72 peaks of Heng Shan. The main hall is dedicated to the god of Heng Shan and the temple behind contains three goddesses, including the mother of the mountain god, the mother of the Jade Emperor and the goddess who gives sons. In the carvings on the balustrade of the main hall are many symbols associated with Buddhism. Of particular interest are the riderless horse which is a symbol of Ma (which means horse) Zu Dao I, founder of the Southern Mountain School of Buddhism in the 8th century, and a stag and crane. The stag and crane are symbols of longevity.

From this temple the route up the mountain begins and the 20 monasteries and temples can be found, though not all are in good condition. The temple of the Safekeeping of the Tripitaka – Cangjiang Dian – is a modern construction built on an old site. The Tripitaka is the three fold Canon of Buddhist texts acknowledged by all the main schools of Buddhism.

Next comes the Zhong Lei temple and further on the Middle Way pavilion, a welcome rest. Off to one side from the main path is the cave temple of Guan Yin, a particularly fine and unusual rock temple to the goddess of compassion. The Zhang Feng Si temple lies close by; founded in the early-7th century as the Lovely Heaven Temple, it was renamed and restored in the 18th century. The four iron statues of the four heavenly Kings are similar to those at Song Shan, though not as old, as these date from 1522–67 AD.

On to the bridge where the immortals meet, a prerequisite for any Daoist mountain, and then comes the Observatory built in the 14th century and one of 27 created at the time. It is known as the Wang Ri Tai. The path leads on to the Huo Shang Miao – Temple of the God of Fire – a 16th century building with an unusual dedication. I know of no other such temple in China. From here it is a climb to the top of Zhurong Feng – the highest of the 72 peaks. Here is the temple of offerings and above, the temple of the mountain god himself – the Zhu Jung Tian.

The Fu Yan Si temple at the base of Reng Bo Feng peak, was founded in 568 AD, but rebuilt in the Qing. Here is a magnificent statue of the mountain god in bronze which is thought to date from the 10th century.

Finally the Nan Tai Si – Southern Terrace Temple – also dates from the 6th/7th century but was completely rebuilt in the early years of the 20th century. The monastery has many treasures but is particularly important as a pilgrimage place for Japanese Buddhists who belong to the School founded by the Chinese monk Xi Qian who lived here in the mid-8th century. To the north of the monastery is the Fang Guang Si, founded in 503 AD but much altered and restored.

BUDDHIST MOUNTAINS[2]

Wu Tai Shan

Wu Tai Shan, Five Terrace Mountain, is the northern Buddhist mountain and is especially associated with Manjushri – Wen Shu – the bodhisattva of wisdom, and the special guardian of Tibetan and Mongolian Buddhism. This explains why so much of the architecture of Wu Tai Shan looks Tibetan, or at least, non-Chinese.

The mountain is in Shanxi and consists of four peaks surrounding a high basin from the centre of which emerges the fifth peak. It is a very large area and the temples are scattered around it. Given that there is no clear direction for the pilgrim paths which run out to the four peaks, I will simply list the main temples.

Unlike Daoist mountains, Buddhist mountains do not seem to have as much local detail on the paths. Indeed, the paths function as primarily routes from monastery A to monastery

240

B, whereas on Daoist mountains, the paths are full of stories, incidents and legends and are a part of the Way itself.

Manjushri is thought to have taught here and it was this which brought into being the first monasteries in the 6th to 7th centuries. I know of no tradition of this as a Daoist mountain beforehand. The close proximity of Heng Shan means that Wu Tai Shan may have been a blank spiritual mountain until its association with Manjushri.

For Mongolian Buddhists (who follow Tibetan Buddhism) this mountain is the most important in the world. Until recently families would travel for months to bring their dead here for burial. It will be interesting to see if the revival of Buddhism in Mongolia and the freedom to travel more revives any of this tradition of pilgrimage.

Manjushri can be easily recognized in that he holds a sword to smite ignorance and a palm leaf book. He is usually of fierce mien and is often seated upon a rather elaborate lion.

Travelling towards Wu Tai Shan you come to the Nan Chan Si – South Meditation Temple – in Wu Tai Cheng. This is famous for its hall built in 782, containing statues which date from the same period. It is the oldest wooden building in China. As virtually all Buddhist temples and statues were destroyed in the great persecution of 841–5, this survival is of immense importance. The central Buddhas include Sakyamuni and, on his right, Manjushri seated on his lion.

Nearby is the Yan Qing Si – Great Celebration temple – built in the 12th century and combining arcane tribal decorations with Buddhist imagery. The main feature here is the text of a sutra carved on a seven metre pillar and dating from 1035.

In Wu Tai Xian itself, the Guang Ji Si – Temple of Extensive Compassion – is essentially Qing, though the main temple is in part 14th century and the statues inside are contemporary. Again, the fusion of tribal design with Buddhism is most noticeable here.

Most famous of the temples on the edge of the mountain is the Fo Guang Si – Temple of the Buddha's Radiance. The great hall dates from 857 and is the second oldest wooden building in China – a fact which was only discovered in the 1930s. The great hall was built to celebrate the ending of the great persecution and unusually, the temple complex faces west not south. Whether this was in respect to the West as the spiritual direction from which Buddhism came, is unclear.

The Manjushri Hall dates from 1137 and has fine new statues of Manjushri and attendants. In the Eastern Hall, the figures are Tang dynasty from the late-9th century, though the five hundred lohans date from the 15th century. The wall paintings are Tang and give a vivid picture of the religious matrix from which Buddhism re-emerged after the persecution.

Further on towards the mountain is the Jin Ge Temple – Golden Tower – founded in 770 AD and covered with gilded tiles which have given it its name. Inside is a particularly large Guan Yin with a Thousand arms and eyes. Look in the centre of the hands for the eyes.

At the base of the central peak, in the bowl formed by the other peaks, lies the pilgrim town of Tai Huai, where the Ta Yuan Si – Pagoda Temple – is noticeable for its enormous 50-foot Great White Stupa. Here one first encounters the full range of traditional Tibetan/Mongolian architecture and artifacts. To walk properly in devotion around the Great Stupa, you should walk with your right hand held out towards the stupa. The prayer wheels are spun to send the prayer to the bodhisattva and thus to earn his assistance in overcoming the struggle of birth and death.

Behind the temple is the Sutra Library built originally in the 15th century but much adapted and housing one of the world's most dramatic and unusual libraries, not just because of the contents but because of the vast revolving bookcase structure within.

Behind this strange building is the Xian Tong monastery, the temple of Fine Penetration which is supposed to date from 70 AD, but this is highly unlikely. The present buildings date from the 14th and 15th centuries. The bronze images here, both statues and castings on pagodas, are of the highest quality and depict bodhisattvas and Buddhas galore, surrounded by other figures from general Chinese folk lore. The bronze pavilion, cast in the 16th century, is outstanding and the detail of the casting is breathtaking. The temple is famous for its links with the school of meditation founded by the Chan master I Xuan in the 8th century.

Beyond this is the Pusa Ding – Hall of the Bodhisattva. This fine temple supposedly marks the place where Manjushri used to sit when preaching and its beautiful coloured roof tiles are meant to mark out its special nature. As the focal point of official visits there are many interesting stele in a variety of languages, noting visits by emperors and kings.

A complete monastery including teaching halls, temples and library is the Luo Hou Temple, or the Temple of Rahu's Footprint. Rahu is the eldest son of the Buddha and is particularly linked with the sun and moon. The temple is the best preserved on Wu Tai Shan. It is famous for the model of the eighteen lohans crossing the sea on a lotus petal inside which are the four directional guardians or Buddhas who appear when the mechanical devices of the statue operate.

Behind this temple is the temple of Yuan Zhao – True Countenance – which dates from the Ming dynasty. The stupa in the middle contains the ashes of the Indian monk who founded the temple. The Three Buddhas here are the past, present and future Buddhas (see page 89) and the temple belongs to the Yellow Hat school of Tibetan Buddhism of which the Dalai Lama is head. Indeed this temple is associated with the early teachings of the founder of that tradition, Tsong Khapa.

In the temple of the Ten Thousand Buddhas – Wang Fo Ge – is a strange little hall dedicated to calming the Dragon king of Wu Tai Shan. The Dragon king is part of Daoist and folk religion lore. Apparently, the Buddhists felt it important to get him on their side, hence his own special hall.

The best statue of Manjushri is to be found in the Shu Xiang temple. It is nine metres high and was made in the 15th century.

The Nan Shan temple has three sections, all dating from the late-13th century but much restored. The centrepiece here is

243

the main hall which is reached by 108 steps – the same number as there are beads on a string of Buddhist prayer beads – available at any good stall anywhere on any of the mountains! The eighteen lohans date from the Ming dynasty but perhaps of greatest interest is the life story of the Buddha, painted in very Chinese style and dating from the Ming. A delightful place.

The Zhen Hai Temple – Calm Waters – contains equally fascinating paintings and sculptures of Buddhist deities and scenes from the life of the Buddha but all dating from the Qing dynasty. It is like a picture book of popular Buddhism, c. 1800.

The mountain has its share of grottoes such as those of Guan Yin and the Diamond Sutra, all with interesting carvings. Other temples further out from the central bowl are often less elaborate and less well cared for, such as the Jade Blossom Temple or the Chu Lin monastery.

Wu Tai Shan is so full of temples and sites it is hard to know what to include and what to leave out. I leave the pilgrim traveller to decide how to take in one of the largest collections of temples he or she is likely to find in one place under Heaven!

Jiu Hua Shan

Jiu Hua Shan – Nine Flower Mountain – in Anhui, is the Southern mountain of Buddhism. This is the mountain of the bodhisattva Ksitigarbha, deity of the dead and of the Earth, known in Chinese as Di Zang and to whom prayers are offered for escape from the Ten Hells (see page 62). This is the mountain of the dead, and rivals Tai Shan in its cult of the dead. The mountain's temples were all destroyed by the Taiping rebellion in the late 1850s and early 1860s. This Christian inspired but later dictatorial peasant rebellion was the world's greatest peasant revolt and lasted for 20 years, nearly overthrew the Qing and cost approximately 20 million lives. The Taiping destroyed all temples in their reach and thus the buildings on Jiu Hua Shan all date from the later 19th century, though they are on ancient sites. The mountain rises to 4696 feet at its top peak, the Ten Kings Peak – referring to the Ten Kings of Hell.

The pilgrim path starts in the village of Shan Gen with the

archway First Heavenly Gate – Yi Tian Men. Beyond this is the Gan Lu Si – temple of Sweet Dew. This is a Daoist dedication, for the sweet dew referred to is supposed to be a vital ingredient in the elixir of life. This was much sought by External School Daoists in their quest for immortality (see page 43). Today you can buy it bottled! Here one begins to encounter the statues of Di Zang along with the usual Buddhas and bodhisattvas such as Guan Yin.

After the Second Heavenly Gate comes the monastery of Huacheng – Temple of Transformation. Its founder was Bei Du, an Indian monk who arrived in 401 AD. In pictures he is depicted travelling across the waters in his alms bowl – which probably means he came from India by sea! The library – Cangjing Lou – escaped the Taiping destruction and its design dates from the 8th century, though the building itself dates from 1430. Here is a large statue to Vairocana the Supreme and Eternal Buddha, known in Chinese as Pi Lu Fo. Seated upon a lotus cross-legged he wears a five-leaved crown to show his enlightenment. He is associated with the Chan school of Buddhism.

The Roushen Temple contains valuable manuscripts and a reconstructed 17-metre wooden pagoda upon which the Ten Kings of Hell are depicted.

All round the Huacheng temple are temples and pagodas too numerous to list fully.

Next comes the Qi Yuan Si – Temple of the Garden of Adoration. This is the biggest temple on Jiu Hua Shan. It is a major centre for the ceremonies for the dead, as are all the temples on the mountain.

Next comes the Bai Sung An – Hermitage of the Hundred Years. The hundred years refers to the age of a monk, one Hai Yu who lived and died here in the early-17th century. His mummified and preserved body can be seen still.

A steep climb above this is the Wan Fo Si – Temple of Ten Thousand Buddhas, a simple building of no great interest. Above this is Guan Yin Si – Guan Yin's temple – so named because of the rock nearby which is supposed to look like the goddess.

From here on, the mountain has just small temples, none of which are particularly significant, but all of which have a charm and a naturalness which is sometimes lost in the larger temples. The mountain is very busy religiously and seems to have survived the Cultural Revolution fairly well. It is still a centre for the Buddhist dead and I suspect will long continue to be so, such is the strength of the veneration of the dead in China.

1 For details of the Daoist Sacred Mountains Tai Shan and Song Shan, see chapter 7, Sacred Mountains.
2 For details of the Buddhist Mountains Pu Tuo Shan and Emei Shan, see chapter 7, Sacred Mountains.

GAZETTEER OF SACRED PLACES

This list does not claim to be exhaustive – far from it. However, it does contain most major or significant sites. I would welcome letters offering additions to the list, with as much detail as possible.

ANHUI PROVINCE

Hefei
Temple of the Palace of Bao – Bao Gong Si
At the western end of Baohe Gongyuan Park. Founded in the 14th century, this Confucian temple is named after a respected government offical and built on the site where he studied.

Temple of Clear Teaching – Ming Jiao Si
A Buddhist temple founded in the 8th century and rebuilt in the mid-19th century.

Wuhu
Temple of Universal Well-Being – Guang Hi Si
Northwest of Wuhu on the southwest side of the Reddish-Brown Mountain. Founded in the 9th century, the three halls date from the Qing Dynasty.

The Mountain of the Nine Blossons – Jiu Hua Shan
One of the four sacred Buddhist mountains, Jiu Hua Shan (see pages 244–6) is 150km southwest of Wuhu.

The Yellow Mountain – Huang Shan
Situated 150km south of Wuhu, it is believed that the legendary Yellow Emperor used alchemy in an attempt to discover the Elixir of Life here.

Meng Cheng
The Ten Thousand Buddha Pagoda – Wan Fo Ta
In the Huai Bei area 95km northwest of Beng Bu. A stele records that this 13-storey octagonal brick pagoda was founded in the Song Dynasty.

Ji Xi
Zao Chi Zong Temple
Founded in the mid-19th century, the temple has frescoes of the Taiping rebellion.

Zhengdian
Said to be the home village of Lao Zi, founder of Daoism and author of the *Dao De Jing* (see page 3).

BEIJING

The major sacred sites are listed below; in fact old Beijing itself is a sacred site laid out according to the strict rules of feng shui.

The Forbidden City
Entering through the Tian Men gate, to the left is Sun Yat Sen park, the site of the Ming Dynasty Temple of Earth and Harvest. To the right is the People's Cultural Park with the Temple of the Imperial Ancestors, rebuilt in 1544. The main gate to the palace is the Meridian Gate where the Emperor would proclaim the new calendar each lunar year (see page 115).

The three great halls in the Forbidden City are those of Supreme Harmony, Perfect Harmony and Preservation of Harmony, a trinity which reflects the Three Buddhas and the Three Pure Ones.

Temples of Heaven and Earth

The complex dates from 1420. The tiles of the Temple of Heaven are blue to reflect the colour of Heaven, the tiles of the Temple of Earth are yellow to reflect the rich yellow soil of China. The main buildings of the Temple of Heaven are round, reflecting the shape of Heaven and the main buildings of the Temple of Earth are square. The greatest building in the Temple of Heaven is the Hall of Prayer for Good Harvest founded in 1420, rebuilt 1889 and set on three round marble terraces matched by a three-layered temple roof representing the Six Levels of Heaven. The Emperor sat on the circular stone in the centre of the temple surrounded by four pillars symbolizing the four seasons. To the east is the Altar of the Sun and to the west the Altar of the Moon. They are known as the Ritan. The Emperor made Spring Equinox sacrifices at the Altar of the Sun and Autumn Equinox sacrifices at the Altar of the Moon. In both places the sacrifice terrace is square and the enclosing wall is circular as in old Chinese coins.

Outside the Forbidden City on Qiong Hua Island of Beihai is a temple complex built in 1651 to celebrate the first visit of a Dalai Lama and the White Dagoba here commemorates it. East of the lake is the Altar of Silkworms where the Empress offered sacrifices. The whole area is a maze of old temples and false walls can be seen in front of buildings. They are demon-stopping walls to block evil forces. A good example is the Nine Dragon Wall, built in 1417 (the temple behind no longer stands).

Confucian Temple – Kong Miao

Built in 1306, it is the second largest Confucian temple in China. At its centre is the Dacheng Hall, the formal shrine to Confucius with his spirit tablet in the centre (see pages 160–63).

249

The Palace of Peace and Harmony – Yong He Gong
The largest Tibetan Monastery in Beijing, built in 1750, it only recruits monks of Tibetan or Mongolian ancestry. The founder of the Yellow School of Tibetan Buddhism is honoured in the Hall of the Wheel of Law. An 18-metre wooden statue of Wandala Buddha stands in the Tower of Ten Thousand Fortunes.

Temple of the Cypress Grove – Bailin Si
Founded in 1347, rebuilt in the Qing Dynasty. It houses 78,230 woodblocks for printing the major Buddhist scriptures, the Tripitaka.

Mao Mausoleum – Mao Zhuxi Jiniantang
In Tian An Men Square. Housing the embalmed body of Mao Ze Dong, the mausoleum covers an area of over 20,000m².

Temple of the White Pagoda – Bai Ta Si
On the north side of Yang Shi Da Jie. The first pagoda was built in the 11th century to house relics, it was restored by Khubilai in the 13th century. The temple was rebuilt in 1457. The fourth hall of the temple contains a good collection of Buddhist sculptures and tankas.

Growth of Intellect Temple
At the eastern end of Lu Mi Cang Hu Tong. Acclaimed for its dark blue tiles, the temple was built in 1443.

Eastern Church
On the east side of Wang Fu Jing, south of Chun Shu Hu Tong. The present church, built at the beginning of the 20th century, is on the site of earlier Catholic churches. The site was originally occupied by Father Adam Schall's 17th century house.

Saint Michael's Church
On the corner of Taj Ji Chang Street, this church is recognizable by its two gothic towers. Built by the Lazarist fathers in 1902.

Long Life Temple

In the western district, go north from the east end of Liu Li Chang Street. This temple was built in 1441 on the site of an earlier temple.

Temple of Everlasting Spring

In the northwestern district. The first street to the west in Xuan Wu Men gate leads to Chang Chun Si Jie, the street named after this temple. The temple is occupied by a factory and by private accommodation.

Recompense the State Temple – Baoguo Si

Take a narrow lane north from Guang An Men Da Jie. Dedicated to Guan Yin under the Ming. The temple is not currently open to the public.

The Mosque on Niu Jie Street

The street runs into Guang An Men Da Jie Street at its northern end. This has always been a Muslim neighbourhood and the Mosque – the Temple of Prayer – is halfway along the street. The complex, founded in the 12th century, contains a prayer hall whose decorations combine western and eastern influences, and an observation tower used for astronomical purposes.

Temple of the Source of the Law – Fa Yuan Si

North of the Islamic Association of China. Historically, this Buddhist temple is the oldest in Beijing (7th century), although few of the present buildings date back even as far as the 18th century. Buddhist novices study here and the complex includes a series of halls and courtyards.

Dong Si Mosque

Left off the Dong Si Nan Da Jie. This mosque covers an area of 10,000m² and was first built in 1356 and restored in 1447.

The Northern Cathedral – Bei Tang
To the north of Xi'anmen Da Jie. The first church was consecrated in 1703 and this is the third church on this site, extensively restored in 1985, when it re-opened.

The Temple of Universal Rescue – Guang Ji Si
Near the crossroads of Xi Si with Dong Si. A Buddhist religious site since the 12th century, the temple has undergone extensive rebuilding including restoration work this century.

The Temple to Protect the Country – Huguo Si
The buildings were altered from a Prince's Palace to a temple in the Yuan Dynasty and is currently in need of restoration.

Temple of the Kings of Medicine – Yao Wang Miao
Northeast of the Temple of Heaven. This temple, founded in the Ming Dynasty, is dedicated to all famous Chinese doctors.

Temple of Peaches – Han Tao Gong
South of the former Dong Bian Men gate. This temple was dedicated to the Queen Mother of the West.

Temple of The Five Pagodas – Wu Ta Si
Behind the zoo in the southern suburbs. All that remains of the larger temple complex is the Five Pagodas building, which was modelled on an Indian design and constructed in 1473.

White Cloud Daoist Temple – Bai Yun Guan
Near the northern wall of the Jin town. Founded under the Tang, it was extensive in the Yuan Dynasty and became the centre of Daoism for northern China. The temple is headquarters of the China Daoist Association.

The Temple of Celestial Peace – Tian Ning Si
The pagoda of this temple can be seen south of the White Cloud Temple. The present 58-metre pagoda dates from the early-13th century, but the temple itself no longer stands.

The Great Bell Temple – Da Zhong Si
Situated 1.5km northwest of Xi Zhi Men gate. Built in 1733, the temple bell was cast in 1406 and is 7-metres high, 3-metres wide and weighs 116,000 lbs. Lotus and Diamond Sutras are inscribed on its side.

The Yellow Temple – Huang Si
Off Huang Si Lu. The present building dates back to 1652. The eastern part of the temple was used for religious ceremonies and the western part was used as a place of residence for visiting Tibetan and Mongolian Buddhist dignitaries. The white marble stupa is covered with fine carvings from the life of the Buddha.

The Eastern Peak Temple – Dong Yue Miao (The former Taishan Temple)
On the north side of Chao Yang Men Wai Jie. Dedicated to the god of Mount Taishan and his daughter. Founded in the Yuan Dynasty, it was rebuilt in 1698.

Southern Cathedral – Nan Tang
Next to Xuan We Men gate. Built on the site where Matteo Ricci lived and died. Permission for a church was given by the Emperor to Father Adam Schall in 1650 and the church was built in 1703. The church is now active and used by national catholics.

The Western Church – Xi Tang
On the south side of Xizhi Men street. Founded in the 18th century, the members were expelled during Jaiqing's persecutions in 1811. A new church was consecrated in 1867, demolished in 1900 and rebuilt soon afterwards.

The Temple of Great Transformation – Guang Hua Si
In the Back Lake area. Founded in the Wanli period, the Temple was restored in 1634.

The Temple of Great Wisdom – Dahui Si
(Also known as the Great Buddha Temple)
South of the village of Weigongcun. Founded in 1513, the Great Hall retains its timber construction.

Outside Beijing
The Ming Tombs
Burial site of the Ming Emperors.

Wo Fo Si – Sleeping Buddha Temple
14th century. Major site of statues.

Western Hills
Many temples and monasteries including the 8 Great sites – 8 temples which are all closed at present as this is a restricted zone.

Quing Emperors tombs
Temples and tombs from 17th century onwards.

FUJIAN PROVINCE

Xiamen
Nan Pu Tuo Temple
On the southern outskirts of Xiamen town, next to the University. This Buddhist temple was originally built in the Tang Dynasty and has recently been restored (see map on page 166).

Quanzhou
Kaiyuan Temple
On Xi Lu in the northwest of the town. Founded in the 7th century, the temple became increasingly important for Buddhist study and by the Song Dynasty a thousand monks lived here.

Qingzhen Mosque

South of the Overseas Chinese Hotel. Originally built in 1009, the shell of the oldest mosque in Eastern China still remains and it is posssible to go inside. There is also a small museum in the grounds of the mosque and there are plans for a full renovation (see page 315).

Muslim Tombs

The Muslim tomb on Ling Shan is said to be the burial place of two Tang Dynasty Muslim missionaries to China (see page 314).

Qing Yuan Shan

There are Buddhist monasteries on this mountain which are now occupied by the army. There is also a statue of Lao Zi which is the largest sculpture on the mountain and one of the largest statues of Lao Zi in China.

Fuzhou

Fuzhou was a centre for Catholic and Protestant missionary activity in 19th and 20th century. Marco Polo records Nestorians in the town and claims there were 700,000 Nestorian households in southern China. The museum houses a set of Christian inscriptions.

Kaiyuan Buddhist Temple

On Xijie. Founded in the Tang Dynasty, the largest building in the complex is the Ming Dynasty Great Hall which houses statues of Guan Yin, the Buddha and 18 Lohan.

Wu Shan

Originally a Daoist retreat, this hill is now a picnic spot. There are few remains of the temples, although there is a Tang Dynasty relief of the Buddha carved on the southeast slope and inscriptions carved into the rocks. At the foot of the hill stands the 35-metre high Black Pagoda founded in 941 AD.

255

Yu Shan

Known for its inscriptions cut into the rock, which date from the 10th to the 19th century. At the foot of the hill stands the seven-storey White Pagoda, rebuilt in 1548 after the original 10th-century wooden pagoda burnt down. At the top of the hill is Guan Yin Hall, built in 1713.

Hualin Temple

On the southern slopes of Pingshan, north of the town. Founded in the Tang Dynasty, the oldest building that remains is the Sumptuous Hall of the Great Hero.

Hongtang Golden Mountain Temple

Founded in the Song Dynasty on an island in the Wulong River it includes a Guan Yin Hall, The Hall of Great Compassion and an 11-metre pagoda.

Temple of the Bubbling Spring – Yong Quan Monastery

14km east of town on Gu Shan, also known as Drum Mountain. Founded in 908, the monastery is famous for its extensive collection of Buddhist sutras including several hundred which are said to have been written in blood.

Hua Lin Temple

Just outside the town on Bei Bing Hill. This temple was founded in the Tang Dynasty. The central hall is square and is fronted by a terrace built in Song Dynasty style.

Tai Ning
Gu Lu Yan Hermitage

14km southwest of Tai Ning at the foot of a cliff. This Song Dynasty hermitage contains four rooms where the remains of fescoes and inscriptions can still be seen.

GANSU PROVINCE

Maiji Shan
35km south of Tianshui, the mountain is famous for its sculptures and grottoes. Wall paintings, clay figures and stone sculptures, dating back to the Northern Wei and Song Dynasties, are found in the caves.

Lanzhou
Thousand Buddha Caves – Bing Ling Si Shiku
Built 60-metres high into steep cliff walls, the 183 caves in this area contain hundreds of statues and sculptures plus a variety of murals. The earliest caves date to the Northern Wei Dynasty, although most of the carvings were worked on in the Tang Dynasty. One of the features of the caves is a 27-metre statue of Maitreya Buddha.

White Pagoda Hill – Bai Ta Shan
White Pagoda Hill is on the north bank of the Yellow River. Named after the 17-metre Yuan Dynasty pagoda at its peak, it is now a park with temples and mosques.

Five Springs Mountain – Wu Quan Shan
There are several temples on this mountain including the Chongqing temple founded in the 14th century, the Mani temple, the Dizang temple, the Cave of Three Teachings and the Tower of A Thousand Buddhas.

Xiahe
Labrang Monastery – Labul Leng Si
Built in 1709, this is an active monastery and a centre of Buddhist learning.

Dunhuang
Mogao Caves
Carved caves dating from 366 AD and also famous as a site of

sealed caves filled with ancient texts, all written prior to the 11th century AD (see page 209).

Anxi
Yu Lin Buddhist Caves
Situated 68km south of the town. Also known as the Ten Thousand Buddha Gorges, they are part of the large group at Dunhuang. There are 41 caves carved from the cliffs in the style of the Mogao Caves.

Jiuquan
Wen Shu Shan
Situated 15km west of the town. A series of Buddhist caves cut out of earth on two sides of the hillside. Elaborate gateways and halls have been built in front of many caves. Notable sites are the Thousand Buddha Cave, the Old Buddha Cave and the Ten Thousand Buddha Cave. Work began in the 5th century in this area which became a flourishing centre of Buddhism.

Yumen
Chang Ma Caves
Situated 60km southeast of Yumen. There are three groups of Buddhist caves known as the Xia Jiao, Da Ba and Hong Shan.

Confluence of the Rivers Pu and Ru
Qin Yang and Zhen Yuan Caves
Buddhist caves carved at a site near the confluence of the rivers. There are more than 200 caves containing a wide range of statues although many are in ruins.

Gu yuan
Yuan Guang Monastery and the Xu Mi Shan Caves
Situated 45km northeast of the town. The Monastery is at the foot of the Xu Mi Mountains and the Xu Mi Shan caves nearby are believed to date from the 5th century with later additions.

The Tibetan Autonomous District of Gan Nan Cang Zu Zi Zhi Zhou
There are hundreds of religious buildings in this Buddhist area. Many monasteries are built on a large scale near the towns and follow Tibetan Buddhist traditions. One of the largest monasteries is the La Bu Leng monastery which governs more than 40 others. There are also mosques scattered throughout this region.

GUANGDONG PROVINCE

Guangzhou
Temple of the Six Banyan Trees – Liu Rong Si
On Liurong Lu to the west of Jiefang Beilu. Rebuilt at the end of the 10th century, the temple is headquarters of the Guang Zhou Buddhist Association. The 50-metre pagoda in the temple complex is the tallest in the city.

Bright Filial Piety Temple – Guang Xiao Si
On Hongshu Lu. Originally a 7th-century building, the temple was rebuilt after a fire in the mid-17th century. Hui Neng trained as a monk here in the 7th century.

Five Genies Temple – Wu Xian Guan
On Huifu Xilu which is west of Jiefang Zhonglu. The Ming Taoist temple was rebuilt after a fire in 1864. The original temple bell weighs 5 tons and is 10cm thick. The bell clapper is missing so if the bell should ever sound it would be a sign of great trouble and it is therefore known as 'Calamity Bell'.

Sacred Heart Cathedral – Shengxin Dajiaotang
On Yide Lu close to the river front. The church was completed in 1888. This impressive granite building, known by the Chinese as 'The House of Stone', is the largest Roman Catholic Cathedral in China.

Temple of Light and Children's Love – Guang Xiao Si
Close to the Temple of the Six Banyan Trees. The royal residence here was turned into a temple in the West Jin Dynasty. Restored many times, the stone pagoda dates from 676 and the two iron pagodas date from the Five Dynasties.

Hua Lin Temple
Off the north side of Xiajiu Lu. Founded in 526 by Damo, an Indian Buddhist monk, the temple was rebuilt and restored up to the Qing Dynasty. The main hall contains 500 lohans, one of them said to be Marco Polo.

Chen Family Ancestral Temple – Chen Jia Si
In Zhongshan Lu. Built to honour the ancestors of the Chen family, this Confucian temple is famous for its carvings and sculptures.

Huaisheng Mosque – Mosque in Memory of the Wise Man
On Guangta Lu south of the Temple of the Six Banyan Trees. Believed to have been established by a Muslim missionary to China in 627 AD. He is said to be the prophet Mohammad's uncle – whose tomb can still be seen in the bamboo grove behind the Orchid Garden on Jiefang Beilu (see page 314).

White Cloud Mountain – Baiyun Shan
The many temples and beauty spots on this mountain range make this area famous, although the temples have now been abandoned or destroyed.

Foshan
Daoist Ancestors Temple – Foshan Zu Miao
At the south end of Zumiao Lu. Built in the late-11th century but rebuilt under the first Ming Emperor who was a Daoist and so converted it into a Daoist Temple. The building consists of interlocking wooden beams held together without nails or other metal. The temple is dedicated to the North or Dark Emperor.

The Hall of the Goddess of Mercy – Guanxin Dian
Built in the 17th century, the temple is dedicated to Guan Yin and houses a 4-metre bronze statue of the goddess.

Shantou
Temple of the Mother of the Heavenly Emperor
On Ma She (Ma Yi) Island on a site that has always had religious significance. This Daoist temple was built in 1985 with money provided by the overseas Chinese community. In the village nearby is the Temple of the Dragon of the Sea, a small temple popular with local fishermen.

Lingshan Temple
Near Chaoyang, south of the town. Buddhist temple founded during the Tang Dynasty, although most of the present structures date from the Qing.

Chaozhou
Han Yu Temple
A Confucian temple built in honour of a master of literature who was banished to this town after producing anti-Buddhist material.

Kaiyuan Temple
Founded in the 8th century to house Buddhist scriptures, this active Buddhist temple is being renovated.

Zhanjiang
Lengyan Monastery
On the banks of Lake Huguagyan, 20km southwest of the town. Dates from the Song period and is one of a number of old buildings on the lakeside.

Zhaoqing
Seven Star Rocks – Qixing Yan
There is a range of temples and caves on the Seven Star Rocks, which are seven hills rising from Star Lake.

The Dingua Shan
Situated 18km northeast of the town. This area has been a popular pilgrimage destination for more than 1,000 years. Amongst the Buddhist temples on this mountain is Qingyun Si Temple which contains a bronze bell weighing 1,100 lbs. There is also the Temple of the White Clouds, founded in the Tang era, approximately 5km from the Qingyun Si Temple.

For Hong Kong and Macau, see end of the Gazetteer.

GUANGXI PROVINCE

Guilin
Guilin Caves
A popular tourist destination. In the many hills around the town there are temples, hollows, caves and grottoes, some containing inscriptions or sculptures. Many have Daoist and Buddhist associations; others are linked to Chinese myths and legends.

Liuzhou
Ancestral Temple of Prince Liu – Liu Huo Si
In Prince Liu Park in the city centre. The original Daoist ancestral temple was built in 821. Stone slabs inscribed by 9th to 13th centuries scholars are housed here.

GUIZHOU PROVINCE

Guiyang
Temple of Great Fortune – Hongfu Si
This Ming Dynasty monastery is in Qianlingshan Park, northwest of Guiyang.

HEBEI PROVINCE

Chengde
Imperial Summer Villa and Outer Temples
This is in a park which covers 590 hectares and contains an Imperial Summer Palace. To the north and northeast of the palace grounds there is a range of Buddhist temples, those which survive were built between 1750 and 1780.

Shanhaiguan
Meng jiangnu Temple
Near Shanhaiguan by the break in the Great Wall. This Daoist Temple was reconstructed in the Song/Ming Dynasties. It recalls the story of Lady Meng whose husband was forced into a construction gang. One winter she went to find him but discovered that he had died from overwork. As she wandered the Great Wall looking for his remains, the wall suddenly collapsed revealing his bones.

Shijiazhuang
Temple of Good Fortune and Festivities – Fu Qing Si
Founded in the Sui Dynasty, the temple is dedicated to the daughter of the Emperor Yang Di who converted to Buddhism after the death of her father.

Vairocano Temple – Pilu Si
Situated 10km northwest of the city. Founded in the Tang period, the Sakyamuni Hall, decorated with Buddhist frescoes, and the Vairocana Hall, decorated with hundreds of religious images and scenes from Chinese life, date from that time.

Temple of Lavish Prosperity – Long Xing Si
In Zhengding, 14km north of Shijiazhuang. There is a set of temples and monasteries in the town and the largest is Long Xing Monastery which is famous for its 20-metre high bronze statue of Guan Yin, housed in the Temple of Great Mercy. The statue was cast almost a thousand years ago.

Beidaihe
Temple of Guan Yin

Built close to Lotus Rock Park, this small collection of 300 year old temples has been restored recently.

Handan
Shigu Shan

Situated 25km southwest of Handan. There are seven caves in the southern foothills and nine on the west side of the mountain, 15km further on. The early caves date to the 6th century and the later ones to the Ming Dynasty. In total there are approximately 3,400 statues.

Wuhan
The Temple of Regained Perfection – Guiyan Si

In the southwest part of Han Yang. This temple dates from the late Ming and early Qing Dynasties. The Lohan Hall houses 500 Buddhas and a statue of the Buddha with 1,000 hands and eyes; the Pavilion contains Buddhist sutras.

Hong Shan

In the Wuchang district. Hong Shan has several temples and pagodas including the Baoting Temple, the 43-metre high Lingji Pagoda and the 11-metre high Xingfusi Pagoda.

Temple of Eternal Spring – Chang Chun Guan

Not far from Hong Shan, in Dong Hu on the shores of the Eastern Lake. The ancient temple was destroyed in the Taiping Rebellion and rebuilt at the end of the 19th century.

Xiangfan
Temple of Great Virtue – Guang De Si

Situated 13km west of Xiangfan. The original Han Dynasty buildings were rebuilt in the 15th century. There are five 15th century pagodas on this site.

Wu Dang Shan

Situated 150km west of Xiangfan. This Daoist mountain range stretches for more than 400km. The Tang Dynasty Temple of the Five Dragons is the oldest and the other temples followed between the 10th and 13th centuries, but many were destroyed. Ming Dynasty Emperors ordered Daoist temples to be built on this mountain which resulted in 38 monasteries and 72 temple halls as well as other religious structures. Amongst the remaining buildings is the Golden Hall on the Heavenly Pillar Peak which was built with gilded bronze in 1416.

Zhang Jia Kou
Cloud Spring Monastery – Yun Quan Si
Founded in 1393 on the mountainside just outside the town.

Lai Yuan
Great Wen Shu Temple – Wen Shu Da Dian
This Liao Dynasty wooden temple contains a Buddhist pillar dating from 960 and a bell dating from 1114.

Xin Cheng
Kai Shan Si
In the northeast of the town. Only the Liao Dynasty temple remains from the Kai Shan Monastery which was founded in the Tang or the Song Dynasty.

Qu yang
Temple of the Northern Sacred Mountain – Bei Yue Miao
The emperors of China offered sacrifices here to Heng Shan. Originally part of a much larger complex, only one of the great ceremonial temples and an octagonal pagoda remain. The Temple of Tranquil Virtue was built in 1270. The frescoes in the temple depict real life and imaginary scenes, including court figures and Daoist demons. There is an important collection of steles around the temple.

Zhaoxian
Monastery of the Stone Buddha – Shi Fo Si
An unusual hexagonal pagoda, several columns and stone Buddhas remain from the original monastery. An inscription on the pagoda indicates that the monastery was built in 1275.

The Cypress Monastery – Bo Lin Si
Near the east gate. Founded in the Han Dynasty, the monastery was given its name in the Qing Dynasty and the building is in Ming Dynasty style. There is a 7-storey Yuan Dynasty pagoda near the temple.

Xingtai
Kai Yuan Period Monastery – Kai Yuan Si Zhuan Ta
In the northeast corner of the town. Founded in the Tang Dynasty, the monastery includes a Yuan Dynasty pagoda built by order of the Emperor in 1215. Northwest of the monastery there is a Tang Dynasty Daoist column covered with inscriptions relating to the *Dao De Jing*.

Monastery of Celestial Tranquillity – Tian Ning Si
In the northwest corner of the town. Two Tang temples remain from this Qing Dynasty monastery. A Buddhist column and pagoda erected nearby, date to the Tang and Yuan Dynasties respectively.

Feng Feng
Mount Xiang Tang Caves
These are two collections of Buddhist rock carvings approximately 14km from each other. The southern group is near the village of Peng Cheng, near the Monastery of the Echoing Hall, and the northern group is near the village of Hu Cun near the Monastery of Eternal Joy. The earliest date from between 550 and 560 AD and continue up to the Ming Dynasty.

HEILONGJIANG PROVINCE

Harbin
Temple of Paradise – Jile Si
On Dongda Zhijie in the centre of Harbin. Built in 1924 the complex includes four halls and a 7-storey pagoda.

Church of Saint Nicholas
One of Harbin's 17 churches, this wooden Russian Orthodox Church was built in 1899 (see page 323).

Temple of Confucius – Wen Miao
This temple of Confucius on Dongda Zhijie was built in 1926 and houses statues of Confucius and other scholars.

Longquan
The Temple of Prosperity – Xing Long Si
These are the ruins of the capital of the kingdom of Bohai which was invaded and destroyed in 926. Remains of the Qing Dynasty temple can be seen.

HENAN

Anyang
Site of the Chang Dynasty capital, Ying, where famous oracle bones were found. Remains of the original city wall can still be seen to the east.

Kaifeng
Jewish Community
There are plans to rebuild the synagogue and build a Jewish museum in the town, since several hundred Jews have lived here from at least 1163 AD.

Temple of the Chancellor – Xiang Guo Monastery
Established in 555 AD, this Buddhist temple has been destroyed and rebuilt many times. The current buildings date from
1766 and include the Great Treasure Temple, the Octagonal
Palace with Glazed Tiles and the Palace of the Sutras.

The Iron Pagoda – Tie Ta
In the northeast of the town. This 13-storey brick pagoda is
all that remains of the monastery which stood here. Built in
1049, it has been carefully restored.

The Monastery of Celestial Purity – Tian Qing Si
In the southeast of the town. This 30-metre 3-storey pagoda is
all that remains of the original monastery and 9-storey pagoda. It dates from the Northern Song Dynasty.

Dong Da Mosque
Built in 1922, this is one of Henan's most active mosques.

Luoyang
White Horse Temple – Bai Ma Si
Once the centre of Buddhism in China, this was the first Buddhist temple in the country, founded more than 1900 years
ago (see page 168).

Long Men Shiku Caves or Dragonsgate Grottoes
From the end of the 5th century to the end of the 7th century
more than 100,000 images and statues of the Buddha were
carved in the caves and cliffs of this impressive site on the
banks of the River Yi. The site also has 1352 grottoes and 3680
inscriptions carved in the rocks (see pages 211–13).

Song Shan
Situated 50km southeast of Luoyang, this is one of the five sacred Daoist mountains and there are many temples and other
religious sites in this area (see pages 192–7).

Tie men zhen
Village of the Stone Buddhas (Shi Fo Xiang) and Hong Qing Monastery
Situated 2km south of the town. It is believed that the carvings in the six hewn caves behind the monastery date from the Northern Wei Dynasty. These carvings include armies of flying demons.

Gong Xian
Northern Wei Buddhist Caves
The caves and temples are at the foot of Dali Shan on the bank of Yiluo River. Building began in 517 AD and continued until the Song Dynasty. There are over 7700 Buddhist sculptures in 256 shrines.

Qin Yang
Xuan Gu Shan
There are six groups of Buddhist carvings in a cliff face which are thought to be around 1,000 years old.

Central Temple of the Monastery of Great Light –
Zhong Fo Dian Da Ming Si
Situated 6km southeast of Qing yang. This wooden Yuan Dynasty temple was once the central temple of a large monastery.

Tang Yang
Yue Fei Temple
Founded in 1450, this temple honours the famous general deified by the Chinese.

Fu Qui Shan and Da Pei Shan
Southeast of Tang Yang. The Monastery of the Thousand Buddhas is on Fu Qui Shan and carvings of the Buddha and bodhisattvas cover the walls of two small rock caves. Nearby stands the Daoist Temple of the Princess of the Coloured Clouds. On nearby Da Pei Shan stands the Monastery of Celestial Tranquillity. A 25-metre stone Buddha is all that remains of

269

the Northern Wei buildings. Other buildings in this area include the Temple to Lu Dong Bin and the Temple to Yu The Great.

Lin Ru
Wind Hollow Monastery – Feng Xue Si
Situated 8km northeast of Lin Ru. Buddhist monastery founded in the Tang and restored in the Ming and Qing Dynasties. The pagoda dates to the 8th century.

Huai Yang
Tomb of Fu Hsi
Believed to be the tomb of one of the great mythical emperors of China. The 30-feet mound of earth is north of the town. Several Qing Dynasty temples and gateways surround the tomb.

Zhen Ping
Bodhi Monastery – Pu Ti Monastery
On the slopes of Xing Shan north of the town. Founded under the Tang, it was rebuilt in 1681 and houses a valuable collection of Buddhist sutras.

Lu Yi
Birthplace and burial place of Lao Zi (see page 115)

HUBEI PROVINCE

Wuhan
Temple of Regained Perfection – Guiyuan Si
On Cuiweiheng Lu where it meets Cuiwei Lu. This is an active Buddhist temple dating from the late Ming and early Qing Dynasties.

Cheng Xiang Bao Ta
On She Shan hill. Built in 1343, the base of this white stone 30-metre stupa is decorated with Buddhist motifs.

Temple of Eternal Spring – Chang Chun Guan
On the shores of the Eastern Lake. According to legend, Lao Zi used to meditate on the site of this temple. The current temple was rebuilt at the end of the 19th century and a community of monks and nuns live here.

The Yuan Gui Si Temple
In the southwest district of Han Yang. This Qing Dynasty Buddhist temple is well known for the Hall of the Five Hundred Lohan.

Jun Xian
Wu Dan Shan, south of the town, is dotted with religious sites. Many date from the Ming Dynasty and include the Jin Dian (Golden Hall) Daoist temple and the Zi Xiao Gong, which dates from 1413.

HUNAN PROVINCE

Changsha
Temple of the Beginning of Blissful Happiness – Kaifu Si
Buddhist temple founded in the Tang Dynasty. The Mahavira Hall has been restored recently and a small community is in residence.

Changsha Catholic and Protestant Churches
These churches are located close to each other, south of Kaifu Temple.

Henyang
Heng Shan
50km north of the town, this is one of the five great Daoist mountains of China (see pages 238–40).

Shao Shan
Mao Ze Dong's House
Chairman Mao was born here and the house is now a Maoist shrine and exhibition centre.

Daoist Hermitage
A Daoist Hermitage stands on one of the peaks surrounding Shao Shan.

INNER MONGOLIA PROVINCE

Hohhot
The Lama Temple of Xilitu Zhao
In the old town, this large wooden monastery gate and The Great Hall of Sutras dates from the Ming Dynasty.

Da Zhao Monastery
In the old town. This monastery dates from the Ming Dynasty and houses the Great Hall of the Sutras.

Great Mosque – Qing Zhen Si
At the old north gate of the town. Founded in the Qing dynasty, the mosque houses a collection of Qurans which are 200 years old.

Temple of the Five Pagodas – Wu Ta Si
In the south of the town. Only the Diamond Pagoda remains from this early Qing Dynasty temple. It stands on a large terrace and consists of five beautifully carved pagodas; the central one is more than 32 metres high. The inscriptions on its base are in Chinese, Mongolian, Tibetan and Sanskrit.

Wu Su Tu Zhao Monastery
Outside the town. This is a Ming Dynasty Buddhist monastery including the 3-storey Great Hall.

Xiao Zhao Monastery
Built in the Qing Dynasty, this Buddhist monastery has a fine pavilion with glazed roof tiles.

E Mu Qi Zhao Monastery
This monastery dates from the Qing Dynasty. The monastery has been built on a large scale, particularly The Hall of the Sutras and the Hall of the Buddha.

Baotou
Willow Tree Monastery – Wudang Zhao
Set in a hilly area 70km northeast of the city. Built between 1621 and 1722, the monastery complex covers more than 50 acres and originally belonged to the Gelukpa Tibetan Buddhist tradition.

Kundulun Monastery
Founded in the Qing Dynasty, this Buddhist temple is built in Tibetan style. The White Pagoda and the Awang Fu, 'The Gateway of Honour', are also part of this complex.

Bayinhot
Yan Fu Si Monastery
Founded in the Qing Dynasty, this monastery is built on a large scale. Extensive Tibetan style paintings and carvings decorate the pillars and walls of the temple.

Ulanhot
Mo Li Temple
This is a Qing Dynasty temple. The ceiling of the Great Hall of the Sutras is divided by supporting beams into sections, each of which is intricately decorated with Buddhist paintings.

Jia Lan Shan Monastery
In A la Shan Banner[1]. This Qing Dynasty complex extends up a hillside forming two groups connected by walkways. It is built in Sino-Tibetan style.

273

Guang Zong Monastery
In A la Shan Banner. This is regarded as the counterpart of the monastery above and has also been constructed in Sino-Tibetan style.

A Sake Zhao Monastery
In A Sake Banner. Built in Qing Dynasty style and housing the Great Hall of the Sutras.

Wu Shen Zhao Monastery
Wu Shen Banner. Built in the Qing Dynasty, this fine monastery is notable for the beauty and design of its Great Hall. A forest of pagodas stands in its grounds.

Silinhot
Bei Zi Maio Monastery
This Chinese style monastery contains the Great Hall of the Sutras which is approached through a wooden hut and then through a Mongolian tent. Mongolian flags and symbols have been fixed to a terrace built on stone and earth mounds in this monastery. This unusual feature is known as the ao bao.

Guang Fu Monastery
In Da Er Han and Moa Ming An Banners. This large Buddhist monastery is built around the Great Hall and employs striking Tibetan decoration and design.

Han Bai Temple
In A Be Ga Banner. This Buddhist temple built in Chinese style is known for its stone pagoda and for the Great Hall of the Sutras, beautifully decorated with paintings.

La Ma Ku Lun Miao Temple
In Yue Wu Zhu Mu Qin Banner. The halls of this large temple exhibit a variety of Tibetan and Chinese designs.

Buddhist Cave Monasteries
In the Ba Lin Banner. The ancient citadel of the Liao Dynasty is near the town of Lin Dong. Four groups of cave monasteries are sited in this Banner; the largest is 29km from the ancient citadel. Over 100 caves have been found, some natural and others rock-cut. There are also two large temples south of the citadel – the Qian Zhao temple and the Hou Zhao temple.

JIANGSU PROVINCE

Yangzhou
The Muslim Hall – Hui Hui Tang
Close to Dong Guan Jie is a Qing Dynasty mosque and the tomb of a Muslim teacher who died in the town in 1275. According to an inscription he was a descendant of the Prophet.

Shi Ta Pagoda
On Shi Ta Lu. This five-storey, six-sided pagoda was originally part of a temple built in 840.

Temple of Heavenly Peace – Tianning Si
At the foot of Plum Blossom Mountain in the north of the town. Founded in the Jin Dynasty, it was the temple where Buddhist scriptures were translated by a Nepalese monk in 418.

The Temple of Bright Light – Daming Si Temple
Situated 4km northwest of the town. The original temple was founded in the 5th century, although the existing structure was built in the 19th century. The monk Jianzhen studied there. In 742 AD he was invited to Japan to teach Buddhism and he began his journey. On his sixth attempt he made it to Japan and died there 10 years later.

Mao Shan
South of the city, some 50km. Home of Mao Shan Daoism, the mountain has numerous fine Daoist temples and monasteries.

Zhengjiang
Jin Shan
The mountain is one of the vantage points overlooking the Yangtse River. The Buddhist temple here rises up the hillside and is connected by staircases. There are also four caves on the mountain known as the Buddhist Sea, White Dragon, Morning Sun and Arhat. The seven-storey Chishu pagoda is at the summit.

Suzhou
North Temple – Bei Si Ta
At the north end of Remnin Lu. The temple complex has a 1700 year history and houses a nine-storey wooden pagoda.

Daoist Temple of Mystery (Temple of Secrets) – Xuan Miao Guan
In the centre of Suzhou Bazaar. Founded in the 3rd century and rebuilt in later dynasties. The Sanqing Hall, built in 1181, is supported by 60 pillars and contains Daoist statues and steles.

Cold Mountain Temple – Han Shan Si
Situated 1km west of Liuyuan (the Garden of Mr Liu), this Buddhist temple has been destroyed and rebuilt many times. The present buildings date from the end of the 19th century. Two interesting features are the saffron walls of the temple and the humpback bridge over the canal nearby.

Two Pagoda Temple – Shuang Ta Si
On Ding hui Si Gang. Originally founded in the 9th century, two Song Dynasty brick pagodas were added and restored after the last fire in 1860.

West Garden Temple – Xiyuan Si
Situated 500km west of Liuyuan (the Garden of Mr Liu). This Buddhist temple was completely rebuilt in the late-19th

century on the site of the original Ming Dynasty temple. The Lohan Hall houses more than 500 gilded Buddhist statues.

Temples on Ling Yan and Shang Fang hills

The road to Taihu leads to these hills. The temple of the Rock of Spirits is still active and houses an exhibition of Buddhist art in China including statues and bronzes. On the way to the temple there is a small cave known as The Guan Yin Cave.

Protection of Sages Temple – Bao Sheng Si

Situated 40km southeast of Suzhou in Jiao Zhi. Founded in 503, the present structure dates from 1860 and houses five Song Dynasty Lohan.

Changzhou
Temple of Heavenly Tranquillity – Tian Ning Si

Founded at the beginning of the 10th century and recently restored, this large active temple is the headquarters of the Buddhist Association.

Lianyungang
Kong Wang Shan

Situated 2km south of the city. There are more than 100 Buddhist sculptures cut into the mountain. They date from the eastern Han period and are amongst the oldest Buddhist sculptures in China.

Hua Guo Shan

Situated 15km southeast of the city. The Sanyuan Temple on the mountain dates from the 7th century. According to legend the King of the Monkeys in the book *Travels in the West* lived in the cave of Shuilian Dong (Water Curtain Cave) on this mountain.

Yuntai Shan

Situated 20km east of the city. It is said that this mountain was the inspiration for the Mountain of Flowers and Fruit in the book *Travels in the West*.

Yixing

Temple of Confucius – Kong Miao

Situated 14km west of Lake Taihu. A 17th century archway leads to the Temple of Confucius which houses a good collection of statues.

Jiujiang

Lu Shan

South of Jiujiang, this mountain area, associated with Buddhism, has more than 90 separate peaks. One of the most important religious sites on the mountain is the Donglin Si (The Temple of the East Wood). The School of the Pure Land, a Buddhist sect, was founded here by the monk Huiyuan, who built the temple in 381.

Nanjing

Temple of the Valley of Spirits – Linggu Si

In the east of Nanjing, the temple is close to the Beamless Hall in Linggu Park. The temple has a memorial hall to Xuan Zang, the monk who carried Buddhist scriptures from India. In the hall there is a model of a pagoda which contains part of his skull.

Confucius Temple – Kong Miao

On Gongyuan Lu. This temple was built in 1869 on the site of the original temple, destroyed by fire in the 12th century. The temple houses an exhibition of local folk art.

Qi Xia Shan

Situated 20km northeast of the city. There are approximately 300 caves and niches carved into the stone of this hill. The most notable is the Three Saints Hall which has a 10-metre figure of the Buddha with bodhisattvas in attendance. The dates for the carvings range from the middle 5th century to the Ming Dynasty.

The Qi Xia Si (Temple of the Dwelling of Evening Clouds) is also in this area. Founded in 483, the temple was destroyed by fire in 1855 and the present buildings date from the late Qing Dynasty. The five-storey pagoda nearby was built in the 7th century.

Xuzhou
Xinghua Temple
South of Xuzhou on the east of the Yunlongshan River. The temple houses 5th century rock-cut statues.

Zhenjiang
The Golden Mountain – Jin Shan
The Monastery of the Golden Mountain, founded in the 4th century, is built on this hill.

Jiao Shan
Dinghui Monastery, founded in the Eastern Han Dynasty, is built on this hill.

Bei Gu Shan
The Ganlu Temple (Temple of Refreshing Dew) on this mountain was founded in the year 265 but has since been destroyed and rebuilt several times.

Wuxi
Saint Joseph's Church
Built in the 17th century, it is the focal point of the lively local Catholic community (see page 320).

· JIANGXI PROVINCE

Nanchang
Temple of Blue Clouds – Qingyunpu
Opinions vary as to when this Daoist temple in the south of
the city was built but it is at least 1350 years old. The three
main halls house a museum exhibiting the paintings of Zu Da
and his pupils.

Temple of Great Peace – Da'an Si
On Yuzhanghou Jie. Founded in the 4th century, this temple
houses a large iron vessel made in the period of The Three
Kingdoms (220–263 AD).

Lu Shan Mountains
Gu Ling
This village area was popular as a summer resort for emperors
and scholars and many of the buildings remain. The religious
sites include The Cave of the Immortals, The Round Temple
and several pagodas in the surrounding area.

Longhu Shan
Dragon Tiger Mountain
Home of the Daoist Celestial Master from *c.* 400 AD to 1927.
Many fine temples.

LIAONING PROVINCE

Shenyang
The Imperial Temple – Huang Si
On Huang Si Lu. This large Buddhist temple was built in 1638
and restored in 1726.

Dandong
Feng Huang Shan
Situated 52km northwest of Dandong is the town of Feng-chang. The mountain, Fenghuangshan, is scattered with temples, monasteries and pagodas found in the Tang, Ming and Qing Dynasties.

Gu Shan
Daoist Temples of Dagu Shan
This mountain is 90km southwest of Dandong, near the town of Gu Shan. A group of Tang Dynasty Daoist temples have been built on the mountain.

Anshan
Qian Lian Shan
Known as the Thousand Lotuses Hill, this was originally a 10th century Buddhist hermitage. There are Buddhist and Daoist monasteries here, some of which are still active.

NINGXIA PROVINCE

Yinchuan
Yinchuan Mosque – Qingzhen Si
Near the south gate, this mosque is the largest in the city.

The West Pagoda – Xi Ta
Southwest of the town. The original buildings were destroyed and a 64-metre pagoda was rebuilt in 1820.

The Treasure Pagoda – Hai Bao Ta
In the north of the town. Founded in the 5th century, it has 11 storeys and is 54 metres high.

281

Zhougwei
Gao Temple – Gao Miao
Founded in the 15th century. The temple is well known since it caters for three different religious traditions – Buddhism, Confucianism and Daoism.

Tongxin
Great Mosque – Qingzhen Da Si
Built during the Ming Dynasty, it is constructed of wood in Chinese style.

Xumi Shan
Situated 50km northwest of the town of Guyuan, the mountain peaks contain 132 caves in which more than 300 Buddhist statues have been carved dating from the Northern Wei to the Sui and Tang Dynasties.

Xiji County
This area is 60km west of Guyuan and is known for its range of tombs and Buddhist statues dating from the Han Dynasty.

QINGHAI PROVINCE

Xining
Ta Er Monastery
Situated 25km southwest of the town, this extensive Tibetan monastery houses palaces, temples, pagodas and pavilions. The monastery is known for its traditional Tibetan yak butter sculptures.

Great Mosque – Qingzhen Da Si
On Dongguan Dajie. Built almost 600 years ago, it is one of the largest mosques in this part of China.

Le Du
Qu Tan Monastery – Qu Tan Si
Situated 19km south of the town which is east of Xining. The
original monastery was built at the beginning of the Ming
Dynasty. Following periods of restoration, its richly decorated
walls, beams and colonnades can still be seen.

SHAANXI PROVINCE

Xian
Big Wild Goose Pagoda – Da Yan Ta
At the end of Yanta Lu on the southern side of Xian. The original pagoda was built in 652 AD to house Buddhist scriptures
carried from India by the monk Xuan Zang (see pages 103–5).

Small Wild Goose Pagoda – Xiao Yan Ta
On Youyi Zilu west of the crossroads with Nanguan Zhengjie.
Built at the turn of the 7th century, this pagoda was used to
house Buddhist scriptures carried from India. Although the
top of the pagoda was destroyed by an earthquake in the six-
teenth century, 43 metres still stand.

Great Mosque – Xing Zhen Da Si
In the Muslim quarter of Xian 300 metres northwest of the
Drum Tower. The present building dates from the 18th century although the Mosque is believed to have been established
many centuries earlier.

Temple of the Eight Immortals – Ba Xian An
East along Changle Xilu and through the street market by the
large gateway. The temple is to the right at the end of the market. It was founded in the Song Dynasty and extended in the
following centuries to become one of the largest Daoist temples in Xian. It has recently been restored.

City God's Temple – Cheng Huang Miao
Take the narrow lane which runs off Xidajie 257 which goes down through the Muslim quarter. This Daoist temple was built in 1433, although the main hall dates from 1723.

Temple of Da Xing Shan
This Buddhist temple, south of the Pagoda of the Small Wild Goose, was reputedly founded in the 3rd century, although it was rebuilt and extended several times during the Ming to Qing periods.

The Temple of Kindness and Goodwill – Guang Ren Si
Near the walls in the northwest corner of the town. Built to house Tibetan Buddhist monks in 1705, restored in 1952. There are good examples of gold leaf statues in the central hall and a library of Buddhist manuscripts.

The Forest of Steles
Near the south gate of the city. A remarkable collection of steles (over 1,000 pieces) including the text of the Twelve Classics, memorial steles including one which refers to Nestorian Christianity, steles containing the Classic of Filial Piety as well as many other fine examples of calligraphy, drawings and maps. The area in which many of them are housed is now a museum although it was a Confucian Temple.

Bao Qing Temple Pagoda
In the south of Shuyuanmen Jie. The Buddhist temple was founded in 705 and a pagoda was added 25 years later.

Temple of the Recumbent Dragon – Wo Long Si
In Boshuling Jie outside the city walls. This Buddhist temple was founded in the Sui Dynasty and according to legend it is named after a Song Dynasty monk who was called 'The Recumbent Dragon' because he regularly had a sleep in the temple. There is an extensive library, including Pali Buddhist texts.

South suburbs of Xian
In the Tang dynasty a set of temples was built in this area. Those that remain include The Bull's Head Temple on one of the slopes of the Shaoling Yuan Hill, the Temple dedicated to Du Fu, east of the Bull's Head Temple, and the Temple of Flourishing Teaching southeast of Du Qu. There is a 7-storey pagoda at the Huayan Temple on the slopes of Shaoling Yuan Hill.

Hua Shan
One of the five Daoist sacred mountains. It is 120km east of Xian (see pages 5–8, 229–34).

Yaoxian
Situated 29km north of Xian. This town is notable for its collection of ancient steles, the oldest dating back to the 5th century BC. There are over 200 steles, and 76 are housed in the local museum, specially built for them. Nearby, on the Mountain of the King of Medicine, there are three Buddhist cave temples which house sculptures dating from the Tang Dynasty.

Huang Ling
Tomb of the Yellow Emperor
The legendary emperor is said to be buried here, hence the name of the town. The building itself is 48 metres in circumference.

Fu Xian
Stone Cavity Monastery – Duan Jia Zhuang
Situated 63km west of the town, lie the remains of the Stone Cavity Buddhist Monastery. Seven rock caves house a range of statues and inscriptions which date from the Tang to the Ming Dynasties.

Yanan
Buddhist Cemetery and Caves and Daoist Hermitage
There are three Buddhist caves at the foot of Qinglian Mountain which contain Song and Jin Dynasty statues. There is also a Buddhist cemetery on this mountain which is sited not far from the road on the left side of Yan Shui River. The oldest grave is from the early-16th century. A small Daoist hermitage stands on an outcrop above the bend in the Yan Shui River.

Lin You
Situated 14km south of the town is a set of Buddhist caves on a very steep cliff containing hundreds of Tang Dynasty Buddhist statues. West of the town on another cliff are 15 Buddhas from the Tang Dynasty. 3km southwest of the town are two more Tang Dynasty rock caves which contain statues of the Buddha. The largest is 4 metres high and all have been well preserved. These statues are associated with the Monastery of Merciful Goodness.

Bin Xian
Situated 10km northwest of Bin Xian are the caves of the Big Buddha Monastery. Carved in the rock, these caves contain Buddhist statues, the largest of which is 29 metres high.

Han Cheng
There are six Daoist temples in this local area and a few miles south of the town is the tomb of the great historian Si Ma Qian. His tomb lies inside the Funerary Temple of the Great Chronicler.

Qi Shan
Situated 150km west of Xian. This is the ancestral sacred mountain of the Zhou tribes and the site where some say the Yi Jing texts were first given. Zong Yang Temple commemorates King Zhou's son (see page 177).

SHANDONG PROVINCE

Jinan
Daming Hu Lake

In the northeast of the town and inside the city walls. There is a small set of temples built around the lake.

Nanda Mosque

On Libai Si Jie. The mosque was founded in the Yuan Dynasty. The windows have detailed decorations incorporating Arabic calligraphy.

Thousand Buddha Mountain – Qian Fo Shan

Situated 2.5km south of the city. This Buddhist mountain is dotted with grottoes around its base and the cliff face has an extensive group of carvings created between 581 and 600 AD. The Xingguo Temple below the carvings houses sculptures of Emperor Chun and his two wives (the daughters of the legendary Yao).

Shentong Monastery

Near the village of Liubu, 33km southeast of Jinan. The remains of the Shentong Monastery include the 15-metre high Four Gate Pagoda, built in 611. Nearby is the Tang dynasty pagoda of the Dragon and the Tiger. The Thousand Buddha Cliff above the pagodas has more than 200 rock carvings dating from the Tang Dynasty.

Nine Point Pagoda and the Guan Yin Monastery – Jiu Ding Ta and Guan Yin Si

This site is close to the village of Liubu. The Tang Dynasty pagoda was restored this century. There is a group of Tang Dynasty rock carvings around the old monastery.

Divine Rock Temple – Ling Yan Si

Situated 75km from Jinan in the northwestern foothills of Taishan. The temple complex served many Imperial dynasties from the Tang to the Ming and 200 stupas have been erected near the temple in memory of the priests who directed the monastery.

Tai An
Tai Shan
This mountain, also known as Tai, is one of the most sacred mountains in China and the foremost of the Daoist sacred mountains (see pages 179–85).

Dai Temple
A large temple, enclosed by walls at the foot of Tai Shan.

Qufu
Confucian temples and complexes
The birthplace of the teacher and sage Confucius, who lived from 551 to 479 BC. The present Confucian temple dates from the Ming Dynasty and is on the site of the original Confucian temple (see pages 157–8).

Qingdao
Lao Shan
Situated 35km northeast of Qingdao. This mountain is associated with the Elixir of Immortality and was regarded as the place where magic herbs grew which could grant eternal life. Religious buildings on this Daoist mountain include a monastery known as Taiqing Palace, founded in the Song Dynasty, the present buildings date between 1573 and 1620. The Huayan Temple on the eastern slopes is the only Buddhist temple on the mountain.

Zhan Shan Temple
This temple in the east of Qingdao town was built in 1934 and is the only Buddhist temple in the town.

Yantai
Penglai Palace
Situated 60km north west of Yantai, this castle built on a cliff top features in Chinese myths, particularly those related to the Eight Immortals. It is thought that the castle is at least 1,000 years old (see page 122).

Ling Yan
Funerary chapel of Guo Ju – Guo Ju Si
This small stone building can be found at a place called the Mountain of the Chapel of Filial Piety. Dating from the 1st century, it is the oldest extant example of Chinese domestic architecture.

Liao Cheng
Shanxi Merchant Guilds Hotel – Shan Shan Hui Guan
Situated 1km from the east gate. This is an 18th century building which contains three Daoist temples.

Lin Zi
Southeast of Lin Zi, near the village of Wang Jai Zhuang. Two sets of carvings and three small caves make up the Buddhist rock carvings in the caves at Cloud Gate Mountain. There are further caves and carvings on nearby Camel Mountain. This Buddhist art dates from the Northern Zhou Dynasty to the beginning of the Tang Dynasty.

Shanghai autonomous city
Jade Buddha Temple – Yu Fo Si
In the northwest of the city. Founded in 1882 and famous for its bejewelled jade Buddhas.

Ignatius Cathedral – Xujianhui
On Puxi Lu in the Xujiahui area. The whole area was given to the Jesuits by a wealthy convert in the early-17th century and became a Jesuit town. Built in 1906, the cathedral is used for worship.

Jiading Confucian Temple – Jiading Kong Miao
In the northwest of the city, this Song Dynasty Temple is only two thirds of its original size yet it still covers an extensive area.

Long Hua Temple and Pagoda
Close to a bend in the Huangpu River. The pagoda is said to have been constructed in the 3rd century and like the surrounding temple has undergone rebuilding over the centuries.

Temple of the Town Gods – Cheng Huang Miao
In the Mandarin Gardens at the heart of the bazaar area. Every town used to have a Temple to the Town Gods and this one, founded in the Song dynasty, is one of the few survivors.

Temple of Serenity – Jing An Si
On Nanjing Lu in the western district. The temple is opposite a park of the same name and is still a place of pilgrimage for Buddhists.

SHANXI PROVINCE

Tai Yuan
Temple of Respect and Kindness – Chong Shan Si
On a lane west of Jianshe Beilu in the southeast of the town. The original monastery is thought to date back to the 6th or 7th centuries and the current buildings date from the 14th century. The central statue is Guan Yin with 'One Thousand Hands and Eyes'. The temple also houses an important collection of sutras.

Twin Pagoda Monastery – Yong Zuo Si
The monastery is not far from the railway station. Built at the turn of the 17th century this monastery is well known for its identical octagonal brick pagodas which are 13 storeys high.

Jin Si Temple

Situated 25km southwest of the town, close to Xuanwang Hill. This group of Buddhist temples is thought to be a thousand years old or more. Within the complex is the Mirror Terrace, originally an open air theatre. Nearby The Bridge Where the Immortals Meet crosses the Canal of Zhibo. On the far side are the iron figures standing on the Terrace for Iron Statues which were cast in 1097 AD. A large statue of the mother of Prince Shuyu is the focus of the Sacred Lady Hall and offerings are still made to her. There are 44 life-size terracotta statues of female attendants on the walls around her (see page 176).

Long Shan

Situated 20km southwest of Tai Yuan in the area of the Jin Si Temple. There are shrines, carvings and the remains of religious buildings on and around this mountain. There is a set of Tang Dynasty shrines at the summit of Long Shan which are still in reasonable condition.

Meng Shan

North of Longshan near the village of Luochang. All that remains of the monastery that was here are two 6-metre pagodas.

Temple of Jin Minister – Jin Dai Fu Si

Situated 5km north-west of Tai Yuan. The existing buildings date from the Yuan dynasty.

Monastery of the Scented Forest – Fang Lin Si

Situated 8km south of Tai Yuan, north of Mazhuang. Founded in 1069, it was rebuilt and added to in the Ming and Qing Dynasties.

Tian Long Shan

Situated 40km southwest of Tai Yuan. There are 25 Buddhist shrines dating from the Northern Qi, Sui and Tang, cut into the rock near the peaks of the mountain.

The Hanging Temple – Xuan Zhong Si
Situated 60km southwest of Tai Yuan. Cut into the cliff, this Buddhist temple was founded in 472 AD. The Pavilion of 1,000 Buddhas has survived and was restored in the 1950s.

Old Temple to the God of War – Gu Guan Di Miao
West of Tai Yuan, in the village of Xaio Wei Ying. Originally a Song dynasty temple but rebuilt in the Yuan Dynasty.

Monastery of Endless Happiness (Twin Pagodas) Yong Zuo Si
Near Tai Yuan outside the village of Haozhoang. The monastery is well known for two Ming Dynasty pagodas in its grounds. Beneath them is the temple made of brick to imitate wooden construction.

Monastery of the White Cloud – Bai Yun Si
Built on the rocks south of Tai Yuan near a place called Hongtugou. It was founded in the early Qing Dynasty.

Shuanglin Monastery
Situated 97km south of Tai Yuan. The monastery is famous for around 2,000 painted clay figurines and statues, the majority of which date from the Song and Yuan Dynasties.

Temple of The Perfumed Cliff – Xiang Yan Si
Situated 40km southwest of Tai Yuan. The temple lies west of Qing Xu. Built entirely of stone in 1190, this Buddhist temple is sometimes called the Temple Without Beams.

Tai Gu
This town, which is 48km south of Tai Yuan, is surrounded by its original Ming Dynasty walls, and still maintains a great deal of its original character. There are several temples in the town including The Temple of Confucius, The Temple to the Earth, The Temple of the Town God and four Buddhist monasteries.

Ping Yao

Situated 48km south of Tai Gu. Like Tai Gu, this town has retained much of its original architecture and the local temples house a fine range of statues. Religious buildings include the Temple of Confucius, The Daoist Monastery of Qing Xu Guan, The Imperial Temple, The Temple of Yu Lu's Wife, The Qing Liang Monastery, The Zhe Guo Monastery, and the Si Xiang Monastery. The Two Forests monastery is 6km southwest of the town. Amongst its four temples is the Thousand Buddha Temple with an outstanding collection of sculptured deities, arhats, hermits and worshippers.

Wu Tai
Wutai Shan

Situated 95km from Tai Yuan, this is the Northern Buddhist Holy Mountain (see pages 240–44).

Guangji Monastery

Inside the city walls of Wu Tai, in the west of the town. Founded in the Song Dynasty the temple houses an unusual 3-metre bronze statue of Guangji or Guan Di, the god of war (see pages 70–71).

Nan Chan Si Monastery

North of the town Dongyezhen on the road to Wu Tai. This Buddhist monastery includes a Tang Dynasty temple.

Foguang Monastery

Southwest of Wu Tai Shan, north of Doucunzhen village. Founded in the Northern Wei Dynasty, it houses a good collection of Tang Dynasty frescoes and statues.

Jinge Temple

Situated 15km south of Tai Huai village. Founded in 770 AD, it has recently been restored and houses a large collection of Buddhas and buddhist deities.

Hongtong
Temple of Great Victory
Situated 200km southwest of Tai Yuan. The 47-metre, 3-storey pagoda was built in the Ming Dynasty.

Rui Cheng
The Monastery of Eternal Joy – Yong Le Gong
South of Tai Yuan, 59km from the town of Yun Cheng and 3km north of Ruicheng. This temple complex was moved from its original site in the town of Yong Le because of the construction of the Sanmen gorge dam (see page 108).

Zhao Chang
Monastery of Widespread Victory – Guang Sheng Si
Situated 19km southeast of the town at the foot of Huo Shan. The monastery is famous for its frescoes, a 13-storey glazed tile pagoda and for the collection of sutras which was discovered here (now in Peking National Library). The Dragon King Temple contains frescoes dating to 1325.

Datong
Yungang Buddhist Caves
Situated 16km west of Datong. This extensive and impressive set of caves (over 50) carved into the southern cliffs of Wuzhoushan contains more than 50,000 statues. The stone caves were carved out between 453 and 525 AD and display a fine range of symbols and artistic styles from China and beyond (see pages 213–14).

Guan Yin Temple
This temple stands on the road to Yungang. Founded in 1038 and rebuilt in 1652, it contains stone carvings dating from the Liao Dynasty.

Heng Shan
One of the five sacred Daoist mountains of China, 75km from Datong (see pages 234–8).

Huayan Buddhist Upper and Lower Monasteries

On the west side of the old city, on a side street off the west side of Daxi Jie. The Upper Monastery was rebuilt in 1140 and the Mahavira Hall survives from that date. It is one of the largest Buddhist halls in China and is also one of the few temples facing east since the monks' special respect for the sun means that most temples face south. Bojiajiaocang Hall, built in 1038, is in the Lower Monastery. This smaller hall is famous for its Liao dynasty clay figures representing the Buddha and bodhisattvas and for the small structures lining the walls constructed to house Buddhist sutras.

Shan Hua Monastery

In the south of the town, it was founded in the Tang Dynasty. The original complex covered almost 14,000 square metres, but today only four of the original ten buildings remain.

Wooden Pagoda of Ying Xian

Situated 70km south of Datong. This 67-metre pagoda is said to be the oldest wooden pagoda in China and was constructed without the use of nails.

Shuo Xian
Chong Fu Monastery

Situated 112km southwest of Datong. This monastery was founded in the Tang Dynasty and rebuilt in the Jin Dynasty. There are good examples of Jin sculpture in the main temple.

SICHUAN PROVINCE

Chengdu
Temple of Wuhou – Wuhou Si

In Nanjaio Park, south of the city. Founded in honour of Zhuge Liang, a famous soldier and prime minister in the state of Shu.

Qing Yang Gong
North of Wuhou Si. Founded in the Later Han Dynasty, this is the most ancient and largest Daoist temple in Chengdu. The oldest buildings which survive, date from the Qing Dynasty (see page 174).

Manjushri Temple – Wenshu Yuan
Named after the God of Wisdom and founded in the Tang Dynasty (see pages 86, 167).

Chengdu Catholic Cathedral
Northwest of the Exhibition Centre. Built in 1884 and reopened in 1979.

Qinzhen Mosque – Qinzhen Si
South of the bell tower, in the old town. It dates from the 18th century. The prayer hall remains and is almost 26 metres long.

Guan Xian
Two Kings Temple – Erwang Miao
This Qing Dynasty Daoist temple was constructed on the foundations of a 6th century building. The creators of the Chinese system of irrigation, Li Bing and his son Li Erlang, are honoured in the pavilions of this temple.

Temple of the Slayer of the Dragon – Fulong Guan
In the north of a small island in the Minjiang River. According to legend a dragon inhabited the river and caused severe flooding. Li Bing and his son succeeded in chaining this dragon and so the floods were controlled. The present buildings date from the Qing Dynasty and a stone statue here dates from the year 168.

Monastery of Divine Light – Baoguang Si
Situated 18km north of Chengdu in the town of Xindu. This is an active and popular temple which was originally founded in the Han Dynasty. There is a fine collection of Buddhist

calligraphy and art and 500 Qing Dynasty clay figurines depicting Buddhist deities and figures.

Qing Cheng Shan
Situated 56km west of Chengdu. This mountain has over 37 peaks and is regarded as a sacred Daoist site.

Emei Shan
One of the four Buddhist sacred mountains (see pages 202–6).

Leshan
Grand Buddha Statue and Temple – Leshan Da Fo
At 71m, one of the largest statues of the Buddha in the world. Work began on carving this Buddha in the cliff face in 713 AD and finished in 803 AD. The statue stands high above the confluence of the Dadu and Min Rivers.

Wulong Monastery
This Tang Dynasty monastery is close to the Grand Buddha and contains Buddhist calligraphy and art.

Chongqing
Lohan Temple
Off the south side of Minzu Lu. Founded in the Song Dynasty the temple contains rock carvings of the Buddha and Lohans.

The Yangtse River
Stone Treasure Stronghold – Shibaozhai
This 18th century pagoda-shaped wooden temple is constructed on the rock on the northern bank of the Yangtse.

Dazu County Caves
Dazu county is famous for its range of religious art, particularly its spectacular Buddhist cave sculptures. Examples are found throughout the county, although the largest groups of sculptures are at Beishan and Baoding.

Situated 2km from Dazu, the 290 caves at Beishan make

use of the natural features of the area. Approximately 10,000 figures have been carved over a period of 250 years, beginning in the late Tang Dynasty.

Baoding is 15km northeast of Dazu. There are approximately 10,000 sculptured figures on this site which were carved over a 70-year period beginning in 1179.

Kangding
Local Monasteries
There are several monasteries in the town, many of which are being renovated. The most active for worshippers is Manwusi on the north bank of Zhepuo River. The Kangding Da Monastery has five pavilions and is built high on a mountain above the town.

Ganzi
Ganzi Monastery
North of the town's Tibetan area.

Dege
Bakong Scripture Printing Monastery
This monastery dates from 1740 and houses hardwood printing plates of ancient texts covering the arts, sciences and religion.

Guang Yuan
Imperial Favour Temple – Huang Ze Si
West of the town. The original date of this Buddhist temple is unknown and the wooden structure has disappeared. Caves and niches containing Tang Dynasty style carvings of the Buddha and Buddhist figures still remain.

Thousand Buddha Cliff – Qian Fo Yan
Outside the town of Guang Yuan. At the beginning of the 8th century thousands of Buddhist statues were carved out of the rock at this site but today there are only about 400 left.

Ba Zhong
Buddhist Sculptures
A set of Buddhist sculptures dating from the Tang Dynasty has been cut into the rock.

TIANJIN MUNICIPALITY

Tianjin
The Grand Mosque – Qingzhen Da Si
In the northwest corner of the old city off Dafeng Lu. Built in the Chinese style at the beginning of the 18th century, the wood carvings in the mosque combine Chinese and Islamic motifs.

The Temple of Great Compassion – Dabei Si
On Tian Wei Lu. The original buildings were founded in 1669. It is the headquarters of the Buddhist Association of Tianjin, and houses a Cultural Relics Hall which exhibits Buddhist relics including a fine collection of statues, some from the 3rd century.

The French Church – Laoxikai Jiaotang
Situated 1km west of the Friendship Guesthouse, this early-20th century church is the largest in Tianjin. The groundplan of the church follows the shape of the Cross of Lorraine.

Jixian
Monastery of Solitary Joy – Dule Si
Situated 120km north of Tianjin town. The two wooden temples which form this Buddhist monastery were built in 984 although there was probably a Tang Dynasty monastery here before. They are amongst the oldest wooden structures in China.

Tian Cheng Temple
On the northern slope of Pan Shan (near Jixian). The temple dates from the Tang Dynasty, although the buildings were destroyed in the 1940s and rebuilt in 1980.

XINJIANG UIGHUR PROVINCE

Turfan
Emin Mosque
In the east of the town. Built in the late-18th century the mosque is known for its decorated brick minaret approximately 40 metres high.

Bezeklik Thousand Buddha Caves – Baizikelike Qian Fo Dong
Situated 48km northeast of the town. There are 67 caves, although only fragments of the frescoes remain since the caves have been damaged.

Ruins of Goachang
Situated 45km southeast of Turfan. Nestorian remains were found in a temple northeast of the city walls and sacred writings belonging to the Manicheans have been recovered here, along with remains of Buddhist monasteries.

Kuqa
Thousand Buddha Caves – Qian Fo Dong
The caves are in a restricted area. The best caves are at Kizil and out of 236 caves only 74 still have murals in a reasonable condition. The style of the art owes much to Indian and Iranian traditions. Many of the murals and manuscripts have been removed. Since Buddhism flourished in this region, there are many other caves and religious sites scattered across the area.

Kashgar
Id Kah mosque – Aitiga Qingzhen Si
Id Kah is one of the most notable of the mosques built in the 18th century in the architectural style of neighbouring Pakistan.

Grottoes of the Three Immortals – San Xian Dong
Situated 10km north of the town. Restored during the Qing dynasty. The walls of one cave contain 70 Buddha images thought to be 1700 years old.

YUNAN PROVINCE

Kunming
Mosque
On Zhengyi Lu, in the centre of the city. The mosque is over 400 years old.

Temple of Perfection and Success – Yuantong Si
On Yuantong Jie. This temple has more than a thousand year history although it has undergone many restorations.

Golden Temple – Jin Dian
Situated 11km northeast of the town on Phoenix Song Mountain. The current Daoist building dates to 1671 and most of the structure has been constructed from bronze.

Pagoda of the West Temple and Pagoda of the East Temple
Founded in the Tang Dynasty, these pagodas are in the south of the city and were rebuilt in 1880.

Bamboo Temple – Qiongzhu Si
Situated 12km northwest of Kunming. An inscription in the main hall is dated to 1316. This Buddhist temple is notable for its large collection of late-19th century clay figures.

Western Hills Temples
There is a set of temples on the Western Hills, on the west side of Lake Dian, including the Huating Temple rebuilt in the 14th century, the Taihua Temple, built in the Ming Dynasty, and the Sanqingge Temple, built in the Yuan Dynasty.

Cao Xi Temple
Situated 15km southwest of Kunming, at An Ning. This Tang dynasty temple was built by Dali princes and restored during the Yuan and Qing Dynasties.

Dali
Three Pagodas Temple – San Ta Si

On a hillside outside Dali, the pagodas are amongst the oldest in China. The tallest is 16 storeys and originally built in the mid-9th century.

Goddess of Mercy Temple (The Big Stone Temple) Guan Yin Tang

Situated 5km south of Dali, the temple is believed to have been built on the site of a large stone placed here by the bodhisattva Guan Yin to protect the city.

Gantong Temple – Gantong Si

Situated 6km south of Dali, this temple was founded in the Eastern Han period and restored in the Ming.

Shen Yuan Temple

Situated 10km north of Dali, this temple was founded in the Tang dynasty. A 1706 text carved in a door claims to record the history of the Bai state.

Jianchuan
Shibao Shan Grottoes

The town is 92km north of Dali. Near the village of Shaxi is a group of cave temples known as the Stone Rock Hill Caves. There are three groups known as the Stone Bells, Lion Pass and Shadeng Village.

Xiaguan
Juzu Shan

A sacred Buddhist mountain 103km east of Xiaguan. According to tradition, Buddhist practice was established here in 833 BC.

Wei Bao Shan

Situated 70km south of Xiaguan, the mountain is well-known for its Daoist temples, including the Ming dynasty Jade Emperor temple which still retains its temple frescoes.

Lijiang

The Mu Shi family, powerful local rulers in the Ming and Qing Dynasties, left behind a collection of temples and palaces near Lijiang. Their religious traditions combine Buddhist and Daoist, Muslim and Dongba influences. Surviving examples are the Gui Yi Tang in Lijiang, the Da Jue Gong near the town of Shu He and the Ta Bao Ji Gong north of Lijiang in Biasha.

Yufeng Si

On Shangri Moupo mountain. This Buddhist monastery belongs to the Karmapa sect of Tibetan Buddhism.

Damenglong
White Pagoda Temple – Fei Long Bai Ta

Just outside the town, this temple was built in 1204 to honour Sakyamuni Buddha who, according to legend, visited this area and left behind footprints. One of the footprints is said to be under a stupa in the grounds.

Menghan
Wat Ban Suan Men

Southwest of Menghan, this Buddhist temple is a fine example of Dai architecture, and is said to be more than 700 years old.

Xishuangbanna

This area is populated by the Dai people. It is an active Buddhist area with local temples in the town and villages. Common features of the local temple architecture are the division of the temple into three parts: the temple, the monks' accommodation and one or two pagodas. The temple, built on rising ground, is encircled by a wall with a gate to the east or south. Many monks learn modern Thai since most religious textbooks come from Thailand. Religious buildings in this area include the Meng Hai Temple 29km south of Jinghong, the Mengzhe Temple 10km west of Menghai and the Menghan Temple 10km southeast of Jinghong.

Lu Xi

This town near the Burmese border contains a Buddhist Temple known as the Da Jin or the Mian Temple. The temple is built in Burmese style and it is called Mian since this is the Chinese word for Burma.

Zhao Tong
Miao Christian Tombs

At the nearby Stone Gateway are the tombs of two Methodist missionaries who created the first alphabet for the Miao language in the early-20th century. The tombs are in Miao style with Christian motifs and are national monuments.

ZHEIJIANG PROVINCE

Hangzhou
Temple of Inspired Seclusion – Lingyin Si

The temple is at the foot of the hills west of Hangzhou and Northern Peak lies behind it. Originally constructed in 326 AD, the present buildings date from the Qing Dynasty. The Great Hall in the complex houses a 20-metre high statue of Sakyumuni carved from 24 blocks of camphor wood in 1956. Nearby the temple is The Peak That Flew From Afar, carved with 330 sculptures and graffiti ranging from the 10th to the 14th centuries.

There is a road at the back of this temple leading to Shang Tien Chu temple which is under construction. It is on the site where the earliest statue of Guan Yin is said to have been discovered and on the route leading to this temple there are many house shrines dedicated to her. On the way to this new temple there are two temples known as the Lower and Middle temples.

Temple of Yue Fei

On Huanhu Lu west of the Shangri-La Hotel. This is the temple where Yue Fei is believed to be buried.

Six Harmonies Pagoda – Liu He Ta

Southwest of the city, close to the bridge crossing the Qiantang River. This octagonal pagoda, built in 970 AD, is named after the Six Codes of Buddhism.

Mosque – Feng Huang Si

On Sun Yat Sen Avenue. Steles in the mosque indicate the dates that the mosque was restored. The first one is dated to 1492 and the last one to 1743. It underwent further restorations in 1953. Part of the old prayer hall still remains and the Mihrab is believed to date from the Ming Dynasty.

Great Buddha Temple – Da Fo Si

At the foot of Bao Shi Shan, north of West Lake, a 9-metre carving of the head and shoulders of the Buddha is to be found cut out of rock in the courtyard. It gives the appearance of the Buddha rising from the ground.

Ge Hong Summit

The peak next to Bao Shi Shan. It is said that the renowned alchemist Ge Hong experimented here with cinnabar in order to create an elixir of life in the 4th century. A temple has been built in his memory.

Yan Xia San Dong

On the south side of West Lake. This is a set of three caves. The second cave contains more than 500 small sculptures carved out of the rock. The third cave contains a collection of Luo Han carvings and is guarded by two notable statues of Guan Yin. All date from the 10th century.

Wenzhou
Temple in the Heart of the River – Jiang Xin Si

A temple has been built on two islands that were joined together in the Ou River. Originally each island had its own Buddhist temple and pagoda.

Miao Gua Temple

At the base on Song Tai Shan. This Tang Dynasty temple was restored in 1988.

Ningbo
Protect the Nation Temple – Bao Guo Si

Situated 15km outside Ningbo in the Lingshan area. The Song Dynasty main hall, Mahavira Hall, is the oldest wooden building in the Yangtse Delta area.

Ayuwang Temple (Asoka Temple)

Situated 20km east of the town. The temple was founded in 522, and the miniature Sheli Pagoda it houses is famous for the bone of Sakyamuni it is said to contain. The pagoda is regarded as one of the reliquaries made by the Indian Buddhist ruler, Asoka.

Tiantong Temple

Situated near Ayuwang Temple. The temple was founded around the beginning of the 4th century and rebuilt in the Tang Dynasty. It became a huge Buddhist complex that housed several thousand monks. Even today the hundreds of rooms that remain, cover an area of 44,600 square metres and monks still live here. According to tradition Dogen and Yonsai came to study Buddhism here and returned to Japan to found the Soto and Rinzai sects.

Tian Tai Shan

Many of the Buddhist monasteries dotted on this mountain date back to the 6th century and the small pagodas around them mark the burials of respected monks. It is the home of the Tiantai Buddhist sect. Gouqingsi monastery, founded in 598, at the foot of the mountain is the largest monastery and the founder of the Tiantai school, Zhi-yi, is buried in a pagoda nearby.

Xin Chang
Temple of the Town Gods – Chen Huang Miao
This 15th century Daoist temple is 48km northwest of Tiantai in the village of Xin Chang. There is a stage which would have been used for religious performances.

Big Buddha Temple – Da Fo Si
This temple is also in the village of Xin Chang (see above) and houses a 3-metre Buddha which is believed to date from the 5th century.

Pu Tuo Shan
Situated 96km east, off the coast of Ningbo, the island is one of the four Buddhist sacred mountains and is particularly associated with Guan Yin, the Goddess of Mercy (see pages 198–202).

Huzhou
Temple of the Iron Buddha – Tie Fo Si
In the west of the town this 14th century temple is also known as the Temple of the Goddess of Mercy due to the 2-metre statue of Avalokitesvara in the main hall. The statue dates to 1022.

Shao Xing
This area is surrounded by several temples including the Ying Tian Temple Pagoda, The Bao Guo Temple and the Temple of Yu the Great which is 5km outside the town at the base of Guiji Shan (see page 24).

In 1997, Hong Kong reverts to China and in 1999, Macau reverts as well. The importance of both places is that traditional Chinese religion has continued undisturbed despite the upheaval of mainland China. In particular, Macau has preserved religious life and temples in a continuous line since the mid-16th century. Apart from the major temples, door gods, house gods, street shrines abound, almost all of which have been lost in China itself.

HONG KONG

(Please note, spellings are phoneticized Cantonese, not pinyin.)

Hong Kong Island
Tiger Balm Gardens, Tai Hing District. A Chinese Disneyland of mythology and religion featuring models of the gods, goddesses and heroes of ancient China. Gaudy but fun!

Shin Wong – City God Temple, Shaukiwan tram terminus. This is the city god shrine for the area.

Tin Hau – Goddess of the Sea Temple – Causeway Bay. Tiny but ancient (for Hong Kong) Daoist temple with 15th-century bell and seafarers' charms.

Pak Tai – Temple of the Dark God of the North who is here worshipped as the seafarers' deity. Mid-19th century sailors' temple. Hopewell Centre, Wanchai.

Sui Pak – True Buddha Temple, Hopewell Centre, Wanchai. Popular for its healing powers.

Man Ho – Civic and Military – Temple, Hollywood Road, Sheung Wan. Oldest temple in Hong Kong and a classic Daoist temple. See also nearby for small hillside shrine to earth god.

Saint John's Cathedral, Central. Anglican cathedral of the mid-19th century. Interesting memorials to expatriates.

Stanley Village
On the south side of the island, street shrines and earth god shrines can be found all over this area. This village retains all its traditional temples such as:
　Tin Hau – Sea Goddess temple, *c.* 1760.
　Kwun Yum (Guan Yin) – Goddess of Mercy Temple with 6-metre statue of the goddess.

Kowloon

Tin Hau – Sea goddess temple, Market Street, Yaumati. Largest such temple in Hong Kong.

Wong Tai Sin Temple. By entrance to Wong Tai Sin MTR station. Large and busy Daoist temple dedicated to this local deity. Good place to find fortune tellers and to see religious life in practice.

Mosque, Kowloon Park. The centre of the Islamic community and a busy place. Nearby is also the Sikh Gurdwara, centre for the large Sikh population.

New Territories

In all the villages there are temples and often Ancestral Halls. Look also for shrines to trees, special rocks, other natural features and earth gods.

Mui Fat – Ten Thousand Buddhas Monastery, Lam Tei, north of Tuen Mun. Over the top glitzy Buddhist monastery.

Tin Hau – Mother Goddess Temple, Shui Tan. Built 1722. Note Ancestral Hall in the same village, now used as a school.

Temple of the Ten Thousand Buddhas, Shatin. On the hill above the town, a large complex with garish but dramatic statues of Guan Yin, Lohans and the Three Buddhas. Also feng shui burial grounds.

Tao Fung Shan, Shatin. Also on a hill above Shatin, study centre founded 1927 for Christian-Chinese religious dialogue. Beautiful buildings and interesting workshop producing crockery with biblical scenes in Chinese style.

Tap Mun Island. Tin Hau temple. Many of the islands have small villages with interesting temples.

Lantau Island
Po Lin Monastery. This has the enormous seated Buddha statue which can be seen as you fly into Hong Kong. The monastery itself is a perfect example of a Southern Buddhist monastery. Founded in 1927

Trappist Monastery of Our Lady of Joy. Christian monastery of these silent brothers. Best known in Hong Kong for their milk.

Cheung Chau Island
Pak Tai Temple, 1783, centre of a famous Bun fight each year, a form of Hungry Ghosts Festival.

Tin Hau Temple. Late 19th-century and still in active use by sailors.

MACAU

A-Ma – Sea Goddess Temple, at southern tip of mainland. Oldest temple in Macau. A delightful collection of small temples climb the hill. Founded in the Ming dynasty. The temple gave its name to Macau – A-Ma Cau.

Central Macau. This area contains many small temples and churches such as:
   Saint Domingo's Church and monastery, 1588, with rich 17th-century furnishings.
   Saint Augustine's Church, 1586.
   Saint Joseph's Church and seminary, rebuilt in the 1760s.
   Saint Lawrence's Church, founded c. 1560 and a favourite subject for artists.
   Saint Paul's Church facade. The most important architectural remains of Japanese and Chinese Christianity of the early 17th century. Only the facade of this church remains, built by Jesuits and Japanese and Chinese converts in 1635. The facade combines Christian and Japanese/Chinese mythology and
310

symbolism. A new museum is being opened in the ruins – caused by a fire in 1835.

Kun Yam (Guan Yin) – Goddess of Mercy Temple. Excellent example of southern Buddhist temple, very active and filled with fine statues. Note in particular the thriving funeral business with chapels, mourners' rooms and many paper models of gifts to be burnt for the dead. Founded in the Ming Dynasty. North of mainland Macau.

Lin Fong – Lotus Temple. Ming dynasty, and a fine example of a southern Buddhist temple. Hall dedicated to Guan Yin, Guan Di and Tian Ma – Mother of Heaven. North of mainland Macau.

Tai Soi Temple, Daoist. Classic southern Daoist temple with multi-layered halls rising above, around and on top of each other. One of the best-preserved Daoist temples in existence and full of the pantheon of Daoism. Note especially the Carpenter's Hall with its Carpenter gods and sedan chairs for escorting the god on his peregrinations. Central Macau.

Taipa Island
Pou Tai Un Temple, Buddhist. Rather overdone new temple with enormous statue of Amitabha Buddha.

United Chinese Cemetery. Near the new airport. Fascinating collection of statues, inscriptions and rituals to be seen here every day.

Taipa village has a fine Pak Tai temple and a Tin Hau temple as well as a Christian cemetery.

Coloane Island
Chapel of Saint Francis Xavier. The Jesuit who first touched China's coast and missionized the Japanese. His humerus is housed here and it is a centre of Chinese Catholic devotion.

Sam Seng Temple. Qing dynasty temple.

Tam Kong Temple. Commemorates the last Song dynasty Emperor who was hounded by the Mongolians to the ends of China – namely this area – and died by throwing himself into the sea. This temple contains many seafaring items.

---

1   Banner means a section of a town and comes from the Mongolian term by which families belonged to a tribal banner. When they settled in towns, the term Banner was applied to the sector or section each group occupied.

OTHER RELIGIOUS TRADITIONS IN CHINA

ISLAM

Islam, known as Yisilan Jiao, is a religion of considerable significance to many of the minorities within China, where it has been their traditional faith for many centuries. There are relatively few converts to Islam in China, either now or historically. Most Muslims have migrated into China bringing their faith with them. In particular, the ten minority groups who constitute the bulk of Chinese Muslims (the Huis, Uygurs, Kazars, Tartars, Kirgizs, Tajiks, Uzbeks, Dongxiangs, Salars and Bonans) are all migrants from either north or west China and it is these areas which still have the majority of Muslims.

Islam is believed to have been brought to China very early in the life of the faith. It entered China through sea trade with Arabia which was well established at this time. Legend says that the first missionaries were sent around 618 AD, which means before the traumatic expulsion of Muhammad from Makkah and the proper beginning of Islam. If such missionaries were sent then, they probably came bearing the message of monotheism per se, rather than Islam as we know it, for none of the formative experiences by which the faith was formed had really taken place, and indeed, the Qur'an was still in the process of being dictated to Muhammad.

Nevertheless, this tradition holds to this day and in Quanzhou, Fujian, the tombs of two of these missionaries on Lingshan are still a site of Muslim pilgrimage.

One very well established tradition says that the maternal uncle of Muhammad came as a missionary to China, to Guangzhou, in 627 AD. Saad bin Waqqas received permission to build a mosque on the wharfside, for use by the many thousands of Arab sailors who frequented the port and to serve as a basis for missionary activity. Founded in the year of his arrival, it is the oldest mosque in China and still stands. Its highly distinctive Tang dynasty minaret also served as a lighthouse.

Officially, the first formal contact between Islam and China came in 651 AD when the third Caliph Uthman ibn Affan (577–656) sent an envoy to the Tang dynasty emperor. However, Islam was never accorded official status in China, existing as it did primarily amongst the non-Chinese. An interesting anecdote illustrates this. In 1700, advisers to the Emperor Kangxi of the Qing dynasty urged upon him a ban on all Muslims in Beijing. The Emperor was told that the Muslims gathered at night in the mosque for the purpose of planning the overthrow of the Emperor. The Emperor apparently decided to find out for himself. One night he dressed up as a Muslim and attended the last prayers of the day at the Libai mosque, the oldest mosque in Beijing, dating from 996 AD. The Emperor listened to the prayers, heard the imam preach and concluded that there was nothing to worry about here. The very next day he issued a decree making it a crime to create trouble for the Muslim communities. This edict, with the Emperor's signature, is still to be seen at the Libai mosque in Beijing.

However, Kangxi was perhaps a little too easily comforted, for later, his dynasty was to be almost toppled by Muslim rebellions in the mid-19th century in northwestern China. Again, in the 1920s, when China effectively fell apart, Muslim insurrectionists and warlords under the famous Ma family, virtually broke away from the Republic and were only crushed by a considerable Republican army.

314

But these are unusual incidents in what has been on the whole a fairly peaceful co-existence of Chinese and Muslim minorities, with if anything, the wrongs being done by xeno-phobic Chinese against the Muslims.

Islam in China has produced no new schools or traditions, nor thinkers or doctrines. The Muslims belong on the whole to the Sunni tradition, the majority expression of Islam world wide.

What is distinctive about Chinese Islam is not any new developments in theology, but the wonderful architecture which has arisen from the interaction between the faith and Chinese arts over the last 1300 years. The minarets are usual-ly in the form of Chinese pagodas or towers with one or two exceptions such as the Huaisheng mosque in Guangzhou. The main prayer halls look like either Daoist temples or the recep-tion halls of Chinese palaces. The minbar – the arch denoting the direction of Makkah and the Kaba, are in styles varying from classic Arabic to classic Buddhist. But perhaps what strikes most visitors are the gardens contained within the walls of the mosques, peaceful oases, which while reflecting tradi-tional Chinese design have a special holiness about them, an aura of calm. Unlike busy Chinese Buddhist or Daoist temples where incenses and prayers are offered all day, mosques tend to be quiet places of study or reflection, moderately busy only at the main prayer times five times a day.

To visit such a mosque, as for example the Great Mosque (Qingzhen Si) in Xian or the Phoenix Mosque (Feng Huang) in Hangzhou, is to enter a world of study and calm, where Islam seems to have mellowed into the Chinese way but added something distinctive.

Today there are some 20 million Muslims in China. It is claimed that there are 23,000 mosques, but I find that a hard figure to believe, likewise the figure of 40,000 imams and teachers. However, being a religion of ethnic minorities, whom the Chinese have taken care not to offend in recent years, it is possible that they have received better treatment than the faiths of Daoism and Buddhism. Many mosques were

315

destroyed or damaged during the Cultural Revolution, but proportionately less than those of Daoism and Buddhism. A healthy wariness of many of the ethnic minorities by the ruling Han Chinese has ensured this.

The Muslims today are able to exist without many restrictions, and all big cities will have their Muslim area with halal butchers and restaurants, Islamic schools and mosques. If there is a concern, it is that the Muslims belonging to ethnic groups often in poor farm land areas are falling behind in the race for prosperity. This in turn concerns the Communist Party because it fears Islamic fundamentalism coming in from Iran via the new Islamic states in the former Central Asian USSR countries. However, so far there has been little evidence that such fears are warranted and Muslims live and trade across China.

CHRISTIANITY

The Nestorians

Christianity first arrived in China in the sixth century AD via traders coming from Persia. Officially, it is dated to 635 AD when the Nestorian bishop Alopen was received formally at Court by the Emperor and was given exactly what Buddhist missionaries were given, namely a monastery and translation facilities in order that the Christian books could be translated into Chinese.

The Nestorian Church is a fascinating branch of Christianity about whose existence most Westerners are unaware. Yet in the 10th to 12th centuries AD, it is arguable that the Nestorian Church was the largest church in the world. Certainly its geographical spread was greater than any other Church at that time, stretching as it did from Syria to China; from Turkistan and Mongolia to India.

The Church takes its name, though it was never one it used, from the Archbishop of Constantinople, Nestorius, who was deposed in 431 at the Council of Ephesus for heresy and who

316

died in obscurity around 450 AD. His crime was that he spoke out against the emerging theology from Egypt which wished to call the Virgin Mary the Theotokos – the Bearer of God. This, Nestorius claimed, smacked of goddess worship and he spoke out against it strongly. He wished to stress the human within Christ and not to overstress the divine. Thus he wished to call the Virgin Mary the Christotokos – The Bearer of Christ.

In taking this position he ran up against the Patriarch of Alexandria, Cyril, who was about as tough a politician as you could imagine. It was an unequal contest and Nestorius and his followers were duly anthamatized at the Council in 431.

The religion spread throughout the Middle East, incurring the condemnation of the Roman Emperor, the Greek Orthodox church and the Oriental Orthodox churches of Syria, Armenia and Ethiopia, who eventually drove the Nestorians into Persia. Here the scholars were welcomed with open arms by the Persians on the grounds that 'my enemy's enemy is my friend'. A major new Theological Academy was established at Nisibis and the Persian Church became Nestorian as a way of showing that it was not linked to the Christianity of the Roman Empire.

Thus established in Persia, the Nestorian Church began one of the most remarkable missionary adventures of Christianity – nothing rivalled it until the explosion of Christianity from Europe in the 16th century onwards. Nestorians were soon to be found preaching and converting from the steppes of Central Asia where they converted many tribes to the faith; to India where they strengthened the Thomarist Church reputedly founded by Thomas the Apostle in 54 AD; to Arabia where amongst other things it was discussions with a Nestorian monk that converted the Prophet Muhammad to monotheism; to Afghanistan where there were archbishoprics and major conversions and finally into China and Mongolia. And all this was done by a Church which was not an imperial one, had no state backing and never sought to be the state religion. It was also a Church which was unaffected by the notions of evil and sin, guilt and remorse which the Western Church was soon to be affected by through the teachings of Saint Augustine. Quite the reverse. This was a Church which stressed that human beings are essentially good.

The Nestorian Church in China of the 7th to 9th centuries was never large but it was widespread and had many churches and monasteries. When the Great Persecution of 841-5 broke upon Buddhism, Manichaeism and Christianity alike, over 3,000 Nestorian monks were forced to revert to lay life and the monasteries and churches were closed.

The headquarters of this remarkable first venture of Christianity into China was the Imperial capital of Changan, now Xian. Here you can see, in the Museum of the Forest of Steles, the Nestorian Stone, erected in 781 AD and recording in Chinese with notes in Syriac, the coming of Christianity to China and the core teachings of the faith. It is a fascinating document, telling of a form of Christianity which is radically different from conventional Western understandings. I have discussed these teachings, provided translations of Nestorian Chinese texts and the history of the Nestorians at length in *Living Christianity* (Element Books, Shaftesbury 1993).

Apart from the Nestorian stone in Xian and remains in the museum at Quanzhou, Fujian, there is little left in China to be seen of this first wave of Nestorian Christianity. It does appear that Nestorian churches survived the Great Persecution on the coast where traders from Arabia came – just as the early Muslim sites are all coastal ports – hence the remains in the Museum of Overseas Trade in Quanzhou. But there was a second wave of Nestorian Christianity in the north, brought this time by conquerors. The Mongols of Genghis Khan and Khublai Khan who swept into northern China in the mid-13th century established the Yuan dynasty which lasted from 1280 to 1368. Many of the Mongolian tribes were Christian, converted by Nestorian missionaries over the previous 3–400 years. The mothers of both Genghis Khan and Khublai Khan were Christian princesses.

When Marco Polo visited China in the late-13th century, he found Nestorian Christians and their churches in virtually every major city he visited. We also have an extraordinary account of the pilgrimage of two Nestorian Chinese monks from Beijing – Mar Jabalaha and Rabban Sauma, one of them being the Archdeacon of Beijing – to Jerusalem in the 1280s. They never got there for one of them was elected Patriarch of the Nestorian Church and died in Baghdad, the centre of the Nestorian hierarchy, while the other went on to visit the kings of Europe, ending up celebrating Easter Mass for King Edward I of England, in France in 1289.

Catholicism

About the same time the Nestorians were going West on pilgrimage the Catholics set off for China. The first to reach China was a Franciscan, John of Monte Corvino, sent by the Pope to the Great Khan in response to a request from the Khan that Christian priests be sent. He was given space in the Forbidden City of the Mongols in Beijing to build a cathedral in the closing years of the 13th century. Other Franciscans came to assist him until at least 1330. But although their correspondence mentions many thousands of converts, this church disappeared and only a few tombstones have been found to record their existence. Foster Stockwell claims that the present Beitang – South Cathedral – in Beijing is built on the site of the Franciscan Cathedral, but I have seen no evidence to prove this, interesting notion though it is and perhaps not entirely unlikely.

The start of the churches which are today functioning and growing in China came with the Jesuits in the late-16th century. Banner carriers of the post-Reformation Counter Revolution of the Catholic Church, the Jesuits were at the cutting edge of modern science and attitudes in the late-16th and 17th centuries. They enjoyed the challenge of relating to new cultures, and China provided one of the most challenging. The Jesuits produced a stream of highly talented men who won the friendship of the Emperors and gained unprecedented influence and control in the bureaucracy and scholarly classes of China. Greatest amongst these was the first Jesuit missionary to China, Matteo Ricci, known in Chinese as Li Ma Dou. He arrived in China in 1582 and immediately started his study of Chinese, both language and culture. When he died in 1610, in a special house provided by the Emperor, he was acclaimed as one of the greatest Chinese scholars of his day by the Chinese.

The Jesuits established major centres of conversion within China, and unlike Islam, there were Chinese converts including leading figures in the academic and courtly circles. To this day there are entire villages and small market towns which are almost entirely Christian and have been since the early-17th century. The greatest monuments to the Jesuits and the coming of Catholicism in China are at Macau, where the facade of the old Cathedral was carved by Japanese Christians aided by Chinese Christians in 1635, and in the surrounding 17th and early-18th century churches such as Saint Augustine's, Saint Lawrence's, Saint Antony's and the church and seminary of Saint Joseph.

The South and East Cathedrals of Beijing are worth visiting, especially the South which is built on the site of Matteo Ricci's house and according to Stockwell is also the site of the 13th/14th century Franciscan Cathedral.

In Wuxi, Jiangsu Province, the majority of the citizens are Christians and fishermen. Their great church of Saint Joseph and the Catholic cemetery are of great interest for the community goes back to the 17th century.

The Jesuits, followed by other Orders such as the Dominicans and Franciscans, were very successful in the 17th century and the Jesuits in particular managed to combine elements of traditional Chinese life such as veneration of ancestors, with Catholic teachings. To this day, the festival of Qing Ming – the Festival of the Dead and a traditional time to venerate ancestors – is a great festival in old catholic strongholds such as Wuxi or Quanzhou. However, other Orders disliked this and accused the Jesuits and their converts of being syncretistic. This row about whether the rites of the ancestors constituted an affront to Christian teachings simmered on throughout the 17th century until in 1715 the Pope decreed that it was wrong for Chinese Christians to venerate their ancestors. This was the Rites Controversy. It effectively ended Imperial patronage of Christianity, which had come close to converting the Emperor. It brought persecution and the expulsion of all but technologically useful Jesuits, and the Catholic communities of China were without contact with their fellow religionists outside China for over a hundred years. They survived by outwardly conforming to traditional Chinese religion but inwardly keeping the faith. When the Catholic missionaries returned in the 1840s many of these communities were still functioning.

Due to language issues, the Catholic Church in China is treated as a separate religion from 'Christianity', by which the Chinese mean Protestants and Orthodox Christians. Thus Catholicism is listed as a religion in its own right in Chinese documents and classifications of religions in China.

Today, the Catholic Church is split. After the Liberation in 1949, China refused to allow the Vatican to have any influence over Chinese Catholics in areas such as appointments of bishops and archbishops. The missionaries were expelled, often in very violent ways. The relationship between the new State and the Catholic hierarchy was not good. Then in 1957 the Chinese Patriotic Catholic Association came into existence, as a pro-Communist state Church. This organization has since taken over all the dioceses and has appointed the bishops without consulting Rome. Thus the official Catholic Church in China is not recognized by the Vatican. This also means it is caught in a time warp. The reforms of the Second Vatican Council of the 1960s have passed China by, and you can easily hear a full Tridentine Latin mass in any of the cathedrals of China!

The Catholic Church suffered greatly under the Cultural Revolution and almost all churches were closed and used for other purposes. Since 1979, many of these have been restored to the Church and new ones are being opened.

The unofficial Catholic Church has gone underground since the late 1950s and it is still largely so. There are signs of greater rapprochement between Rome and the Patriotic Catholics but there is also a long way to go. It is impossible to find reliable figures for the number of unofficial Catholics – some say there are 10 million but this is highly unlikely. Official Catholics number around 4 to 5 million, with perhaps another million unofficial Catholics.

Protestantism

In the mid-19th century there were more Protestant missionaries in China than in the whole of the rest of the world. China has always exercised a particular fascination for Protestant Christians and literally thousands poured into China during the 19th century. They brought with them much that was good and much that was bad. They brought the divisions and arguments of Europe, so that scores of different denominations had their own churches in the same cities in China. They also brought a largely working class or lower middle class understanding of Christianity. This contrasted strongly with the highly educated Jesuit missionaries of the 17th century who enjoyed engaging with Chinese culture. Many Protestants saw China and anything Chinese as inherently bad. This, fused with the links of the spread of missionaries – both Protestant and Catholic – during the 19th century with gunboat diplomacy by the Western powers and the carving up of China by the West, meant that Christianity in China (Protestant and Orthodox) was seen by many as an imperialist anti-Chinese religion, and with some justification.

Nevertheless, substantial churches were established by the time the missionaries were expelled in the early 1950s. In the wake of their departure, many of the Chinese church leaders met to create a new organization to combine all the main Protestant denominations. This is called the Three Self Patriotic Movement – the three selves being self-administration, self-financing and self-propagating. This is now the main body coordinating Protestant churches in China.

However, there is also an underground church which feels the Three Self Movement is a sell-out to the State. This is especially true since the ravages of the Cultural Revolution which closed virtually all Protestant churches, forcing Christians to meet secretly in their homes. This 'house church' movement is arguably one of the strongest expressions of Christianity in China today, organized without buildings or structures.

Since 1979, churches have been given back and some new ones built. Officially there are some 6 to 7 million Protestant Christians – an eight to nine fold increase over the number in 1949. However, some estimate that with unofficial Protestants, the number is much nearer to 30 to 35 million. Some commentators even claim as high as 70 million. What is clear is that along with Catholicism, 'Christianity' in China is now very popular with young people, rivalled only by Buddhism, because of Christianity's links with the West. This reversal of attitudes has meant tremendous growth for the churches.

Orthodoxy

The Orthodox Church found itself inside China when areas of Siberia were absorbed by the Chinese state in the late-17th century. To begin with, the Orthodox Churches simply ministered to the needs of Russians in the Chinese Empire and thus the oldest Orthodox churches are found in cities in the far north such as Harbin – where a few rather bedraggled churches still exist, some just about functioning. In Urumqi, Xinjiang, there is a functioning Orthodox church and in Shanghai and Beijing, the Orthodox church has opened again. However, this is almost entirely a faith which looks to the needs of Russians as few Chinese were ever converted to Orthodoxy. What remains is a rather sad and struggling little community.

JUDAISM

When Judaism reached China is unclear. Almost certainly some Jews entered China during the Han and Tang dynasties (*c.* 206 BC – 907 AD) travelling the Silk Route and coming from the big Jewish communities in the Persian and Islamic Empires. The earliest written record dates from 718 AD and is a document found at the Dun Huang caves in 1901 which relates to the sale of sheep. It is now in the British Museum. Records for Guangzhou record Jews in 877, which is hardly surprising, and it can be fairly safely assumed that just as Nestorian churches and Arab mosques were to be found in all the major ports on the south coast of China at this time, so were Jews and synagogues. Jewish communities are definitely recorded in the Sung dynasty (960–1280 AD) in Beijing, Quanzhou, Luoyang, Ningbo, Hangzhou, Nanjing and Yangzhou.

However, it is the Jewish community of Kaifeng which is of greatest interest because records still exist along with the original Scrolls of the Torah which the community used. The community appears to have arrived in Kaifeng during the 10th century, though the steles still to be seen in the Kaifeng Museum claim they arrived in 10 BC.

The synagogue was first built in 1163 on land given by the emperor. In 1489 there were 70 families, as recorded on the oldest of the steles, dated from that year. The other two steles date from 1512 and 1619 and record the fluctuating fortunes of the community. In 1904 only six families remained. However, recent figures claim that there are 200 Jews in Kaifeng, though none are practising. The synagogue was destroyed by the terrible flood of 1855 which devastated Kaifeng. A patched up version staggered on into this century, but had none of the glory recorded in the drawing done by a Jesuit visitor in 1723, which shows a traditional Chinese temple hall, but with some unusual features internally. It was also enormous – supposedly 400 feet by 150 feet – larger than the largest synagogue in the USA! The Scrolls from the community were purchased by missionaries in the mid-19th century and this probably saved them from destruction or loss. None now resides in China, but the best of the collection can be seen in the Royal Ontario Museum in Toronto.

The site of the synagogue is still to be seen, not least in the name of the street which it stood on, called 'Lane of the People who teach the Scriptures'. Plans are afoot for the synagogue to be rebuilt on or near the original site and for a museum to be established there to celebrate Judaism in China.

MANICHAEISM

There are no Manichaeans left in China, indeed there are none left anywhere in the world. Manichaeism takes its name from the teacher Mani, who lived in Persia in the 3rd century AD and taught a faith which combined elements of Christianity, Zoroastrianism, Buddhism and Hinduism. He taught that the world was caught in a vast cosmic battle between good and evil. He saw the human soul as being part of the good which had become trapped in the grossness of the material world – the bad. Mani's core teaching was that this soul had to be freed from the body in order to reunite with the Ultimate Good – God. Mani claimed that this was what all the great teachers, Jesus, Zoroaster, the Buddha and so forth, had come to teach.

The revulsion against the physical world led to extreme dualism and to extraordinary asceticism. This attracted many in the religious hotchpotch of the late Roman Empire, and Saint Augustine, before he became a Christian, was a Manichaean for ten years. Elements of his Manichaeism remained with him to his death and have entered Christianity through his teachings. For a while it looked as if Manichaeism not Christianity would win the Roman Empire. But Christianity won and Manichaeism in the West died out, but continued in Persia and along the Silk route and in China until at least the 10th century. Manichaean documents have been found in the caves at Dun Huang which were sealed in the 10th century and which illustrate a thriving Manichaean community within China.

Today there are few remains of the Manichaen religion still visible. There are a few inscriptions in the museum at Quanzhou and nearby is a statue of Mani which has been incorporated into the Buddhist temple of Cao An, at Huabiao Hill in Jinjiang County, just outside Quanzhou. The Buddhist temple was built in 1922 on the remains of a Manichaean temple. On the main altar, a statue of Mani, retrieved from the old temple, is still worshipped, but now by Buddhists. In Xingjiang, Uighur

Province (Sinkiang) at Turpan, there are the remains of a monastery at Goachang, but no living place of worship.

TABLE OF DYNASTIES

Xia	*c.*2200BC – *c.*1766BC	
Shang	*c.*1766BC – *c.*1122BC	
Zhou	*c.*1122BC – 770BC	
Spring and Autumn period	770BC – 476BC	NB The term Zhou is often used to cover these two periods as well
Warring States	476BC – 221BC	
Qin	221BC – 206BC	
Han	206BC – 220BC	sometimes dividied into Western Han – 206BC – 24AD Eastern Han – 25AD – 220AD
Wei	220AD – 265AD	collectively known as The Three Kingdoms
Shu Han	220AD – 263AD	
Wu	222AD – 250AD	
Western Jin	265AD – 316AD	
Eastern Jin	317AD – 420AD	

Northern and Southern Dynasties	420AD – 589AD	Southern:	Song	420 – 479
			Qi	479 – 502
			Lian	502 – 557
			Chen	557 – 589
		Northern:	North Wei	386 – 534
			Eastern Wei	534 – 550
			Northern Qi	550 – 537
			Western Wei	535 – 556
			Northern Zhou	557 – 581

Sui	581AD – 618AD

Tang	618AD – 907AD

Five Dynasties	Later Liang	907AD – 923AD
	Later Tang	923AD – 936AD
	Later Jin	936AD – 964AD
	Later Zhou	947AD – 950AD
	Later Liang	951AD – 960AD

Song	Northern Song	960AD – 1127AD
	Southern Song	1127AD – 1279AD

Liao	916AD – 1125AD

Jin	1115AD – 1234AD

Yuan	1280AD – 1368AD

Ming	1368AD – 1644AD

Qing	1644AD – 1911AD

Republic	1912AD – 1949AD

Peoples' Republic	1949AD →

GLOSSARY

Amitabha   The Buddha who presides over a Pure Land,
            a mystical universe where all who pray
            sincerely to Amitabha can be reborn.

Apsaras   Angel-like devotees of the Buddha or of
            bodhisattvas.

Arhat   See *lohan*.

Bank of Hell   Currency notes specially printed to be burnt
notes   at a funeral, to help the dead person pay his
                or her way through hell.

Bodhisattva   One who uses his or her accumulation of
                merit, not to achieve Nirvana, but to help
                others.

Buddha   An enlightened one. See also *Sakyamuni,
            Maitreya, Amitabha*.

Buddha nature   The essential spiritual nature of the Buddha,
                not embodied in a specific form.

Chan   Chinese Buddhist tradition founded by
            Bodhidarma, known as Zen in Japan.

Confucius   Kong Fu Zi, philosopher and scholar who
            lived from about 551 to 479 BC.

Dao	Literally, 'the way'; the natural order of the universe.
Dao De Jing	Classic text of Daoism, supposedly written by Lai Zi. Dates from *c*. 4th century BC.
Deva	A good spirit in Buddhism and Hinduism.
Dharma	The path and teachings of the Buddha.
Eightfold Path	Eight principles taught by the Buddha and followed by Buddhists in order to reach enlightenment.
Feng shui	The tradition of building and landscaping in harmony with the natural forces of the land. Also known as geomancy.
Five elements	The energies that make up everything that exists: in Chinese tradition these are wood, fire, earth, metal and water.
Four Noble Truths	The insights regarding the nature of suffering and people's response to it, that came to the Buddha when he reached enlightenment.
Geomancy	See *feng shui*.
Gong	Literally, 'palace'; used for Confucian, Daoist or Buddhist temples which have an imperial connection.
Guan	From the word to 'look' or 'see'; a Daoist temple.
Guan Yin	Boddhisattva of Compassion also known as Goddess of Mercy. One of the most popular of the Chinese deities.
Lao Zi	Also rendered as Lao Tzu. A legendary teacher and philosopher, thought of as the founder of Daoism. Author of the Daoist classic, the *Dao De Jing*, he is supposed to have lived in the 6th century BC.

Lohan	Also *arhat*; monks who have reached the stage of ending the Eightfold Path and can help others.
Mahayana	Literally, 'great vehicle'; a form of Buddhism in which large numbers of people can achieve salvation by the merits and compassion of bodhisattvas. The main form of Buddhism in Japan, Korea, China, Mongolia, Tibet and the Himalayas.
Maitreya	The future Buddha, usually depicted as fat and laughing, indicating prosperity and happiness.
Miao	Literally, 'palace' or 'residence'; a Confucian temple.
Nirvana	The cessation of desire and of ordinary existence, the ultimate aim of Buddhists.
Pagoda	A storehouse or library for sutras, usually covered with illustrations of Buddhist stories. Some pagodas contain relics.
Qi	Also 'ch'i'; the primal breath of creation, also the 'breath' that sustains life in each living being.
Qi-lin	A creature combining features of a unicorn, lion, dragon and deer.
Que	Pillars.
Sakyamuni	The historical Buddha, known in Sanskrit as Gautama Siddharta.
Sangha	The community of Buddhist monks and nuns, who keep the Buddha's teachings alive.
Shaman	A man or woman who is able to act as intermediary between the physical and spiritual worlds.

Shan	Mountain.
Si	Literally, 'hall'; a Buddhist temple or monastery.
Steles	Inscribed stones.
Stupa	A mound with the centre rising to a small tower, built to house relics of the Buddha or of holy men and women.
Sutra	Discourses traditionally attributed to the Buddha.
Tao	See *Dao*.
Theravada	Literally, 'teachings of the elders'; a form of Buddhism mainly practised in Sri Lanka and Southeast Asia. Based on the teachings in the Pali Canon, it emphasizes the difficulty of achieving enlightenment.
Trigram	A set of three lines, either broken, representing yin, or unbroken, representing 'yang'. There are eight possible combinations, which are used for divination purposes in the *Yi Jing* (I Ching), the 'Book of Changes'.
Yang	The active, positive, hot, male principle in the universe.
Yin	The passive, negative, cool, female principle in the universe.
Zhang Dao Ling	Founder of 'religious' Daoism, 2nd century AD.
Zhuang Zi	Daoist philosopher of 4th century BC and the title of the book of his thoughts and stories.

BIBLIOGRAPHY

The following does not include sources in Chinese, nor does it specifically list Chinese Tourism publications. The Chinese government and the various Provincial governments, along with publishing houses in China, provide a wide range of general leaflets and booklets on most major sites. Unfortunately, the English translations are often poor and only cover a fraction of the information given in Chinese. However, the booklets are improving as more and more Western tourists visit sites.

Guide Books

I have found three guide books to be of particular and distinctive use when visiting China.

Blue Guide China by Frances Wood. This is the best guide to what to see and what you are seeing. Clearly written and informative, it covers most major sites.

Lonely Planet China. Subtitled 'travel survival kit', this is the best guide to where to stay, how to get there, what to buy, etc. It also has good features and maps on some of the major sites, although its coverage is not as thorough as the *Blue Guide*.

Nagel's China. This expensive book is a delightful oddity. Its detail on some sites is quite superb while on others it is of little use. It contains the most detailed introductory sections covering everything from Art and Religion to Games! Highly idiosyncratic, it is an excellent book for the more detailed and passionate traveller who doesn't mind the oddities of its style.

I have one general observation concerning all three of the above books, although less so Nagel's. That is that their coverage of Buddhism is quite good, but that their understanding of Daoism is poor. This affects their commentaries on Daoist sites for it is clear that while familiar with Buddhism, they are not as familiar with Daoism.

General Books

de Bary, Theodore. *Sources of Chinese Tradition* Colombia University Press, 1960.

Birrell, Anne. *Chinese Mythology* John Hopkins University Press, Baltimore, 1993.

Cahill, Suzanne E. *Transcendence and Divine Passion – The Queen Mother of the West in Medieval China* Stanford University Press, 1993.

Ch'en, Kenneth K.S. *Buddhism in China* Princeton University Press, 1964 (frequently reprinted).

Ch'en, Kenneth K.S. *The Chinese Transformation of Buddhism* Princeton University Press, 1973.

Fung Yu-lan. *A History of Chinese Philosophy* vol. I, Princeton University Press, 1952, paperback edition, 1983.

Getty, Alice. *The Gods of Northern Buddhism* 2nd edition, first published 1928, reprinted by Dover Publications, New York 1988.

Hawkes, David (trans). *Songs of the South* Penguin, 1985.

Kwok, Man Ho, Palmer, Martin and Ramsay, Jay. *Tao Te Ching* Element Classics, Shaftesbury, 1994.

Kwok, Man Ho and O'Brien, Joanne. *The Eight Immortals of Taoism* Meridian, New York, 1991.

Kwok, Man Ho and O'Brien, Joanne. *The Elements of Feng Shui* Element Books, Shaftesbury, 1991.

Lau, D.C. (trans). *Analects*, Book XI, Penguin, 1979.

Mannerheim, C.G. *Chinese Pantheon* Finno-Ugrian Society, Helsinki, 1993.

Munakata, Kiyohiko. *Sacred Mountains in Chinese Art* Krannert Art Museum and University of Illinois Press, Urbana, 1991.

Naquin, Susan and Yu, Chun-Fang (eds). *Pilgrims and Sacred Sites in China* University of California, Berkeley, 1992.

Palmer, Martin with Breuilly, Elizabeth (trans). *The Book of Chuang Tzu* Penguin Arkana, London, 1996.

Palmer, Martin. *The Elements of Taoism* Element Books, Shaftesbury, 1991.

Palmer, Martin and Ramsay, Jay. *Kuan Yin* Thorsons, London, 1995.

Palmer, Martin and Ramsay, Jay. *I Ching* Thorsons, London, 1995.

Saso, Michael. *The Teachings of Taoist Master Chuang* Yale University Press, New Haven, 1978.

Saso, Michael. *Blue Dragon White Tiger* Taoist Center, Washington D.C., 1990.

Schipper, Kristofer. *The Taoist Body* University of California, 1993.

Smith, Bol, Adler and Wyatt. *Sung Dynasty Uses of the I Ching* Princeton University Press, 1990.

Soothill, W.E. (trans). *The Lotus of the Wonderful Law – Saddharma Pundarika Sutra* Clarendon Press, Oxford, 1930.

Strassberg, Richard E. *Inscribed Landscapes* University of California Press, Berkeley, 1994.

INDEX

quan - W look, see
verminous".